For almost half a century H. G. Wells was an international phenomenon, the only writer of his time who could command an audience with both Roosevelt and Stalin. His circle of friends included George Bernard Shaw, Rudyard Kipling, G. K. Chesterton, Somerset Maugham and, of course, the young Rebecca West, with whom he had a long-term affair – perhaps the most tempestuous and sparkling literary liaison of the century. Equally illustrious was his circle of enemies, including the indomitable Hilaire Belloc, who destroyed Wells in a vicious and public argument.

Unlike any previous biographer, Michael Coren shows that while many have considered Wells to be on the side of the angels, he was in fact invariably on the wrong side in the major political and literary debates of the age. Drawing on eye-opening new material, *The Invisible Man* delves deep into the paradoxes that characterized Wells – the utopian visionary and staunch advocate of women's suffrage who was also a misogynistic womanizer; the epitome of liberal tolerance who was also a social engineer and thoroughgoing anti-Semite. Wells has hitherto remained untouched by charges of anti-Semitism, but Coren reveals for the first time his disturbing views on 'the Jewish problem' (for instance, he called Jews 'termites in the civilized world'), views he defended vehemently even through the 1930s.

The avuncular author of *Kipps* and *The Time Machine* is depicted, shockingly, as one who advocated concentration camps, racial eugenics and the incarceration or execution of those who did not 'fit in'. *The Invisible Man* is one of those iconoclastic biographies that change our perception of their subjects for ever.

Journalist and writer Michael Coren is the author of the highly acclaimed *Gilbert: The Man Who Was G. K. Chesterton* and *Aesthete: The Frank Diaries of Michael Coren*.

THE INVISIBLE MAN

The Life and Liberties of
H. G. WELLS

MICHAEL COREN

VINTAGE BOOKS
A DIVISION OF RANDOM HOUSE OF CANADA, TORONTO

First published in 1993 by Random House of Canada Limited, Toronto, and in Great Britain by Bloomsbury Publishing Limited, London.

Canadian Cataloguing in Publication Data
Coren, Michael
The invisible man: the life and liberties of H. G. Wells

Includes index.
ISBN 0-394-22332-2

1. Wells, H.G. (Herbert George), 1866–1946 – Biography. 2. Authors, English – 20th century – Biography. I. Title.

PR5776.C57 1994   823'.912   C94-930514-6

PICTURE SOURCES
Bassano & Vandyk Studios: page 5 *top*
Estate of H. M. Bateman: page 6
Mary Evans Picture Library: page 5 *bottom left & right*
The Illustrated London News Picture Library: pages 1 *bottom*, 4 *inset*, 7 *top*
Frank Wells: pages 1 *top left & right*, 2 *top & bottom left*, 3 *bottom*, 4 *top & bottom*

Cover illustration by Steve Martin

Typeset by Hewer Text Composition Services, Edinburgh
Printed by Cox and Wyman Limited, Reading, Berkshire

10 9 8 7 6 5 4 3 2 1

To John and Alison Hayes

CONTENTS

ACKNOWLEDGEMENTS

I would like to thank the librarians at the Harry Ransom Humanities Center at the University of Texas at Austin; the Rare Books Room of the Library, University of Illinois, Champaign-Urbana; the H.G. Wells Collection in the Bromley Central Library, Kent; the British Library of Political and Economic Science, London School of Economics and Political Science, London; the London Library; the Library of St Michael's College, University of Toronto; the Institute of Contemporary History and Wiener Library, London; the British Library, London; the Hilaire Belloc collection at Boston College, Mass.; and the staff and library at the University of Nottingham. Thanks also to Christopher Rolfe of the H.G. Wells Society, the Earl of Longford, the late J.B. Priestley, the late Anthony West, the G.K. Chesterton collection formerly at Top Meadow (now in the British Library) and the Study Centre in Bedford, Lucinda Vardey, Carolyn Brunton, particular thanks to the Ontario Arts Council and the Canada Council for their financial assistance, Greg Gatenby, Dr William Sarjeant, Dr Stephen Hayhurst, Susan Walker, Mon. F. Miles, Iain Benson, Don Fehr, Prof. David Regan, the National Sound Archive, London, David C. Smith, Prof. Moshe Ben-Avi, Aidan Mackey, Thomas Doucette, Dr Irene Dimitri for expert help in Russian translation, Lynda Turchin, Prof. Jay Corrin, Prof. Norman Sherry, David Reynolds, Penny Phillips, Liz Calder, Daniel Richler, Jill Offman, Katherine Govier, Karen Cossar, Douglas Pepper, Noona Barlow, the late Malcolm Muggeridge, Ronald McLoskey, Gregory MacDonald, Prof. Robert Calder, John Raulston Saul, John Bierman, Don Bastion, Alan Coren, Bonnie Lefave, Stanley Lispey, Leanna Crouch, Kenneth Griffith,

Gerry Sherlock, Prof. Ian Willard, Linda Zwicker and the many and various people who have helped me with this project. I am grateful to the G.K. Chesterton Study Centre for permission to reproduce photographs of Hilaire Belloc and G.K. Chesterton, and to Martin Wells for permission to reproduce photographs of his grandfather.

PRELUDE

Conventional literary and political history depicts H.G. Wells as being unerringly on the side of the angels. I disagree with this finding. It is my belief that Wells' influence on his own age, and his legacy to those ages to come, were, taken as a whole, pernicious and destructive. This book recounts Wells' undoubted gifts and occasional bouts of genius but, in the interests of re-balance, pays particular attention to his numerous and various faults. The first quarter of the book focuses on a period of Wells' life which presents him at his worst. Readers should not be unduly repelled. Wells was a man who, like the fine wines he often purported to detest, mellowed with age. This is less a literary biography than a life of a largely invisible man. It has been my intention to restore his authentic visibility.

Richard Perceval Graves in his fine biography of his uncle, Robert Graves, states that 'Biographers also have a duty to be sympathetic to their subjects. As soon as I begin to discover that a biographer is treating his subject with malice, envy, dislike or contempt, I begin to suspect the quality both of his motives and of his human understanding.' I prefer a sympathy with the truth, and if in the pursuit of such I lose sympathy for my subject, it does not in any way tarnish or lessen my motives and sense of empathy. How may we write the lives of the Hitlers, Stalins and other evil-doers if we are only allowed to compose biographies of those with whom we sympathize? When I set out to write my life of H.G. Wells I had nothing but affection and admiration for the self-made man of so many achievements. It was only during my three years of research for the book, when I came across a plethora of negative facts and events which had been omitted from previous biographies, that I realized two things: that Wells was possibly not the man I had thought; and that other biographers had been far too selective in their inclusions.

Introduction

13 October 1936. Herbert George Wells was seventy years old. His frame had become a little fleshy, his hair had thinned and his moustache now contained streaks of grey, but that same sparkle in the eye, disarming cheek and seductive self-confidence were still very much in evidence. He had aged well. And he had aged triumphantly. Literary London was about to gather to celebrate in style. In a single summer, that of 1934, Wells had met both President Roosevelt and Premier Stalin, and nobody had considered the meetings to be in any way unusual. He was, without any fear of hyperbole, one of the most famous literary figures in the world. He was the author of a dozen best-sellers, and twice as many books of international influence. He was a man of letters, a popular historian, a political activist, a predictor of the future, a Cassandra and a guide, a doyen and a guru. His was a household name, and the households ranged from working-class tenements to palaces and offices of state. King Edward VIII had been a particular fan.

He was notorious as a lover. Young women, his friends announced, could still tremble at a glance; for the wrong reasons, his enemies rejoined. Wells' radio broadcasts were listened to with profound respect. Although his voice was, and always had been, shrill and weak, his words broke the barriers of class and education. He somehow spoke to all; and was listened to by most. He was HG. Any extension of the name was considered to be quite redundant.[1]

'Hundreds of people came to it,' said Somerset Maugham of Wells' birthday party. 'Bernard Shaw, a magnificent figure with his height, his white beard and white hair, his clear skin and bright eyes, made a speech. He stood very erect, his arms crossed, and with his puckish humour said many things highly embarrassing to the guest of the evening.'[2] Shaw was not the only speaker. Wells was International President of PEN, the pressure group of 'poets, playwrights, editors, essayists, novelists', and it was under the auspices of that organization that the party was held. The Savoy Hotel was the chosen location, and it was a spot Wells knew intimately. His close friend Arnold Bennett had had a dish named after him in the hotel restaurant. Wells did not receive such an honour, but the set meal of the party was at least as grand a commemoration. J.B. Priestley presided, the speakers included J.M. Barrie, Julian Huxley, Arthur Bliss and André Maurois. It is recorded in the files that Mr Priestley omitted to pay four pounds, seven shillings and sixpence for his tickets.[3]

The guest list reads like a who's who of British publishing: Jonathan Cape and Hamish Hamilton, Vera Brittain, Philip Guedalla and Maynard Keynes, A.A. Milne and A.D. Peters. Of the five hundred present, other, less obvious names ranged from Lord and Lady Mountbatten to the Chilean Ambassador. Then there were the PEN representatives from more than twenty nations, among them New Zealand, Colombia, Finland, South Africa, Hungary, Iraq and Germany. Those who were unable to attend sent contrite telegrams. 'In profound appreciation of your lifework penetrated as it is by the ideas of cooperation in all phases of intellectual activity and thus interpreting also the ideals of the PEN club international movement,' the Swedish branch offered in congratulation. The Japanese were more taciturn. 'We delegates of Nippon PEN club congratulate you sincerely on your anniversary day,' wrote Toson Shimazaki from a cabin on an ocean cruiser. Cartoonist David Low sent a simple and hopeful 'Long Life' in his telegram.[4]

The entrance to the Savoy was crowded with photographers and many of the guests had to push their way through the scrum; such celebrity in the literary world was novel. The evening was brisk, but not too cold. Some of the younger men had decided not to wear their coats. Wells was more careful, and arrived in the fur-collared heavy coat and small trilby hat which he habitually favoured; the formal evening wear underneath, with which he never grew accustomed, was less to his liking. Once inside they were greeted with a tastefully decorated dining-room and what one guest remembered as an almost 'overwhelming cloud' of cigar smoke.[5] The meal, for which PEN members paid twelve shillings and sixpence, non-members fifteen shillings, was later thought to have been rather hurried. A selection of Huitres Natives, Saumon Fume, Coupe Yvette au Sherry, Creme Madrilene, Mignon de Sole Sylvia, Noisette d'Agneau Fines-Herbes, Pommes Chateau, Salade d'Automne, Souffle Glace sur Rothschild and Petit Fours. How unfortunate, one sombre wit was heard to stage-whisper, that HG's French was so extremely poor.[6]

Wells drank his coffee and stood up. He was not a good orator. Unlike many speakers, he gave his best at the beginning, and his perorations were invariably strained and dissonant. He took his expected deep, voluble breath and then began from a typed speech. 'It is a fine thing to be entertained by a great crowd of friends,' he said, 'and I cannot tell you how much I enjoy being praised and in having my importance so generously and so delightfully exaggerated.' He paused, sipped from a glass of water in front of him, and then continued in a slightly more rapid delivery. 'I feel uplifted and expanded. It is hard to speak without embarrassing emotion of those life-long friends who have done me the honour of coming tonight. Yet all the time I will confess that the mellow brightness of this occasion is not without a shadow. I hate being seventy.' A uniform laugh from the assembled guests. 'To make this festival perfect you should have discovered that there had been a mistake somewhere and that I was — say forty-five. With another thirty or forty to go. Tonight I am very much in the position of a little boy at a lovely party, who has been given quite a lot of jolly toys and who has spread his play about the floor. Then comes his nurse. "Now Master Bertie," she says, "it's getting late. Time you began to put away your toys." I don't in the least want to put away my toys . . . '[7]

The toys would last for another ten years, but would give Wells diminishing amounts of pleasure. His physical health would not break until two years before his death, but his emotional well-being declined rapidly in the late 1930s. This evening in London was the pinnacle of his success and of his reputation. After the lavish party Wells and a few close friends, warmed by the fine wines they had imbibed, exited from the Thames doors of the Savoy Hotel, and Wells gazed at the river and the land beyond. It was the county of Kent, in which he had been born, in another century and in very different circumstances. As he frequently insisted on telling those he met for the first time, Mr Wells had come a very long way indeed.

1 Early Days

The early story of Herbert George Wells is one of triumph over enormous odds and seemingly insurmountable obstacles. He liked to boast to friends that while he may not have been born in a manger, his rise to influence and fame was almost miraculous. His family was poor and troubled; there was no helping hand to guide young Wells towards the best books. This quintessentially self-made man, however, always acknowledged that more than anyone else it was his mother who shaped and moulded him. 'We had no servants; no nursemaids and governesses intervened between us,' Wells wrote in his autobiography. 'She carried me about until I could be put down to trot after her and so I arose mentally, quite as much as physically, out of her.'

Sarah Neal, 'a little blue-eyed, pink-cheeked woman with a large serious face',[1] was almost forty-four years old in 1866 when Wells was born; friends and relatives had warned her that she was too old to live through another pregnancy, but she gave birth to her son with surprising ease and lack of complications. She had grown up in an inn-keeping family in the county of Sussex, where her father, George Neal, of Scots-Irish descent, was something of a local character. Although his inns were respected in the community as oases of good taste and order, financially they were completely unsuccessful, causing a great deal of instability for the family. Despite this he managed to send Sarah to a middle-class school, where she was given a rudimentary but prized education. The small Chichester school, known as Miss Riley's, was rooted firmly in the low-church Protestant tradition – a factor that had a profound influence on Sarah's life thereafter and, consequently, on Wells too. As he later frequently pointed out, his mother's education was notable not by its content, but by its very existence.

Sarah entered domestic service – work she quite enjoyed because she generally liked being around people of the upper classes and cherished the security and elegance of a great house. Structure was the essence of the nineteenth-century family and of English society in general, and in many ways the large, wealthy household in Victorian England requiring a downstairs staff was the perfect microcosm of the layered social system. Moreover, there was a sense of belonging; long-term servants could abandon any worries concerning their lodgings and board, have decisions made by their employers and enjoy vicariously the triumphs and indulgences of an upper-middle-class or aristocratic clan.[2] The disadvantages of this arrangement are self-evident, however; many servants were reduced to the role of working children, and were often treated that way, with few rights and many duties, reliant solely on the altruism and responsibility of their masters.

The obvious and humiliating dichotomy between what is popularly known as upstairs and downstairs left an impression on the young H.G. Wells, who spent several very formative years in this environment. It provided fuel for his imagination; several of his works reflect an experience of a divided world, one half of its population existing in subterranean tunnels and rooms. But it also became a target; his anger at this contrived 'preselection' was seldom far from the surface. His mother Sarah, on the other hand, was usually quite happy in service, for in addition to providing her with a suitable income and a home in generally elegant surroundings, it also coincided with her evangelical belief in the immutability of the establishment and order, which stressed that she must remain in her given position, yet assured her that there were many beneath her station and that their place was similarly unchangeable.

After five years working for a Captain Forde and his wife, Sarah Neal left to become a maid in the house of Fanny Bullock at Uppark in Sussex, where she became a friend as well as an employee of the family. From the magnificent eighteenth-century estate one had an unequalled view of the Sussex Downs, while the servants' quarters, and the corridors which connected them to the main body of the house, were recognizable from the exterior only by a series of sinister-looking fern-sprouting air-shafts. It was at Uppark that the devout and invariably trusting Sarah Neal met her future husband.

Joseph Wells was from a large family with deep roots in the county of Kent. His father was head gardener to Lord de Lisle at Penshurst Place. The profession had been passed down through the Wells family with such pride that those sons who did not pursue horticulture as a trade were nevertheless avid gardeners. However, it was not the family's only recreation, particularly for its youngest son Joseph. Wells recorded in his autobiography:

My father grew up to gardening and cricket, and remained an out-of-doors, open-air man to the day of his death. He became gardener at Redleaf, nearby, to a Mr Joseph Wells, who, in spite of the identical name, was no sort of relation, and in the summer, directly the day's work was over, my father would run, he told me once, a mile and more at top speed to the pitch at Penshurst to snatch half an hour of cricket before the twilight made the ball invisible. He learnt to swim and to handle a muzzle-loading gun and so forth as country boys do, and his schooling gave him reading and writing and 'summing', so that he read whenever he could and kept his accounts in a clear well-shaped handwriting.

Joseph Wells arrived at Uppark following his employer's death and an unsuccessful period as a jobbing gardener and labourer. At first Sarah thought the new man was 'peculiar'. He kept to himself much of the time and was reluctant to join in the fraternal cama-raderie of the house, which was the basis of Sarah's social life. But as she got to know Joseph her opinion began to change. She began to admire his abilities and appreciate his particular attractiveness. He was a man of the soil, a powerful and robust figure who over-whelmed Sarah with his self-confidence and sanguine, optimistic attitude towards his future. Within a few months they were in love. Sarah insisted that for the relationship to continue they must get married. They asked their employers for permission (such a request was still necessary from those in service) and received it; a match between a maid and a gardener was seen as an ideal arrangement.

But that was the only sense in which the arrangement was ideal, for in every other respect they were fundamentally different. Joseph possessed an earthy wisdom and good looks, yet he was also volatile and restless; he toyed with schemes of emigration and rejected the stability that his future wife so cherished. Sarah longed for a discernible and dependable future, while Joseph Wells refused to contemplate any future that denied him the chance of adventure. Furthermore, Sarah was deeply religious. Although Joseph's early love letters were sprinkled with references to God, the Church, devotion to the evangelical creed and so on, such religious fervour did not last much beyond their courtship. Nevertheless, however incompatible they were, by early 1853 the couple were writing regularly to each other about marriage and children.

Before the couple could get married, however, Sarah Neal had to leave Uppark very suddenly, to care for her ailing mother. Joseph left his post just weeks after Sarah, almost certainly because of her departure. Sarah's mother is a sadly anonymous figure, hardly mentioned in Wells' reminiscences. She was a member of that Victorian generation of fey matriarchs who suffered illness on a bafflingly regular basis, and were constantly in need of care and comfort. On this occasion, however, she was desperately ill and seemed to be near death. George Neal, who was usually there to nurse his wife through these periods, was unable to because he was not well himself. He had earlier been diagnosed as suffering from a nervous breakdown, but in retrospect it was probably the early stages of a brain tumour, combined with cancer of the stomach. His condition grew progressively more severe and at the end of August 1853 he had a seizure and died within the day. The resulting turmoil was recorded by great-grandson Anthony West:

Her [Sarah's] mother at first seemed to be unmoved by the event, but on the day following her husband's funeral she went out of her mind. My grandmother was hit all the harder by her mother's transformation into a violently hostile stranger because of the situation in which she found herself. Her father was over his ears in debt when he died and as soon as they heard of his end, his creditors descended on the New Inn en masse in order to stake out their various claims upon his assets. My grandmother had to fend them off as best she could while making the funeral arrangements, looking after the mad woman, and caring for her twelve-year-old younger brother.[3]

Trying to hold the family together over the next months proved to be exceedingly difficult for Sarah. In November, when her mother died too, she was on the verge of a complete break-down. Joseph came immediately from his temporary home in Gloucestershire to be by her side, where he promptly proposed to her. They married shortly afterwards, on 22 November, in London's St Stephen's Church in Coleman Street.

With no steady income and no home the new couple were off to a precarious start indeed. As a single man Joseph's periodic and capricious spurts of industry were followed just as often by sloth and indifference, and he evidently saw little reason to change his ways now that he was married. Between April 1854 and August 1855 he earned twenty-five shillings a week as head gardener at Shuckburgh Park in the Midlands. Shortly after settling into the new location Sarah became pregnant, which gave her all the more reason to be anxious about her husband's future. She was justifiably concerned that his employment, the family's livelihood, was too dependent on the whim of a single employer. Her worst fears were borne out, for within six months of the birth of their first child, Frances, on 20 February 1855, Joseph Wells was dismissed by his employer – his work was evidently too half-hearted.

For a short time they lived with family in Gloucestershire and Kent, while Joseph applied for and was interviewed for a succession of jobs in London, none of which materialized. By the beginning of the winter in 1855 they decided to purchase, with the aid of a family loan, a china shop in Bromley, then a rapidly expanding town in Kent. The establishment, known as Atlas House, consisted of a yard, three dusty floors and a narrow basement. For the price of fifty pounds the young couple now owned a home, where their children would be born and raised, and a business, which, as it turned out, was much more than they had bargained for.

The image of the small shopkeeper of nineteenth-century England may be charming, but the reality of the life was excessively demanding. One needed the skills of a salesman, bookkeeper and carpenter, none of which Joseph excelled in. He was a jack of some trades, but master of none, and the day-to-day grind of his new business soon lost its appeal. He knew virtually nothing about commerce and very quickly became an isolated figure in the town's commercial community. His natural habitat was the local cricket club – which he rejuvenated and led – and the pubs along the Bromley High Street, where he drank, gambled and spent increasingly long and regular amounts of time. The more time he devoted to recreation, the less he gave to his wife and the shop.

Years later Wells would recount an anecdote that sheds some

light on the condition of his parents' marriage even then. Sarah and Joseph were scheduled to attend a wedding in South London on a Saturday afternoon in May, which meant that they would need to leave for the ceremony no later than 11 a.m. Joseph went out early that morning for cricket practice and did not return home until 4.30. 'Why,' Sarah screamed, 'didn't you come back in time, or at least send someone back here to tell us you were delayed?' ''Cos I was having a much better innings there than I could ever have with you,' he replied.[4]

Such neglect and rejection naturally took its toll on the marriage, which became increasingly enervated and unloving. Sarah was virtual manager of shop and home, while Joseph managed to jettison his responsibilities with alacrity. A sense of mutual hostility, bordering on contempt, was exacerbated by fear of conceiving more children. Frank, their second child, was born in 1857, Fred five years later. The couple began to sleep in separate rooms. Sarah became bitter and sullen, Joseph became detached, apathetic, and began to contemplate leaving the country or selling the shop in order to make a new life elsewhere for himself.[5]

In 1864 the dwindling marriage was dealt a heavy blow. Frances, not yet ten years old, died suddenly from an inflammation in her bowel. Sarah suffered an almost total emotional collapse. She developed a monomaniacal obsession with her deceased daughter, speaking to her as if she were still alive, asking her where she was, thinking she could hear her footsteps and cries. First she blamed herself, then her neighbours, then her husband, for the death of her beloved child. She pleaded with Joseph for support, yet he seemed unable to provide anything more than a perfunctory shoulder.

Sarah and Joseph's marriage had sunk to a desperate level when their fourth and last child, Herbert George, was born, at 4.30 on a Saturday afternoon, 21 September 1866. It had rained most of the day, but the clouds lifted between three and five o'clock, as if to greet this latest world citizen. Unlike the actual delivery, which was straightforward, the baby proved much more difficult than any of Sarah's other children. She had 'never had so tiresome a baby as this one,' she said of him. A perennial victim, the infant constantly had bruised legs, cut eyes, and he became his mother's particular project, in need of safekeeping and protection. This was the source of much sibling jealousy, for the young Herbert was a spoiled child indeed. More than his brothers when they were his age, he threw fits and tantrums, and could usually count on his mother to settle squabbles in his favour. After all, he was younger and weaker.

Wells recounts in his autobiography how his brothers would respond to his antics by throwing him into the attic and smothering him with pillows until he gave in. 'Why they did not suffocate me for good and all,' he wrote, 'I do not know.' Despite this kind of jostling and his parents' unhappy marriage, Wells was quite happy as a child, largely because of his special relationship with his mother. As an adult he would reminisce that for many of those early days it seemed that only he and his mother existed, and that other family members, and the world at large, could be blocked out from his innocent consciousness.[6]

At the age of eight Wells discovered his own area of interest and ambition, quite literally by accident:

My leg was broken for me when I was between seven and eight. Probably I am alive today and writing this autobiography instead of being a worn-out, dismissed and already dead shop assistant, because my leg was broken. The agent of good fortune was 'young Sutton', the grown-up son of the landlord of the Bell. I was playing outside the scoring tent in the cricket field and in all friendliness he picked me up and tossed me in the air. 'Whose little kid are you?' he said, and I wriggled, he missed his hold on me and I snapped my tibia across a tent peg . . . I had just taken to reading. I had just discovered the art of leaving my body to sit impassive in a crumpled up attitude in a chair or sofa, while I wandered over the hills and far away in novel company and new scenes. And now my father went round nearly every day to the Literary Institute in Market Square and got one or two books for me, and Mrs Sutton sent some books, and there was always a fresh book to read.

Sarah supplemented her son's studies with mandatory Bible reading and a variety of religious pamphlets. Although Wells would eventually reject Christianity with all the bitterness and spleen of a forced proselyte, as a child, at least, he consumed most of what his mother and her church offered.

Sarah Wells believed that education was essential not as an end in itself but as the means to realizing success in later life. Her 'clever' son deserved encouragement. Only yards along Bromley High Street was Thomas Morley's Academy, where she enrolled Wells when he was eight years old. The Academy was typical of the plethora of small private schools that were created in the mid-nineteenth century for the children of the lower middle class. Before the turn of the century there was no universal education system in Britain, and with no national standards existing for education, these schools varied enormously, being subject for the most part to the particular tastes of the headmaster. The better ones based their curriculum on principles of patriotic, religious or humanistic duty, of improving the opportunities of 'English, Christian children'. Others were founded simply for financial gain and the flagrant exploitation of a newly monied class of people. Thomas Morley's Academy was somewhere in the middle. Its particular emphasis was on imperial history, the fundamentals of prose style and the importance – though not necessarily the pleasure – of reading. There were thirty boys at the school, between the ages of seven and fourteen, and with greatly varying abilities and aptitudes.

The young Wells' precocity was illustrated by his approach to schooling: it was clear to him early on that what Thomas Morley offered at the Academy was merely a partial education; he would have to teach himself at home. Thus by the Atlas House oil lamp every evening he set up a rigorous, if completely random, agenda for himself, reading anything he could get his hands on: travel and humour books, Wood's *Natural History*, Chaucer, collections of bound copies of *Punch*, which introduced him to the arcane, idiomatic world of English literary comedy. His scattered approach to reading evolved into a more selective reading of the classics, as well as books of science and fantasy.

Unlike his father, Wells did not especially enjoy sports. He was more of a wanderer and a walker. His often solitary jogs and jaunts around Bromley filled his grasping imagination with notions of the possible. Friend, and enemy, G.K. Chesterton would write: 'For young HG the streets of England were paved not with gold, but with adventure.'[7]

Since imperial history was a particular strength at the Thomas Morley Academy, Wells became interested in military history and during his solitary walks he would often map out historic battlefields in the local parks and use the wicket and boundary lines of Bromley cricket pitch to deploy his troops. His earliest attempts at fiction writing occurred during this time too. He would frequently be seen scribbling notes in a tiny leather-bound notepad given to him by his mother which he habitually carried in his trouser pocket.

His first serious effort was an illustrated children's story called *The Desert Daisy*, which described a war involving the royal family, the episcopacy and military leaders – all of whom, ironically, would feel the righteous anger of the adult Wells. The storyline was accompanied by a series of elaborate sketches, most of them signed with the family pet-name for Wells, 'Buss'. He also wrote a series of parodies of *Punch* and other comic magazines of the era. He even tried his hand at historical essays. All of this mostly extracurricular writing was being produced by a young boy barely ten years old. Such academic enthusiasm was sufficiently rare at the Academy for Wells very quickly to become Mr Morley's favourite pupil, which, of course, provoked the hostility of his classmates. Wells' loneliness grew with each passing year at the school.

During his time here the young Wells also began to develop an awareness of the English class structure. Though solidly lower middle class, both of his parents displayed a certain inflated class snobbery. His father's involvement in cricket (although, unlike a gentleman, he played and coached it for money) brought the young Wells into contact with members of the rural gentry; while his mother's powerful perception of her own class standing, compounded by her often enthusiastic approval of the wealthy and powerful lifestyle of her former employers, was fed to Wells for as long as he could recall.

His headmaster too exhibited this same snobbery, emphasizing the all-important difference between the privately educated pupils of his school and the 'rabble' outside the gates. When the boys' gang from the Academy, Morley's Bull Dogs, met the local boys, the Bromley Water Rats, for a brawl, Wells was shocked by the attitudes evident on both sides. The boys from the Academy boasted that they were 'of the middle class', the local Bromley boys spat out the same description as an accusation. These schoolyard scuffles were Wells' first exposure to the subtleties, and antagonisms, of England's class structure. He realized for the first time that the mere possession of an education gave one a certain station in society. The memory of these brawls remained with him and the revelation fuelled his desire to continue his own education, flavouring his later writings and his relationships.

His class origins also influenced his sexuality. As a boy he possessed neither the confidence of upper-middle-class boys nor the 'experience' of lower- or working-class boys. Unlike upper-middle-class boys he had no training in the social graces, and consequently for many years felt uneasy with girls and later on with older women. He grappled clumsily with fantasies and feelings.

Until my adolescence, sex fantasies came to me only in that dim phase between waking and sleeping. I gave myself gladly and willingly to my warfare, but I was shy of sex; I resisted any urge I may have had towards personal romancing and sensuous fantasies. My sexual trend was, I think, less marked or more under control when I was twelve or thirteen, than it was when I was nine or ten. My primary curiosities had been satisfied and strong physical urgencies were still unawakened.

Lacking any 'real' sexual experiences as a child, his inchoate and indistinct sexual desires were given form by the depictions of stately, impossible women in political cartoons in *Punch*, and by gynaecological diagrams of the most meagre kind in Wells' science books. He rarely saw or met girls of his own age, and so was never able to compare his increasingly idealized version of the female form with the real thing. His sexual confusion was compounded by his parents' physical coldness towards one another; their abstinence had by this time become entrenched. Thus Wells' perception of women was based almost entirely on sexual longing. Although this was by no means unnatural, the Calvinistic conscience implanted by his mother produced a tremendous guilt, which he did not entirely expunge until he was into his late teens.

Looking back on his childhood, Wells often referred to two incidents, both in fact accidents, that transformed his life: the first was when he broke his leg at the age of seven and discovered the pleasure of reading; the second was when he was eleven, and occurred not to him but to his father. Joseph Wells' sole financial contribution to the household was by then the few shillings he made from cricket. He ignored the shop and spent decreasing amounts of time with his children. One Sunday in October 1877 while attempting to prune the garden grape-vine, he fell from the ladder, fracturing his thigh. He never really recovered and remained partially crippled for the rest of his life. What little money he was able to make playing cricket was reduced to virtually nothing. A more immediate problem, however, was the succession of medical bills from the local doctor. Though the family was far from poverty, they were forced to adapt their life and diet to take account of their vicissitudes. Wells developed a life-long dislike of thick, doughy bread because of the amount of this cheap food he was forced to eat during his childhood. He had to wear boots that were too small and splitting at the edges, and tuition payments to the Morley Academy were becoming more burdensome for the family. Wells was astute enough to realize that his formal education might soon end. He was not prepared, however, for his mother's plans for his future.

At the age of thirteen Wells was apprenticed off to a reliable, successful craftsman, in a reliable, successful craft. The family had contacts in the drapery trade, and after letters of negotiation had been exchanged with the firm of Rodgers and Denyer in Windsor, Wells was withdrawn from the Thomas Morley Academy and shipped off to begin work.

The working hours at Rodgers and Denyer were exhaustingly long. Apprentices began at half past seven in the morning and finished at eight-thirty at night. Such conditions required that the staff live in, spending their rest time in one of several dormitories that contained ten inadequate beds. The boy wrote his mother a series of consistently bleak letters. In one he described his daily routine:

We lie in bed until 7.30 when a bell rings & we jump up & put trousers slippers socks and jacket over nightgown & hurry down & dust the shop etc.

About 8.15 we hurry upstairs & dress & wash for breakfast.

About 8.30 we go into a sort of vault underground (lit by gas) & have breakfast.

After breakfast I am in the shop & desk till dinner at 1 (we have dinner underground as well as breakfast) & then work till tea (which we have in the same place) & then go on to supper at 8.30 at which time work is done & we may then go out until 10.30 at which hour the apprentices are obliged to be in the house.

I don't like the place much for it is not at all like home.

The underground dining-room was damp and poorly lit, the meals repetitive and bland. The only spare time available to Wells was the cherished hiatus between the end of work and the strict lights-out call at 10.30 – barely two hours to read and write. The moral education of the staff was supervised by older apprentices or junior managers, self-appointed suzerains who were quick to condemn any behaviour they perceived as not in keeping with the reputation of the shop.

The only relief came at weekends, when Wells would go to visit an uncle named Thomas Pennicott, who managed an inn in nearby Surly Hall just outside Windsor. Here Wells was the centre of attention, pampered by his uncle and teased deliciously by his two female cousins. He spent as much time as possible with his cousins at Surly Hall, and these were some of the happiest moments of his young life – 'a perfect heaven to R & D's,' he wrote. But the stark contrast between weekends with his uncle and his giggling girl cousins and the sterile, depressing drapery shop only served to exacerbate his predicament. He tried to view his drapery work as though it were a passing nightmare, but he knew it could well turn into a nightmare that would not end.

Wells' anxiety over his circumstances rapidly escalated to overwhelming fear as he realized that the foundations of his future life were being laid in a suburban drapery shop. He knew that success here would mean a life of servitude and drudgery, and he wanted to avoid that at all costs. So he seemed deliberately determined to fail. He would escape from the front of the shop to the warehouse whenever he could to read and sleep. More serious still, his recorded cash tally began to differ from the actual contents of the till. His employers allowed for small discrepancies in their young staff, but Wells' mistakes rapidly took on a worrying regularity.

When he was dismissed by the firm (with pilfering implied) he was genuinely surprised, and, of course, delighted. His employers produced no evidence to substantiate charges of dishonesty; the ostensible reason for his dismissal was a fist fight with a junior porter. The management of Rodgers and Denyer made it quite clear to Wells that they did not trust him and would not be providing any references. No matter; he was free. It was as if a cloak of darkness had been lifted from his shoulders; all of his former ambitions and dreams were again before him.

He went directly to Surly Hall, where he swam, rested and played with his cousins and uncle, while his family once again took up the question of his future. He of course was not consulted in these discussions. Though Wells would later regret his bovine complacency at Surly Hall while his career was being planned, in reality there was very little he could have done to influence any decisions.[8]

The discussions about Wells' future placed an enormous strain on Sarah. She and her husband had disagreed about almost everything for the past year, and planning their youngest son's career was no exception. Joseph wanted to give his son more of a free rein, let the boy's abilities take him where they might, but Sarah was less optimistic about the opportunities for a boy of Wells' class and background if he were just given a 'free rein'. She, in some way, wanted more for her son's future. They argued endlessly about this, with Joseph sometimes storming out of the house in a heated temper. Sarah habitually blamed her husband for their precarious circumstances; Joseph retaliated by calling his wife a snob and a fool.

Just as their marriage appeared once again to be on the verge of dissolution an unexpected and welcome opportunity materialized. Lady Fetherstonaugh, owner of the great house at Uppark, had recently died and Frances, Sarah's former employer, found the duties of managing the house beyond her constitution. Remembering that Sarah was an ideal leader, she extended an offer of employment as the head manager of the house staff. Sarah was fifty-seven and had been out of service for some time, yet the position at Uppark provided advantages that Atlas House no longer had. In 1880, after she had arranged for some financial help – a tiny pension paid for out of her meagre savings – for her husband, Sarah abandoned Bromley and its misery.

Wells' future was still undecided. An obscure relative, known as 'Uncle' Williams, the brother-in-law of Thomas Pennicott, eventually offered what appeared at least to be an acceptable solution. An itinerant teacher of sorts, he had recently accepted the post of headmaster of Wookey School near the city of Wells in Somerset. Wells could come to the school as an 'improver', a hybrid position combining the roles of part-time teacher and pupil. Although his 'uncle' seemed to Wells a curious character, the opportunity he was offering appeared to be an ideal solution to both his and his family's troubles. It would cost his family nothing, he could stay at the school, pursue an intellectual career, and perhaps even enter the teaching profession.

So, with some incredulity, Wells began studies and duties at

Wookey. Within weeks, however, his initial suspicions became much more pronounced. Uncle Williams, it appeared, had an extremely limited education, and his unorthodox behaviour was more lunatic than eccentric. He would sometimes enter the classroom, shout at the top of his voice about the state of the weather, then make a rapid exit. He would also talk to himself in public and absent himself from the school for long, unexplained periods of time. His day-to-day administration of the school was disorganized, showing a lack of any authentic experience as an educator. After only three months the local authorities, acting on instruction from government education inspectors, closed the school down. The young Wells, the rug once again pulled from under him, returned to Surly Hall, and then back to his mother at Uppark for almost two years.

Wells' stay at Uppark had a major and lasting impact on him, particularly because most of his time there was spent without his father, whose by now essentially plebeian and cynical view of life had become increasingly pervasive and burdensome on everyone. Wells was drifting further from his father and, though respectful, their relationship from here on became increasingly more distant. Wells' book, *Tono-Bungay*, is full of autobiographical recollections of Uppark, its sounds and 'wood-smoke-scented luxury'.[9] He wrote in the novel:

The great house, the church, the village, and the labourers and the servants in their stations and degrees, seemed to me, I say, to be a closed and complete social system . . . the great house mingled so solidly and effectually with earth and sky, the contrast of its spacious hall and saloon and galleries, its airy housekeeper's room and warren of offices . . . I thought this was the order of the whole world.

As the son of the highest-ranking female servant, Wells was free to explore and wander anywhere in the below-stairs quarters, which were a labyrinth of tunnels, surreptitious rooms and closets worthy of the most vivid imagination. He enjoyed a sense of superiority over the other servants, as the son of their leader, but he was liked by them and they generously tolerated his antics and inquiries. The adolescent boy was in virtual heaven; there was no work required of him and he was given a room in the attic with all the time he desired for reading and study.

During his first winter in the house, in December 1880, when heavy snows made the place seem even more haven-like, Wells made his first foray into journalism, conceiving and producing a daily newspaper called, characteristically, *The Uppark Alarmist*. It was a provocative sheet, written entirely by Wells – a striking endeavour for a fourteen-year-old boy. It satirized the staff, and some of the upstairs occupants, and made fun of the entire idea of a stately home. The house staff were divided between those who thought Wells should pursue a career in journalism and those who thought he should be chastised for his insolence.

Wells' lasting image of himself during those days at Uppark was that of the literate teenager suddenly let loose in an aristocratic library. At last he was free to indulge himself in what he loved most, to read whatever happened to catch his interest. It was all there in the library, where he discovered Jonathan Swift's *Gulliver's Travels*, then Thomas Paine's revolutionary works, *Common Sense* and *Rights of Man*. His most important discovery, however, was Plato's *Republic*, which helped give form to many of the undeveloped theories and ideas swirling around in his head.

Such glorious indulgence could not continue, however. Sarah, still determined that her son learn a trade, contacted another family member, Samuel Cowap, a successful chemist, and Wells was once again shipped off to be an apprentice. But this did not turn out to be as bad as his previous work at the drapery shop, for he was now exposed for the first time to practical science, which was not lost on someone as insatiably inquisitive as young Wells.

During his apprenticeship the family arranged for Wells to be tutored by the headmaster of the local Midhurst Grammar School, Horace Byatt. He needed to know Latin for his work with Cowap, which meant that he would get the rudiments, at least, of a gentleman's education. Although he lacked the skills that would make him an outstanding scholar, Byatt was a gifted teacher whose hortatory abilities made him a consummate educator (his talents had served another future author extremely well: while in the Potteries, Byatt taught Arnold Bennett). Wells' progress under Byatt was exceptional. To Byatt's delight and astonishment, he appeared to assimilate and comprehend the intricacies of one of the standard Latin texts, Smith's *Principia*, in little over a month, an almost unprecedented achievement for a student of Wells' age and background.

Sarah struggled to afford the tuition for her son, and was

tempted once more to have young Wells enter a trade such as the drapery profession. 'But this time I went recalcitrant,' Wells wrote in his autobiography, 'not indeed against my mother, whose simplicity and difficulties I was beginning to understand, but against a scheme of things which marched me off before I was fifteen to what was plainly a dreary and hopeless life, while other boys, no better in quality than myself, were enjoying all the advantages – I thought they were stupendous advantages in those days – of the public school and university.' Horace Byatt offered a temporary solution: Wells could stay in his home as a boarder until he completed his education. It was a forlorn cause, as Wells and Byatt knew that the period could be nothing more than a stay of execution.

The dreaded threat of servitude to drapery became a reality once again in May 1881. After Wells had spent only six weeks as Byatt's pupil, Sarah, no longer able to afford the tuition, decided that he should be apprenticed to Edwin Hyde and the Southsea Drapery Store. For the third time before the age of sixteen, the young Wells had to forgo his education to be shipped off to an apprenticeship. The post was arranged through the unwitting altruism of Sarah's employer, who assured Hyde that the new boy was faithful and industrious. Wells maintained at least a pretence of dedication through the trial month of May, so that by June he signed his articles. This period in the drapery business was yet more numbing and repellent than the first. Wells was well aware of what his future would be if he could not get out of this cycle. His mood at the time is recorded vividly in his autobiography:

Retail trade, I thought, had captured me for good. I had now to learn to work and to work faithfully for the profit and satisfaction of my prospective employers to the end of my days. I had been at large for a year and found no other way of living. The last chance had gone. At that moment I could not discover in my mind or in my world, as represented by the narrow side street into which I was looking, the little corner pub or the blind alley below me or the strip of sky overhead, the faintest intimation of any further escape.

I turned around from this restricted outer world to survey my dormitory in much the same mood as a condemned prisoner surveying the fittings of the cell he is to occupy for his allotted term.

It was an appallingly low point in his young life. Years later he confided to J.B. Priestley that it was the first time he had actually contemplated suicide. 'It was not hopelessness which made death so tempting, if only for a passing time,' explained Priestley. 'It was hope; and knowing that hope was so obtainable, and so apparently distant.'[10] Desperate he certainly was. He had a glimpse of where his talents might take him, but his education had been abruptly halted again. Working in sweat-shop conditions for small wages and with no hopes for liberation, he found his young man's dreams were shattered.

His only comfort, still, was candlelit reading sessions in his room. Byatt had irrevocably instilled in him a respect and adoration for learning, a faith that education need not terminate because formal tuition came to an end. Wells made regular visits to the library at Southsea and used the reading room at the local branch of the YMCA to improve himself; he read some fiction, but only as a reward for reading an encyclopaedia or a difficult work of philosophy. In spite of his dislike for drapery work, his existence at Southsea was undoubtedly superior to the one he had led in Windsor. Edwin Hyde was not a cruel employer. Living conditions were acceptable. Hyde provided his workers with substantial meals and a small but deftly selected library. Yet even his reading no longer provided Wells with the necessary escape from his drudgery; rather, it provided a nagging, ever louder call to taste the offerings of the larger life.

He was almost seventeen now, and desperate to grip any lifeline out of the situation. Sarah urged her son to consider the theology of the problem, stressing the importance of the next life in order to minimize his own struggle here on earth. Willing to consider any explanation that would help him deal with his present torment, he attended a succession of local churches, Anglican, low-church Protestant and Roman Catholic, in search of explanations for his misery, but these experiences just confirmed him in his agnosticism.

After two years at Southsea, Wells emerged behaving, as he described it years later in his autobiography, 'very much like a hunted rabbit that turns at last and bites. A hunted rabbit that turned and bit would astonish and defeat most ordinary pursuers.' He had had enough and was determined to make his own way out of this servitude.

In fact the decision Wells eventually made exhibited maturity and judgement far beyond his years. In a letter to Byatt at

Midhurst, he explained his predicament and asked if there were any opportunities for him to return to the school in order to pursue a career in education. Further, in a letter to his mother, he informed her of his intentions, insisting that her plans for him were no longer realistic. Byatt promised Wells a place at his school if he could pass certain exams. He was too old to enter teaching as a student teacher, but he could become an assistant teacher in 'a middle-class school'. Wells wrote to his mother that a place was open at the school, but as he would be more of a student than teacher he would receive no wages. They would have to wait until he could teach on a regular basis. He insisted that he would be able to live on ten shillings a week, and,

estimating clothes to cost 10 pounds a year you would have to pay for me about 35 pounds in the year for one year more. But then, when the start is made there is every prospect of rising to a good position in the world, while in my present trade I am a drapers assistant throughout life. But I must begin at once. If I start at all I must begin next September. Which would you prefer? I leave the matter in your hands . . .

Sarah was understandably anxious about committing a large sum of money to what might be no more than a whim. After all, fifty pounds had already been paid to Mr Hyde of Southsea, who was under no legal or moral obligation to return any portion of the money if Wells broke his indentures. Wells knew the extent of his mother's indecision. In a desperate effort to persuade her he walked seventeen miles from Southsea to Uppark, meeting his mother as she returned home from church – a scene faithfully recreated in *Tono-Bungay*:

The nearer I drew to Bladesover, the more doubtful I grew of the quality of my reception, and the more I regretted that alternative . . . I took a short cut through the Warren across the corner of the main park to intercept the people from the church. I wanted to avoid meeting anyone before I met my mother, and so I went to a place where the path passed between banks, and without exactly hiding, stood up among the bushes . . . My mother looked up, went very white, and put her hand to her bosom . . . I suppose there was a fearful fuss about me. And of course I was quite unable to explain my reappearance.

Sarah pleaded with him to return at once to Southsea; he agreed only on the condition that she promise to consider the matter again, and give a decision. But Wells was sceptical of his mother's intentions, and wrote another letter to his former teacher. Byatt sweetened his original offer: he would now pay Wells twenty pounds for the initial year, with a promise of double that salary thereafter. The new situation would now cost his parents nothing. Sarah's resistance was finally overcome.

Wells now prepared himself for the life he had dreamed of for five years. Although not exactly the school of his dreams, Midhurst had the compensation of the energetic Byatt for its lack of brilliant students and gifted masters. Sixty pupils and two assistant masters greeted the new teacher, who proved a considerate, if not a skilled teacher, liked by parents and other teachers as well as his pupils.[11] There was an effortless approachability about him seldom found in teachers then, partly because he saw himself as little more than a glorified student and therefore never adopted the manners of the conventional teacher.

In his other capacity as a student at Midhurst he won numerous awards, bringing glory and, equally important, financial gain to Horace Byatt and his school. For each academic prize Wells won, two to four pounds would be donated to the school. For this reason, and because of his genuine belief in Wells' extraordinary potential, Byatt purchased Wells new textbooks on a variety of subjects such as geology, physiology, and human and plant biology.[12] That Byatt himself knew little if anything of these disciplines was irrelevant; he would sit by and mark his other students' work as Wells read and memorized new and difficult information at a prodigious rate. Wells became a devotee of the god education. Like the character in his novel *Love and Mr Lewisham*, the young man pinned an intricate schema on the wall of his garret, located over a local sweetshop: sleep, food and play were to be rationed, or sacrificed, as he followed the curriculum he set for himself. In his free time he would take long walks with one of the assistant masters, a man called Harris. 'I insisted on a pace of four miles an hour,' wrote Wells. 'During this pedestrianism we talked in gasping shouts.'[13] No doubt Harris was doing most of the listening. It was an exceedingly gratifying time for Wells. His butterfly mind would land on one subject, extract all the value and interest it held for him and then search for another source of nourishment and challenge.

By the time Wells was eighteen, only a year after he had arrived at Midhurst, he had exhausted all that the school had to offer. A new opportunity arose for him in the form of a national plan to promote the teaching and learning of science.[14] Exams were organized for each school with a graduate headmaster. Byatt entered Wells for every subject he could and was not disappointed, for Wells performed so well on the examination that he was invited to apply to the Normal School of Science in London. He was readily accepted, and awarded a grant of one guinea per week. Such good fortune seemed beyond reality. Furthermore, the college at South Kensington was home to T.H. Huxley, the foremost scientific thinker and teacher in the country. Wells was ecstatic, to say the least. At eighteen he was ready indeed for London's ample welcome.

2 The Shaping of a Life

The London of 1884 was a cornucopian city. It was a period of apparently limitless urban expansion. Here was Conan Doyle's 'great cesspool into which all the loungers and idlers of the Empire are irresistibly drained ... the great wilderness of London'.[1] Many of the more egregious aspects of metropolitan poverty had changed little since Henry Mayhew's monumental report.[2] His descriptions of child destitution particularly affected the Victorian reading classes, with their penchant for tales of the young. His seven-year-old watercress girls would rise before dawn to buy their product from the market, then patrol the streets, earning perhaps 3d per day. One of them explained.

I used to go to school, but I wasn't there long. I've forgot all about it now, it's such a long time ago; and my mother took me away because the master whacked me. He hit me across the face with his cane ... I always give mother my money, she's very good to me. She don't often beat me. She's very poor and goes out cleaning sometimes. I ain't got no father, he's a father-in-law. No; mother ain't married again – he's a father-in-law ... I don't have no dinner. Mother gives me two slices of bread-and-butter and a cup of tea for breakfast, and then I go to tea, and has the same.

To the gauche young man from Kent this was all far more, and far less, than he had anticipated. At the age of eighteen Wells was callow and cautious, a neophyte in London's swirl. He was a little underweight – not a hint of the corpulence of his later years – and had a scrawny, even cadaverous appearance. His skin was pale, as it would be until he was a very old man, and he looked at times almost feminine. He blushed very easily, and when he did he would often rub the back of his hand across his face to try to disguise his embarrassment. He was always nervous, always at the ready, never at ease or at rest, but fidgeting, scratching his head, crossing and uncrossing his legs, pacing, making fists and leaning backwards and forwards when he was sitting down. He had only the most meagre of wardrobes and was forced to wear grubby dark suits and worn shirt-collars. Wells would never be elegantly attired, but at this stage of his life he could barely afford a change of clothes. His hair too was usually unkempt, falling over his drawn face in a voluminous wave. A thin, gappy moustache completed the picture. But nothing could hide or obscure those flashing eyes, always shining and alive, speaking volumes. It was his eyes, friends as well as enemies said, that were irresistible, they were so full of curiosity, so full of promise. What he lacked in worldliness and stature he made up for in ambition and willingness. His self-esteem was contagious: he was, he believed, a hussar for the truth, and for the most part those who came into contact with him concurred.

In the Normal School of Science he had discovered his castle; indeed with its minarets and towers it physically resembled a bastion of his childhood imagination. Although founded as recently as 1879, the college had gained an international reputation as the epicentre for scientific education in Britain. As such it attracted aspiring scientists from all over the country, as well as parts of Europe and the Empire. It stood firmly and proudly, and arrogantly, on what it claimed were the unassailable truths of evolution, as well as on the teachings of its star professor, Thomas Henry Huxley.

Huxley, born in 1825, grew up in a society that held the world and its species to be God's creation. As a ship's surgeon he had worked extensively around Australia, studying marine life on the Barrier Reef, and became a Fellow of the Royal Society in 1851. Three years later he was Professor of Natural History at the Royal School of Mines. He was widely known as an educator of 'working men', adroit and at ease in explaining points of scientific difficulty to uneducated audiences. At the same time his essays, such as 'Evolution and Ethics', made a profound impression on intellectual and political leaders, including the confirmed and abrasive Christian, William Gladstone. First and foremost Huxley was a Darwinist, a friend of Darwin himself and known, affectionately and otherwise, by the sobriquet 'Darwin's bulldog'. It was Huxley who coined the term 'agnostic'. The other side to Huxley's character was less decorous. He was intolerant and choleric, with a proclivity towards arrogant and ill-informed dismissal of opposing views. Lacking Darwin's genius, he compensated with sheer bombast.

His charismatic ability to translate theory into an idiomatic vernacular was, of course, entirely seductive to the young Wells, who, like most eighteen-year-olds, was in need of a mentor and hero. Huxley was a valetudinarian by the time Wells arrived in London, so the newcomer was only able to take one course delivered by his idealized teacher before Huxley retired, but nevertheless the torch of 'scientific progress', as Wells saw it, had been passed. Wells' course with Professor Huxley was an intriguing hybrid of biology and zoology, spiced with plenty of personal recollection and opinion. Wells was genuinely mesmerized.

Throughout his first year at university, Wells was too poor to feed himself properly and was forced to adopt an asceticism with which he was severely uncomfortable. Yet he was determined to devote himself, at whatever cost, to academe. His sole friend was another student, A.V. Jennings, who, according to Wells, 'noted that I was getting perceptibly thinner and flimsier, and almost by force he carried me off to a chop house and stood me an exemplary square meal'.[3] Both men achieved fine results in their exams. In the winter competitions of 1885 Wells took a first in biology and advanced zoology, and a good second in botany.

When, however, T.H. Huxley retired the following year because of old age and exhaustion, for Wells the spell was broken. The terminally ill Professor Guthrie, a pallid and unsuccessful teacher, drifted from theme to theme, losing the attention of his class; teacher G.B. Howes was gifted, but lacked the authority and brilliance of Huxley. Wells' grades worsened steadily, as did his enthusiasm for his studies. He absented himself from the college and became a regular figure at the Dyce and Foster Reading Room in South Kensington, immersing himself in the writings of William Blake and Thomas Carlyle. The balance between science and letters was perceptibly tipping as Wells came to realize that his future as a science teacher was dim and his prospects as a scientific researcher almost non-existent. He was plagued by a roving mind, an inability to concentrate on one subject for very long. The year he spent at the college after the departure of Huxley was academically barren.

Wells was frustrated and even angry at what he saw as his lack of advance; he began to use a phrase which he repeated time and time again through his life and which characterized his ambition and drive, 'no step forward is two steps backward'. His butterfly mind would help him as a novelist, but it hindered him as a student. Yet it was not only the departure of the great Thomas Huxley which was distracting Wells the student. Two other factors played their part: political ambition and romance.

In 1887 Wells failed his final geology exam, more from indifference than lack of intelligence. The outcome was inevitable. He had spent valuable revision time at the college debating society, where although his oratorical skills left a great deal to be desired, Wells' sheer confidence and sense of purpose won him devotees and followers.

This was the era of the debate, when public speeches attracted tens of thousands, and windows were smashed by disappointed partisans unable to find room inside their chosen auditorium.[4] The speeches of nationally known authors were recorded in detail in contemporary periodicals, and frequently printed in book form. 'It was a period when the voice was the cutting edge of the intellect,' said Maurice Baring of Edwardian England.[5] It was also the heyday of socialist aspirations. For someone of Wells' frustrated talents and class origin some desire for political change was unavoidable. The labour movement in all of its many forms was abounding with the energy of the new, and because socialism was still untried it was the panacea of revealed truth for its followers. The culturally conservative working-class leaders of the trades unions, and patrician radicals of the self-proclaimed London intelligentsia, were busily painting an emollient gloss of Englishness over Marxist and mid-European ideology. It was this dashing, tempting atmosphere which captured Wells' thoughts now, when he should have been studying at the college library.

Wells was ever an uneasy combination of English nationalist and socialist cosmopolitan, and in the reformist groups of the 1880s he had discovered his natural habitat. He was attracted as much by the intellectual stimulation as the political activity. Wells revelled in an adult form of his schoolboy education: crammed, erratic and tipped with a dangerous unpredictability. He also relished the opportunity to stress and prove his importance. Socialist activists were relatively few; how abundantly necessary was Wells' participation in an inevitable struggle which would transform society and liberate haberdashers' apprentices everywhere. Nor was he easily discouraged. The punctilios of party dogma, and tedious conflicts of personalities, were meat and drink to a man who had endured long periods of loneliness and intellectual isolation. He received approbation and encouragement from those he had previously regarded as his 'betters'; an Oxford don and early socialist activist named Peterson described Wells as 'an example of the future of our movement, an example of a living reason for optimism'. They encouraged him to disseminate his views, and to do that he would have to write.

In 1885 he read his paper, 'The Past and Present of the Human Race', to the debating society, and next year a more serious piece on democratic socialism. In both he exhibited a powerful understanding of the repeated themes and flows of history, the cyclical, almost predictable nature of power struggles and social change. He read with more authority now, learning to control his volatile voice and use inflection and dramatic pauses to compensate for his lack of volume. He began to create an image for himself, combing his hair in a side parting, using oils to keep it in place. He wore a red flower in his buttonhole, even took to carrying a rather battered second-hand walking stick; he discarded the latter when one of his teachers asked, rhetorically, if Wells was in love. He was ambitious, and relished this new-found influence and power. In December 1886 the *Science Schools Journal* was formed by a coterie of like-minded students. Inevitably, Wells was asked to become its editor. Yet the dull and painful pattern of his early life refused to change. Once again, just as contentment and achievement were in his grasp, reality thrust itself in his way. The registrar of the college complained about his lack of attendance and criticized him for his political and journalistic distractions. As a consequence Wells was obliged to pass the editorship of the *Journal* on to another. He wept for two hours on the day he relinquished the editor's chair.

Wells' personal and emotional life had also taken on a momentum during the second half of his sojourn at the Normal School of Science. His mother had asked an old and trusted friend to give her son lodgings in London. Sarah had evidently been out of touch with this friend for quite some time, for the lodgings were not what Sarah or the young Wells expected. It was a house where moral standards were flexible, and Wells conducted a brief and rather untidy physical relationship with the owner's sister. There was much groping and hurried embraces but the affair was not consummated. He soon found a new home, however, run by an in-law of the Wells family. 'Aunt Mary', as the new landlady was known, was affectionate, maternal and smothering. She introduced Wells to her daughter, a comely girl named Isabel. He was instantly attracted to her. Isabel possessed a striking combination of innocence, grace and, perhaps most important for Wells, availability. They strolled together to her workplace, a small photographer's shop where Isabel worked as a retoucher. Walking became a mainstay of their relationship: through the crowded streets of London's West End, across Hyde Park and the sedate eighteenth-century squares of Bloomsbury, to the Euston Road and Regents Park.

'We were passionate allies who would conquer the world together,' Wells wrote. 'She did her best to follow me, though something uncontrollable in her whispered this was all nonsense.'[6] An ability to follow was an attribute Wells demanded, and assumed, in his women. Isabel was naive and trusting, in awe of this intellectual who lectured her on atheism and revolutionary change. The balance of the couple was appallingly wrong.

Two inexperienced young people drenched with the passions of first love were in no condition to accept rational objections. Wells was told by student friends that he was far too distracted from his studies, and that although he could not recapture early successes, there were still respectable exam results to be salvaged. He rejected their counsel, and left the Normal School of Science in 1887 after failing his exams. The failure did not affect him as it would have done a year earlier. Wells had fully assimilated the view that academic success no longer mattered to him.

Because he could not find a teaching position in London, he had to settle for a post in the little known Holt Academy in North Wales. For the time being at least he had no choice but to leave behind the socialist groups and literary magazines of the city, and of course Isabel, who would simply have to await his return.

Holt Academy had promised advanced educational facilities and a liberal approach to the teaching of science.[7] What Wells actually encountered were antediluvian attitudes and a school composed of decaying huts and inadequate buildings. The gloom of Wells' own primary education had been partially lifted at times by his own initiative, at times by a vivacious teacher. Not so at Holt Academy. The pupils were, in Wells' eyes, lower class and unruly; and Wells' only friend was a European anarchist and anti-Christian with a colourful and ignoble history, described by Wells as 'a cuckold maker, & all that is lovable in a comrade'.[8]

At least his workload at Holt was flexible. Wells had sufficient free time to read, and write. He worked on a selection of short stories and began work on his first real novel, *Lady Frankland's Companion*. His attitude towards writing was changing from casual interest into an addiction. It was not, however, the only addiction that took hold of him in North Wales. In August 1887 he wrote to a friend that his mood had changed and that there was now a reason for optimism. The reason's name was Annie Meredith, whom Wells described as 'a pretty girl, minister's daughter, teacher in a high school. When we met we were enchanted.' While the patient Isabel waited faithfully in London, Wells conducted a surreptitious love affair. It is doubtful that he even wrote to Isabel from Wales; he certainly displayed no contrition on returning to London. The relationship with Annie Meredith eventually broke apart on account of her religious and political commitments. Wells had for once encountered a strong woman who opposed his views; she took the initiative, and left him. Distraught and disillusioned, Wells set his mind to leaving Holt Academy.

Accident overtook intent. Commanded to take part in a rough-and-tumble football match, Wells was violently fouled. He lay on the ground for some time. When he left the pitch he began to vomit, then found that he was urinating copious quantities of blood. A doctor was called and though he could not diagnose the injury, he felt certain that Wells must be in agony. He in fact felt nothing at all, but was prepared to sham the pain in an effort to be invalided out of the school.

Pain, however, did eventually come. More doctors were called, who at first diagnosed tuberculosis, later changing their verdict to include a crushed kidney. The problem, which plagued Wells for over a decade, was never properly explained. London specialists told Wells that diabetes was a factor, and Wells himself thought he may have suffered from appendicitis while at Holt. Whatever the problem, it was evident that he could not remain at the school. If, however, he left Holt before the end of his annual contract he would forfeit the twenty pounds due for six months of teaching. Wells attempted to continue his work. It was hopeless. Within a week he was in a state of collapse. Once again, his mother extended her hand of sanctuary.

For four long months between the end of 1887 and the beginning of 1888 Wells was confined to his sick-bed, during which time he wrote a rather self-mocking, humorous letter entitled 'The House of the Captivity: Valley of the Shadow of Death', explaining to all who would listen that the nearness of death was a terrifying thing indeed.[9]

For nearly four months I was dying with immense dignity. Plutarch might have recorded it. I wrote – in touchingly unsteady pencil – to all my intimate friends and indeed to many other people. I saw the littleness of hate and ambition. I forgave my enemies and they were subdued and owned to it . . . [10]

With time on his hands he began to wonder, and worry, about his future. He contemplated setting up in some form of business with his mother's savings, but soon rejected this idea. He sent query letters to tenuous contacts, including his doctor at Uppark;[11] nobody offered either employment or charity.

By the middle of the year Wells' health was improving and by the late summer he was fit to travel and work. On arriving in London in 1888 he possessed a mere five pounds, and fewer prospects. He found lodgings for four shillings a week in Bloomsbury's Theobalds Road, in half a room with walls so thin that private conversation was impossible. He managed to find work as a tutor, filling empty heads with information, and increased his wages by hack work for some of the new mass circulation magazines in London. His first articles were often unsigned – the decision of the magazines, not of Wells – and were just as frequently hurriedly written and unedited. Gradually he spent more time on his writing and took it more seriously. His byline began to appear. 'I returned to my lodgings with the substance of an article,' he wrote in his autobiography of these first essays. 'My cousin Bertha Williams at Windsor was a typist and I sent the stuff for her to typewrite. Then I posted this to the *Pall Mall Gazette* and received a proof almost by return. I was already busy on a second article which was also accepted. Next I dug up a facetious paper I had written for the *Science Schools Journal* long ago, and rewrote it.'

Isabel was all the while still waiting for the renewal of their love affair. Wells seemed unwilling at first. She was left in a painful state of limbo, neither rejected nor embraced by her once and, as she confidently hoped, future lover. Wells had by this time lost his virginity, almost certainly to a London prostitute. His priapic nature was in full flourish now, and he sought out Isabel once again, to resume their affair. But she no longer saw Wells as the boy of their former courtship. Isabel may have been an innocent, as Wells thought, but she understood the financial demands of marriage and was used to a permanent, if meagre, social status. If the courtship was to continue and flourish, the surprisingly tenacious young woman explained, Wells first had to demonstrate his ability to maintain a household and sustain a job.

Wells solved the latter difficulty by taking a position at Henley House school in Kilburn. He would be paid sixty pounds a year to teach science and mathematics. He received partial board and was permitted to continue his informal studies for a BSc degree and teaching diploma. Henley was the first quality school Wells had encountered. It was run by J.V. Milne, whose son, A.A. Milne – creator of Winnie-The-Pooh – was one of Wells' pupils. A.A. Milne later wrote to his former teacher from Cambridge, asking for an article for the undergraduate magazine. He wondered if Wells could 'remember a small-sized boy with long hair to whom you taught at one time all the geology he never knew?'

A.A. Milne considered Wells a fine writer but a poor teacher. He was 'too clever and too impatient'. His impatience had much to do with the pressure from his coming final exams for his science degree. In July 1889 he took his Intermediates, receiving second-class honours in zoology; the next year he completed the course with a First. Fortune appeared to be moving in his direction. He was published in the highly regarded *Fortnightly Review* and was also offered employment with the University Correspondence College. The pay was over four pounds a week and the pace of the work could be altered according to Wells' alternative commitments. It was now time to put his mind to thoughts of marriage. This time, Isabel was ready to accept.

Wells and Isabel were married at Wandsworth Parish Church on 31 October 1891. They set up home just a few miles from the church. They faced enormous problems almost immediately after settling down to the realities of married life. Isabel was at times irresponsible with money and, though eager to please, was woefully unprepared for this new domesticity. And Wells seemed unable, physically and psychologically, to be faithful to any one woman. The more trusting and artless Isabel appeared, the more her husband exploited her pathetic assumptions of honesty. Wells admitted that 'after six engagement years of monogamic sincerity and essential faithfulness I embarked as soon as I was married upon an enterprising promiscuity ... The old love wasn't at all dead, but I meant now to get in all the minor and incidental love adventures I could.'[12]

This egregious state of affairs reached its nadir when Wells' aunt was temporarily living with the couple. She came home early one day to discover her nephew with a colleague of Isabel's from the photographer's shop, a young woman named Ethel Kingsmill. If the relative was not aware of the circumstances, she would discover the truth before very long; Wells was not ashamed to boast of his conquests.

Wells' adultery was not the sole problem. He abused Isabel emotionally from the first month of their marriage. This abuse would take many forms. Wells would read a newspaper or magazine article that angered him and demand that Isabel agree with him. Her response would be to accept meekly, without comment, Wells' bombastic opinions. Again, Wells would shout and scream at her, ordering her to assume the passion and enlightenment that he had cultivated in himself with such determination over the years. Quarrelling, he believed, was not an anomaly but a pleasurable requirement: 'In the first place and mainly, it is hygienic to quarrel, it disengages floods of nervous energy, the pulse quickens, the breathing is accelerated, the digestion improved. Then it sets one's stagnant brain astir and quickens the imagination.'[13]

Wells rapidly came to understand that he had married a woman who could not help him reach the higher rungs of the literary and political ladder. She was uncomfortable in social settings, had no small talk and would never be the dinner party hostess so vital and common to the late Victorian and Edwardian male literati. And the more Wells aspired to be a part of that elite of literati, the more he realized that it could not be done with Isabel by his side. 'There was no contact nor comparison between our imaginative worlds,' he wrote. 'She could not understand why I mocked and fretted perpetually . . . My unaccountable irritability was a perpetual threat to our peace.'

In one of Wells' classes there was an intelligent and inquiring young woman named Amy Catherine Robbins. She was anxious to learn and, more importantly, anxious to learn from Wells. He gave her private tuition outside the classroom. The juxtaposition of the awkward, fatuous Isabel and the serious, aspiring Catherine emphasized Wells' frustration. He repeated elements of the court-ship of Isabel: he and Catherine would travel home together, they would walk and talk. The budding romance was interrupted, however, by another injury to Wells' health. Walking to Charing Cross one day he began to feel faint, then frightened; when he coughed, he found his mouth was full of fresh blood. He rushed home, where the doctor was summoned at once. Ice-packs and Isabel's good care restored his health, but during his convalescence he had had time to think. Although it was Isabel who sat patiently by his bed and transformed herself into his nurse and his maid, it was Catherine who occupied his waking and sleeping thoughts. He wrote several notes to her, one of which was headed with an affectionate cartoon of the pyjama-clad Wells sitting up in his bed: 'Your unworthy teacher of biology is still – poor fellow – keeping recumbent, though he knows his ceiling pretty well by this time, but no doubt he is a-healing and by Saturday he will be, he hopes, put out in the front parlour in the afternoon.'[14] Isabel added a somewhat pathetic postscript, explaining that Mr Wells would be confined until Sunday.

In January 1894 Wells left Isabel to be with Catherine. 'We were both in reality in flight from conditions of intolerably narrow living,' he wrote in his autobiography, in an attempt to objectify his actions. 'But we did not know how to state that properly, we were not altogether clear about it, and we caught at the phrasing of Shelley and the assumption of an imperative passion.' Perhaps he had believed that Isabel was aware of his goings on and would accept the break with resignation. If so, he was wrong. She was crushed by the betrayal and would take years to recover from the trauma. Catherine Robbins' mother was so ashamed that her daughter could have become involved in so duplicitous and dirty an affair that she broke down, and fell victim to a coma. Wells tried to explain to Isabel that he had not left her for ever and begged her not to divorce him. Such was his domination over his wife that she went so far as to apologize for disappointing him and promised to try harder to be a good wife in the future. But there was no turning back, and a messy and mutually painful divorce took place. Wells was never really in any doubt: he and Catherine shared an ambition to achieve things, to make their mark. It was only Wells, however, who would succeed.

It took time for Wells to begin a professional writing career. He had drifted around the semi-professional teaching community long enough to realize that teaching was the wrong profession for him: it was far too time-consuming, paid very little and did not bring him into contact with any members of the wider literary community. Writing assignments came gradually at first. The role of journalist moved towards him like an unscheduled steam engine, sometimes rushing from station to station with whirling speed, occasionally stopping between stations for annoyingly long and inexplicable periods. But with an intellectual such as Catherine by his side Wells felt sufficiently confident to take on London journalism from the front. Quantity, he knew, was as important as quality in making him known to magazine editors. Byline was everything.

He had read J.M. Barrie's *When a Man's Single* while recovering from his last bout of illness, and the book left an indelible impression on him. Barrie revealed the esoteric secrets of freelance writing in his account of his time at the *Nottinghamshire Journal* and his subsequent magazine writing. He explained that international travel and experience of wealth and power were not necessary for a young journalist. Ignore the great and grand movements of life, wrote Barrie; instead, concentrate on the everyday events of your own existence: these accounts will sell. Like the writings of Dylan Thomas some sixty years later, Barrie's words gave working-class writers an exemplary alternative to the patrician style. The book irrevocably altered Wells' style of writing and gave him confidence in his own prose and grasp of the language. No longer did he write for an imaginary audience composed of university professors and literary critics, but for himself and his peers. He threw off his stylistic mask and let his ideas and imagination speak for themselves.

The *Pall Mall Gazette* was eager to publish Wells' efforts, and Wells was eager to write for the paper. It had, after all, published the writing of Anthony Trollope and Matthew Arnold. Wells became a regular, almost weekly contributor for a brief period. But under its new editor, William Thomas Stead, the paper had lost some of its reputation. Wells was even more avid to appear in the pages of Frank Harris's *Saturday Review*, but Harris did not initially return the enthusiasm. Wells' first meeting with the mercurial editor did not go well. Having submitted a manuscript earlier, Wells went to the editorial offices of the *Saturday Review* in a morning coat and silk hat. He had to wait over an hour for Harris and by the time he was shown into his office he realized that his hat was curling and sweat was dripping down his back. Harris threw the manuscript at Wells, demanding to know what he had meant by all of his scientific pretensions. Stunned, Wells did not attempt to answer; he left the office and beat his hat into a shapeless mess. The hat suffered needlessly. Harris came to his senses when his staff read the Wells manuscript, changed his opinion of the badly dressed young man, and arranged for another meeting. Wells was soon writing for the *Saturday Review*.

Harris's patronage could not have been more fortunate. The *Pall Mall Gazette* lost interest in Wells once its new editor was in place. Wells knew, as did all freelance writers of the era, that the only constants in the industry were books. Editors could change. Magazines and newspapers could die in a night. Wells began thinking of expanding some of his stories to book length. The former editor of the *National Observer*, William Ernest Henley, proved to be an even more important contact. Wells told him about a piece he had written for the *Science Schools Journal*; it bore the incongruously literary title, 'Chronic Argonauts'. Unlike Frank Harris, Henley could tolerate Wells' scientific pretensions and was particularly intrigued by the story's theme of time travel. Henley promised Wells employment on his next magazine. When he took over the editorship of the prestigious literary journal *The New Review* in 1895, he kept his word and immediately asked Wells for the latest version of his scientific fantasy story.

Wells had revised the story at least five times before it reached the far-sighted patron at *The New Review*, but he was still dissatisfied with its shape. Henley, however, had no such anxieties. He had discovered raw talent in the past and took a pride in knowing when to act decisively. A dramatist and editor for a number of years, he had also collaborated with Robert Louis Stevenson. (With one of his feet amputated as a result of tubercular arthritis he was the inspiration for Long John Silver in *Treasure Island*.) Stevenson's descriptive nickname for him was 'Burly'; others spoke of a High Tory of imperialist views and altruistic ways.[15]

Henley's influence on Wells' career cannot be overestimated. He wrote to his young contributor, offering 100 pounds for what would become *The Time Machine*. More than this, he took the liberty of approaching publisher William Heinemann, who eventually paid fifty pounds for the book rights, with a commitment to a first edition of 10,000 and a generous royalty of fifteen per cent. Henley's faith in this little known author was remarkable. Wells was twenty-eight years old, one of a plethora of struggling authors. He was living far from the hub of literary life, in the small town of Sevenoaks, Kent, where he and Catherine had taken sanctuary from London, past relationships and gossip. His appearance was lacklustre, his physical presentation shabby and forgettable. A payment of 100 pounds from a respected magazine to an unknown demanded a great deal of editorial commitment and risk.

Wells was staggered. His capital was trebled overnight. His confidence multiplied. He now felt free to pour out his imagination on the page before him, knowing that publishers and editors would treat his work as the product of a recognized author, not as the hopeful scribblings of a needy journalist. It was as though the floodgates of his mind suddenly swung open, and no power could shut them.

The Time Machine represented Wells' early energies and enthusiasms at their most productive and fertile. The theme of time travel was not new, but in Wells' hands it became accessible and gripping; more than this, it was a metaphor, and a warning. The Time Traveller of the work is given no name, and little description, but he manages to grasp the reader's interest and sympathy almost immediately. In his time-travelling invention he witnesses many future ages, but the most important, and that which receives most attention in the book, is the age of the Eloi and the Morlocks. These two races are descendants of contemporary humanity, living in the year AD 802,701. The former is refined and decadent, to the point where its members have no will or resistance. The other, forced to toil beneath the surface like its proletarian ancestors, has reversed the class equation and feeds on the flesh of the effete surface-dwellers. Wells couched all of this within a story of romance, adventure and individual courage, but the message remained constant. Mankind was not guaranteed a hopeful future, and unless the exploitation of one class of society by another was stopped, any and every future savagery was possible. The hero's closest friend ponders this as he laments the Time Traveller's final disappearance:

One cannot choose but wonder. Will he ever return? It may be that he swept back into the past, and fell among the blood-drinking hairy savages of the Age of Unpolished Stone; into the abysses of the Cretaceous Sea; or among the grotesque saurians, the huge reptilian brutes of the Jurassic times. [He continues:] Or did he go forward, into one of the nearer ages, in which men are still men, but with the riddles of our own time answered and its wearisome problems solved? . . . He, I know — for the question has been discussed among us long before the Time Machine was made — thought but cheerlessly of the Advancement of Mankind, and saw the growing pile of civilization only a foolish heaping that must inevitably fall back upon and destroy its makers in the end. If that is so, it remains for us to live as though it were not so.

The book was written with a delicacy and passion which Wells rarely, if ever, duplicated. The Anglo-Jewish author and activist Israel Zangwill — who would later ostracize Wells because of his remarks about the Jewish people — reviewed the book in the *Pall Mall Magazine*: 'In his brilliant little romance *The Time Machine* Mr Wells has inclined to the severer and more scientific form of prophecy — to the notion of a humanity degenerating inevitably from sheer pleasure of physical comfort . . . There is a good deal of what Tyndall would have called "scientific imagination" in Mr Wells' further vision of the latter end of all things, a vision far more sombre and impressive than the ancient imaginings of the Biblical seers.' R.H. Hutton in *The Spectator* referred to 'a very clever story as to the conditions of this planet in the year 802,701 AD'.

The response was enormous, and enormously favourable, and spurred the author into other projects. Wells worked hard on *The Island of Dr Moreau*, putting flesh to the characters and themes he had conceived in the fields of Bromley and the library at Uppark. Let science have its barbaric but beautiful way with literature, he repeated to himself, and the characters and plots would spring forth with uncontrollable rapidity. His output was prolific. The quirky Frank Harris was now prepared to give Wells frequent work on the *Saturday Review*; another journal offered him the post of theatre critic. After publication of *The Time Machine* in the summer of 1895 came *Select Conversations with an Uncle*. In September came *The Wonderful Visit*, followed shortly by *The Stolen Bacillus and other Incidents*. The critics who had adored the first work were less splendid in their praise of the following three volumes and began to express their concern about such productivity. They were unaware that these books were manifestations of already structured and half-formed manuscripts, mostly worked on and reworked in the past two years. In the following two years came *The Island of Dr Moreau*, *The Invisible Man* and *The War of the Worlds*.

The War of the Worlds, like *The Time Machine*, is not a work of characters and relationships, but totally one of plot and concept. Before the protagonist was the anonymous Time Traveller, now he is The Narrator. He is an innocent, caught up in a chain of events which he can only observe and try to escape. When a force of Martian invaders lands near his home, he is able to record their takeover of the country from beginning to end. Wells cleverly places the action in London and southern English settings, heightening the terror through familiarity and realism. The sense of claustrophobia in the tale is smothering and constant. Once again the nightmare is evoked of the consumption of human flesh – this time not by deformed cousins of the human race, but by alien invaders. The Martians sweep all before them, destroying the best of human scientific and moral resistance with contemptuous ease. Wells inserts into his story the character of a weak curate, who is eventually killed by The Narrator when his screams threaten to give their hiding place away. The invaders are finally beaten not by human ingenuity, but by unseen bacteria, innocuous to humans but deadly to the non-immune Martians.

Wells draws the historical moral that, terrifying and murderous as the aliens were, our encounter with them led us to scientific advances. The underlying lesson of the book, however, is an ethical one. He reminds us that our strength is as nothing to that of others, just as the strength of the colonized peoples of the world is as nothing to that of the European and North American nations. Wells' Narrator reflects of the Martians:

And before we judge them too harshly, we must remember what ruthless and utter destruction our own species has wrought, not only on animals, such as the vanished bison and dodo, but upon its own inferior races. The Tasmanians, in spite of their human likeness, were swept out of existence in a war of extermination waged by European immigrants, in the space of fifty years. Are we such apostles of mercy as to complain if the Martians warred in the same spirit?

Most reviews were supportive but some commentators disliked the tone of the work. One of Wells' least favourite reviews of the book was from the *Critic* in the United States in April 1898 and was in reality quite sympathetic. The piece smelt, he said, of snobbery and misunderstanding. It concluded with: 'The author has written an ingenious and original work. Now and again in the intervals of a colloquial or hysterical style, one comes upon passages of sweetness and virility. The book has the tone of intense modernity, with notes of convincing realism and morbid horror. One misses the simplicity of Gulliver and the epic impressiveness of the stories of Sodom and Mt Carmel. It is an Associated Press dispatch, describing a universal nightmare.'

The plot of *The Invisible Man* again places the extraordinary within the confines of the most ordinary. A young scientist named Griffin discovers the secret of becoming invisible and soon realizes that there are at least as many disadvantages as advantages to the gift: he is bumped and jostled by people in the street, almost run over. Wells was extending and exploding arguments based on the 'if only' dream which he would later apply to a man whose wish was to lose weight: his desire was granted but his body size remained the same, with consequent disasters. Griffin experiences a series of adventures and commits a series of crimes. The piece is an entertainment, with the caveat that science is a weapon, and must be safeguarded lest unscrupulous people exploit it for their own ends. Clement Shorter in a self-contradictory piece in the *Bookman* in October 1897 thought that the story was 'bound to be popular, has not a suspicion of preaching about it, and in a quite unpretentious way will help to pass an amusing hour or so. I have not been fascinated by a new book for many a day.'

The Island of Dr Moreau is perhaps Wells' most terrifying and successful book; successful because it conveys horror and suffering more effectively than anything else Wells ever wrote, and with more verisimilitude than the writings of most other authors. Edward Prendick is the victim of a shipwreck. He manages to find shelter on an island inhabited by a gifted scientist driven out of

Britain as a pariah. Dr Moreau has taken the science of vivisection and animal experimentation to its most extreme degree; on the island he has turned animals into semi-humans, grotesque and pathetic half-replicas known as Beast Folk. The wretched beings are tormented and threatened, terrified of 'The House of Pain' where Moreau conducts his gruesome operations. They occupy a twilight world, making the haunting sounds of agonized animals, but attempting to stand upright and live as humans. The creatures eventually revert to their animal state and kill Moreau. Prendick is forced to live as one of them for some months, until he manages to escape and return to the civilized world. He says:

I could not persuade myself that the men and women I met were not also another, still passably human, Beast People, animals half-wrought into the outward image of human souls, and that they would presently begin to revert, to show first this bestial mark and then that . . . I feel as though the animal was surging up through them; that presently the degradation of the Islanders will be played over again on a larger scale.

The book was acclaimed, if misunderstood. Wells had written more than a consummate horror story; he had attacked the creational theories of the Church and proclaimed the bestial aspect within mankind. He was chagrined at its popular misinterpretation, but the book's sales and the public profile it won him, coming so rapidly after the previous two, eased his disappointment.

This was, in fact, success unbridled. Wells had found his voice and was shouting loud and regularly. This was the most fertile period of his artistic life and never again would he equal such a consistently fine output of fiction. With success came money, respect and, most of all, confidence. He began to spread his wings, attended musical concerns and art galleries, and asked his contacts on newspapers and in publishing to get his name put on to the various fashionable party lists. Success also meant that he and Catherine were able to marry, on 27 October 1895, and set up house. Wells acquired an agent, James Brand Pinker, and an expanding set of literary friends. The speed of all of this perplexed Catherine. She knew her new husband too well, and understood his inability to remain in one place or with one person for very long. She evidently decided to compromise all the way to submission in order to keep her man. Wells arbitrarily decided that he no longer cared for her name Catherine and that from now on his wife would be known as Jane. It was not a request but a fiat. Jane accepted without complaint.

Wells' marriage with Jane was a success if measured in years; as a partnership, however, it was a bitter failure. She was humiliated by her husband from the second year of their time together until her death in 1927. His innumerable sexual affairs became so infamous and so expected that Jane Wells was at times a virtual prisoner in her own home, intimidated by the gossip of London. She was 'poor Jane' and 'silly Jane' to most of Wells' friends, and all of his enemies. It is telling that even her sympathizers used the name given her by Wells himself.*

The feminist critic and novelist Dorothy Richardson, who became an intimate of Wells and a close friend of the family,[16] depicted a married couple in one of her novels, with striking resemblances to Wells and Jane. Wells, at first, denied any authenticity in the portrait, but later admitted that it was unnervingly accurate. The hostess of the novel is anxiously busy when guests arrive at her home. She appears to be foolish, timorous and nervous about how she is regarded. She potters around as her husband holds court. The assembled company compete for attention, each presenting their own weapons of wit and awaiting a verbal parry. The husband remains in the middle, supervising the barbed merriment and ensuring that his own puns and mimicry gain the most approval. He throws comments tipped with vitriol at his ill-at-ease wife, and expects no defence. There is tangible tension between the two, but no balance. She is dominated and harassed by her husband. The author of the book sees through the frail curtain and is 'overcome by painful visions of the two at breakfast, or going home after social occasions'.

In *Mr Britling Sees It Through*, Wells wrote of a woman who was almost certainly his long-suffering wife: 'She went through life outwardly serene and dignified, one of a great company of rather fastidious, rather unenterprising women who have turned

---

* In most biographies of Wells, including the central texts by David C. Smith, and Norman and Jeanne MacKenzie, the index reference is for Jane Wells (née Amy Catherine Robbins). Anthony West uses 'Wells, Amy Catherine Robbins (Jane)'.

for their happiness to secondary things, to those fair inanimate things of household and garden.' Jane had been forced to change, to transform herself into a factotum for her husband. The ambitious young thinker anxious to record her thoughts on paper was now a combination of literary agent, secretary, accountant and maid. She was even asked eventually to referee between her husband's rival mistresses, but was still required to wait patiently for Wells' inevitable return from these sordid and shattering infidelities. Wells often humiliated her in public as well; he once told an assembled group of friends, in his wife's presence, that a man should see the world and leave everything behind, 'wife, and child and things; go all over the world and come back experienced'. One incredulous listener asked the fate of the hapless wives. The reply: they 'will go to heaven when they die'.[17]

Wells needed women as a thirsty man needs water: less for sensual pleasure than to fill a physical requirement. To Wells this meant that women could be used when and where necessary. Many of them were, to be sure, willing partners, but few of them escaped their trysts without pain and a sense of being exploited. 'I met some, in fact many, of Wells' women,' stated J.B. Priestley, 'and all of them were scarred by a sort of love and hate attitude towards Wells. He had never been less than exciting, but also never less than hurtful. From most of them, including I think Rebecca West, I got a sense that they felt used, even abused.'[18]

Jane claimed that she understood her husband's cravings. She understood more. Wells, she had discovered, was emotionally dependent on female approbation and adoration. If any wife has fulfilled the role of loving mother it was Jane Wells. When he returned battered from a scathing criticism, a lost debate or a stinging row with another woman, Jane held out her arms for his succour and stability. Home was safe, Jane was safe, and with her Wells was safe. A son, George Philip, was born in 1901, and another child, Frank Richard, in 1903. His family's growth only confirmed Wells' restless feelings. Family was contrary to excitement, to sexuality. For both of these things Wells would roam far and wide, but for lasting security he made his way home.

Wells was in demand in London now, a cynosure at the social functions of publishers and editors. He was something of an enigma, a man who had materialized from nowhere to develop and expand a genre. His fiction was filled with dazzling possibilities, and terrifying probabilities. Beginning with the publication of *The Time Machine* in 1895, his name appeared in print at least weekly, often every other day. He was described as the English Jules Verne, though the title does neither man justice. Wells' claustrophobic accounts of things to come and things that might be had a basis not in adventure, but in speculation. His scientific fantasy was a literary device used to explore social and political questions. For instance, his Time Traveller witnessed an extension of the class divisions of late nineteenth-century Britain; the book was an indictment of class as much as a journey into the future. *The War of the Worlds* parodied imperialism and the use of amoral power, reminding his countrymen, whose conquests encircled the globe, that there was always a force mightier than they. He based *The Island of Dr Moreau* on the theory of evolution, vividly portraying the agony of physical and spiritual development. *The Invisible Man* shows man exploiting miraculous gifts without ethical reference. The theme which flows through Wells' early work, which binds and even transcends these stories, is the desire for mankind to challenge ancient assumptions. Neither biological nor sociological limitations, argued Wells, are carved in stone. Change was the essence of his vision, and he was determined to spread it, to write more and more. But his self-imposed workload was almost killing him.

In 1897 Wells had at least three breakdowns. The thirty-one-year-old author was ordered by doctors to take a complete rest. His kidney, which was troubling him, might have to be operated on, they warned. Such surgery was difficult and hazardous. Wells obeyed medical orders for a short while, but before long threw himself back into the maelstrom. He often worked at his desk for six or seven hours at a time, with only one break for some sweet and milky tea and some bread and butter. He would shout to Jane or a maid for 'tea and toast, tea and toast', without even looking up from his papers. Wells wrote quickly – often too quickly – and worked on three or four projects at a time. But he was a bad editor, loathed revision, and consequently let howlers creep into his writing. Very few authors, however, have equalled his output. He was capable of starting work before dawn, writing till mid-afternoon, and then going to a restaurant to meet a group of friends.[19]

Wells always placed great importance on his friendships,

although he sometime made it difficult for his friends to return the affection. He now numbered amongst his friends some of the leading writers in Britain, men like George Gissing, Joseph Conrad and J.M. Barrie. Gissing, who was nine years older than Wells, had been particularly impressed with Wells' early story, *The Wheels of Chance*, and was intent on meeting its author. Educated in Lancashire, as a young man Gissing had been caught stealing and been sent to prison for a month. He left England for the United States, but his search was never really geographical. He believed in his literary vocation with such passion that he expressed his confidence as crass arrogance. Although he was a notable writer with a good ear and a fresh style, he found it very difficult to make a living, partly because he refused to write for the more lucrative periodicals, partly because he refused to adapt his work to publishers' and editors' demands. Poverty trailed him, and his personality drove friends from his side. He was twice married to working-class women, whom 'he expected to be eager and grateful' according to Wells. By the time the two men met Gissing had already published seventeen books, but was still in financial crisis and professional and personal trauma. 'It was as natural that my father befriend Gissing,' wrote Anthony West, 'as day follows night.'[20] Wells was one of Gissing's few true friends in London's literary community, but their friendship was disastrous for both of them. In many ways they were too much alike, reflecting each other's errors, especially in their attitudes towards their lovers. They provided each other with moral support when forthright censure would have been appropriate.

Wells' friendship with his agent, Pinker, was often much less harmonious, vacillating between affection and discord. Because of the sales of Wells' books, any agent in the country would have welcomed him as a client. He was not, however, an easy man to deal with. Because of his parents' financial troubles during his childhood, Wells dreaded poverty. He was determined never to be in need. He inundated Pinker with requests for larger book advances, greater royalties and more substantial payments for articles and columns. When Wells wanted to build a house it was up to Pinker, he thought, to come up with the money. Pinker could never do enough to satisfy him.

Wells became increasingly demanding with those around him, increasingly high-strung and nervous, until in early 1899 he had another severe breakdown and had to be confined to bed.[21] Periods of intense activity followed by some form of physical, mental or emotional collapse had become a regular pattern in his life. It was as if a safety valve, a fuse, was incorporated into his character.

It was while Wells was convalescing from this latest attack in New Romney that he became friends with four of the most important and influential writers of the time: Edmund Gosse, Henry James, Joseph Conrad and J.M. Barrie. A quintessentially Edwardian image is one of James and Gosse riding on their bicycles to see Wells on his sick-bed. These men represented the literary era with an unrivalled precision: Gosse, the critic, splendid in his certainty of what was acceptable, what was not; James, the American who adopted Europe, believing in the nobility and responsibility of his craft. J.M. Barrie was the little author who refused to grow up; he wrote, as did Kenneth Grahame, for those who lamented the passing of the times. Wells, for his part, was the shock-trooper of the new political journalism, writing not for the few but for the many. And then there was Joseph Conrad. He was somehow the best of them, the most pristine, the most triumphant. Wells envied Conrad's internationalism, his mastery of languages and his travel and adventure. It was Conrad who encouraged Wells to put down roots, to buy a house of his own and establish a base from which to work, and play.

The literary critic and chronicler Frank Swinnerton recorded an anecdote about the group. Wells, Gissing and Barrie were playing cards – a form of poker, Swinnerton believes – and Gissing was easily winning. After four hours Barrie, the least enthusiastic of the trio, suggested that the game end. No, said Wells, we continue. Another three hours passed and once again Barrie asked for a halt. Again Wells refused. Finally, as dawn on the following day came, Barrie slammed his cards on to the table and walked to the sofa in the corner of the room to rest. Gissing had remained silent through all of this, and had not lost a penny. Even he, however, had begun to wilt by breakfast time, and stood up as if to end the game. Where are you off to? demanded Wells. The game is over, replied Gissing. Then you give in, you give in, from Wells. No, I've taken all of your money, from Gissing. But Wells was insistent. If you leave the table, even if you take all my money, you lose the game. Do you agree? Gissing, exhausted but richer, agreed. Wells stood up and threw his arms in the air. I have won, he shouted, I have won.

The building of Spade House on the Kent coast began in 1899, but was interrupted repeatedly by Wells' running arguments with the architect and builder. For example, Wells wanted every door and banister in the house to be designed either in the shape of a spade or with a spade motif within it. The builder thought this was too expensive, time-consuming and perhaps a trifle vulgar. He was promptly dismissed and a second construction firm was found. This time the work went ahead, uninterrupted for the most part. The opulence of Spade House reflected Wells' blooming confidence; its completion depended entirely upon his literary success. Its building cost close to 3,000 pounds, a small fortune.

Magazine articles and royalties were clearly insufficient for such ambitious designs as these, and this undoubtedly increased the pressure on Wells to write more books. *The First Men in the Moon* was published in 1901 and earned him more money than either he or his agent had expected. The book represents a vehement condemnation of the imperialist tenets of its protagonists. The story is narrated by a hopeful playwright and failed businessman, Mr Bedford. Together with Cavor, an eccentric scientist who has discovered how to break the laws of gravity, Bedford journeys to the moon, where they encounter a race of inhabitants utterly utilitarian in that they exist only to work in a specific job and when their services are no longer required they simply lie supine on the ground. Bedford, who realizes that the moon is full of gold, returns to earth to spend his fortune. Cavor, the man of science, remains among the moon-dwellers, eventually sending messages to earth. There is an obvious dichotomy between the man of wealth and the man of science. It is the former who delivers an eloquent parody of the book of Genesis, when he first sees the surface of the moon:

So, one must imagine, the trees and plants arose at the Creation and covered the desolation of the new-made earth.
  Imagine it! Imagine the dawn! The resurrection of the frozen air, the stirring and quickening of the soil, and then this silent uprising of vegetation, this unearthly ascent of fleshiness and spikes. Conceive it all lit by a blaze that would make the intensest sunlight of earth seem watery and weak. And still around this stirring jungle, wherever there was a shadow, lingered banks of the bluish snow.

Reviewers greeted the book with praise – though Jules Verne was highly critical of it – but added that it was surely time for

Wells to attempt more orthodox work. Typically, he took this criticism to heart. The time was ripe, his friends assured him, to outline his political ideas to the public. There was no longer any need for him to use scientific fantasy as a disguise or a device. Wells was convinced. He began to put in order political and sociological papers and notes which he had accumulated during the last five years. He was determined to stake his claim as a political philosopher and a social commentator who had to be taken very seriously indeed.[22]

3 Anticipating Utopia

Wells published the purest and most succinct account of his ideal political system in 1901. He called it *Anticipations*. It was 'the keystone to the main arch of my work', he explained, and indeed it was. *Anticipations* presented a novel and terrifying picture of a Wellsian utopia. He believed the imagined and desired society he envisaged there would come about within ten years.

The book begins with a long, somewhat tedious analysis of the history and future of locomotion, and goes on to discuss war, social relations and democracy. It is, however, in the crucial and intricate section entitled 'The Faith, Morals and Public Policy of the New Republic' that Wells explores his idealized future. Liberal democracy, he believed, was moribund. When it finally succumbed to the catharsis of historical forces, a new, polished and ethical society would emerge. A renascent class would come to rule, a people 'adapted to the big-scale conditions of the new time . . . an unprecedented sort of people'.

Here was the swirling hybrid of predestinarian and Marxist gleanings and his own radical ideas which Wells had been groping towards in his earlier books. The idea was that one part of the world's population would benefit by killing or enslaving the rest. Civil, economic and political freedom would be severely limited and controlled; racial and social homogeneity would be enforced; the omnipotent state would, by a combination of education and social engineering, produce a world of content and obedient citizens.

This was an extension of the Darwinist theory of evolution through the survival of the fittest, and of a perverse form of utilitarianism and the idea of the greatest good for the greatest number. Both of these theories Wells had eagerly consumed as a teenager and a student, but he adapted them without the moral reference or foundation of Charles Darwin or Jeremy Bentham. Moreover, he had been brought up with his mother's belief in predestination and the God-given right and duty – in fact the theological inevitability – of the rule of the saints. The sentiments contained in these writings were heartfelt, and the product of much thought and reflection. 'Wells didn't think that he was a pessimist, far from it,' wrote J.B. Priestley:[1]

In fact he believed that social engineering was the most optimistic and positive philosophy there was at the time. With hindsight the material contained in *Anticipations* is awful; if we are honest, it was awful when it was written. Yet to some degree it was a product of fashion, of the Edwardian obsession with building a better future, instead of standing by and waiting for things to happen. We only learnt our lessons later.

After the collapse of the established order, a pristine successor would take its place. Wells wrote of the composition of the new order, and of its policies to benefit humanity:

And the ethical system which will dominate the world-state will be shaped primarily to favour the procreation of what is fine and efficient and beautiful in humanity – beautiful and strong bodies, clear and powerful minds, and a growing body of knowledge – and to check the procreation of base and servile types, of fear-driven and cowardly souls, of all that is mean and ugly and bestial in the souls, bodies and habits of men . . . the method that has only one alternative, the method that must in some cases still be called in to the help of man, is death . . . For a multitude of contemptible and silly creatures, fear-driven and helpless and useless, unhappy or hatefully happy in the midst of squalid dishonour, feeble, ugly, inefficient, born of unrestrained lusts, and increasing and multiplying through sheer incontinence and stupidity, the men of the New Republic will have little pity and less benevolence.

Behind the despots of this cleansed state would stand the young, uniformly supportive of the new order and described in a later work as 'boys and girls and youths and maidens, full of the zest of new life, full of an abundant joyful receptivity'. Such rhetoric appears repeatedly throughout the extended chapter, particularly in the context of Wells' ideas on race.

For the most part Wells believed that 'lower' peoples would die out by what the historian Philip Guedalla later described as 'pseudo-natural causes', such as diseases, plagues and their own inability to survive. To ensure such a result the leaders of the New Republic would 'contrive a land legislation that will keep the black or yellow or mean-white squatter on the move'. He goes on to ask: 'And how will the New Republic treat the inferior races? How will it deal with the black? how will it deal with the yellow man? how will it tackle that alleged termite in the civilized world, the Jew?' The question is posed for rhetorical effect, of course, and Wells does not hesitate to answer it. Undesirables would be discouraged, by any means necessary, from procreation.

The Jew, who 'ages and dies sooner than the average European', possesses an 'incurable tendency to social parasitism', and particular care must be taken to expunge any traces of racial identity and pride or religious faith from world Jewry. Later on Wells had more to say about the Jewish people but it is relevant at this point to consider Malcolm Muggeridge's comment that Wells had read some of the works of the Anglo-German race theorist, proto-Nazi and anti-Semite, Houston Stewart Chamberlain. Muggeridge disagreed with J.B. Priestley about the essence of *Anticipations* and wrote that, 'although Wells was not a National Socialist, he told a group of students in 1938 that he had read some of Chamberlain's articles, and his book on Richard Wagner, before he had written *Anticipations*, and that he found some of these ideas – which are undoubtedly pagan – to be helpful. He went on to read, he explained, Chamberlain's *Foundations of the Nineteenth Century* at a later date.'[2]

Chamberlain's volume on Wagner was translated into English by G. Ainslie Hight in 1897, the year following its original German publication. His *Foundations of the Nineteenth Century* was published, also in Germany, in 1899, but its first English translation did not appear until as late as 1910. Chamberlain believed in 'improvement', and in the moral renewal of mankind; not of all men, however, but only the Teutonic race. Wells did not believe in this particular aspect of Chamberlain's ideology, but he did believe that it would be the English-speaking peoples who would lead and dominate the new order. Chamberlain applied the biological idea of species to human societies and races. 'Only thoroughbred races accomplish the extraordinary,' he wrote.[3] He stressed 'decadence and regeneration' and 'racial purity', and argued that if no master race had existed in the past, 'we are determined that there shall be one in the future.'[4] Muggeridge commented:

I do not see anything surprising in Wells adopting ideas of mass relocation and murder. He was a progressive in an era when progress, at least in the material sense, had come to a halt. The empire was in decay, class warfare was on the horizon and Wells believed that life on earth was the only life we had. Pretty bleak. So he opted for schemes which make us shudder today.[5]

It is tempting to believe that Wells was writing with irony when he described the wretched fate of so many people, these 'people of the abyss', or presented a scenario of the worst possibilities, warning his readers of what might befall mankind. This is not the case. Wells emphasized his point time and again in the book, making it clear that the races that did not fit into his elaborate plan had no place in the New Jerusalem:

And for the rest – those swarms of black and brown and yellow people who do not come into the needs of efficiency? Well, the world is not a charitable institution, and I take it they will have to go. The whole tenor and meaning of the world, as I see it, is that they have to go.

Peppered throughout the text are signs of the author's obsession with 'multiplication' of inadequates; the forced movement and isolation of ethnic, sexual, political and moral dissidents; the engineering of humanity so as to create one type of human being, acceptable to H.G. Wells. But there was more, and worse. 'This thing, this euthanasia of the weak and sensual, is possible,' he wrote. 'I have little or no doubt that in the future it will be planned and achieved.'

Nor were the punctilios of such slaughter ignored. In case any members of the elite resist their murderous destiny, they are to be reminded that there is an 'ideal that will make killing worth the while'. The people of his new order

will naturally regard the modest suicide of incurably melancholy or diseased or helpless persons as a high and courageous act of duty rather than a crime. . . . If deterrent punishments are used at all in the code of the future, the deterrent will be . . . good scientifically caused pain, that will leave nothing but a memory.

The lascivious and the lazy, the dark-skinned and the dreamers, the rebels and the religious, the unstable and the unhappy, and all who do not fit deftly into the eye of Wells' needle would be put to death. They may be allowed to live,

only on sufferance, out of pity and patience, and on the understanding that they do not propagate; and I do not foresee any reason to suppose that they [the New Republic's rulers] will hesitate to kill when that sufferance is abused. And I imagine also the plea and proof that a grave criminal is also insane will be regarded by them not as a reason for mercy, but as an added reason for death.

One of Wells' favourite reviews of his book appeared in the journal *Nature*, which stated:

It seems to me that this book should have – even for those whom it cannot fail to offend – more than the interest which attaches to clever fault-finding. It is, truly enough, an unsparing indictment of existing government, society, education, religion, and morality, but it contains also a confession of faith and is full of a spirit of hope and belief in future development.

Sidney Webb thought the book his favourite of the year, and Arnold Bennett was quite bowled over: 'I have been absolutely overwhelmed by the sheer intellectual vigour ... really made me a little afraid of you. Either you have in supreme degree the journalistic trick of seeming omniscience, or you are one of the most remarkable men alive.' Beatrice Webb recorded in her diary that the volume was filled with 'luminous hypotheses' and that it was 'the most remarkable book of the year; a powerful imagination furnished with the data and methods of physical science working on social problems.' Wells himself described *Anticipations* as 'designed to undermine and destroy the monarch, monogamy and respectability. One has to go quietly in the earlier papers, but the last will be a buster.'[6] He wrote to Sidney Dark that 'My biggest thing, my most intimate thing, my first line of battleships is *Anticipations*'.[7]

There were, however, many dissenting voices. The young G.K. Chesterton considered the book 'terrifying, if not horrifying. Mr Wells may be something of a genius, but within every genius there is an element of darkness. It is exhibited here in a book of gloomy, hellish predictions. Mr Wells appears to relish such a future for man, even call for its fruition. Well, well, Mr Wells, I beg to differ.'[8] Arthur Conan Doyle, a doctor as well as an author, wrote that *Anticipations* was 'vile and villainous. Any man who knows science and medicine knows that the book is muddle-headed. Any man who knows humanity knows that the book is horrible.' The review of the book in the *Literary World* of 1 August 1902 was unambiguous in its opinions. The anonymous critic wrote:

If anyone wishes to know what a very cocksure person, 'well up' in two or possibly three of the natural sciences, but comprehensively ignorant of history, ethics and the social sciences in general, thinks mankind will be and do in the year 2000 AD, this is the book for him. The author is a well-known novelist who has dealt extensively with the possible future of men after the manner of fiction, and his novels have had a certain attractiveness for many. Certainly they deserve a wider audience than these *Anticipations*, which are not put in the form of fiction, but seem as purely the construction of a single brain working narrowly and arbitrarily as any novel could well be.

The work is placed before us as a very sober and coldly reasoned sketch of the actual society ... One must be free to remark that this picture throws more light upon the limitations of Mr Wells's own culture than it does upon the probable evolution of society. It is no more reliable than the countless novels of the future unhappily so familiar in recent years and so profitless. The book is a travesty of possibilities.

In general, however, the book was not widely reviewed and escaped mass criticism.

Yet to what extent was Wells simply reiterating the views of an entire group of intellectuals; just how extraordinary were his beliefs and his hopes? There is no doubt that socialist and early fascist thinkers looked to eugenics as a positive force, for change and, as they perceived it, improvement. By the outbreak of the First World War there were small but active movements throughout Europe advocating human engineering. Wells did, however, stand out for several reasons. He was one of the first writers, and certainly the first popular writer, to include racial engineering in his philosophy. There had been monomaniacs in the past who had written about the subject and peppered their work with anti-Semitic obsessions, but none of these was regarded as being on the left, within the bounds of respectability. It was also that very popularity that made Wells' writings unique. The rantings of a fanatic were one thing, but the considered views of a highly and widely respected novelist were quite another.

This goes some way to explaining some of the positive response to *Anticipations*. Sidney Webb, for example, wrote to Chesterton after the latter's attack on the book, and declared that while much of *Anticipations* revolted him, it was imperative that the overall belief in eugenics not be attacked by fellow radicals. He thought Wells 'a man who had fallen over the edge'.[10] The plaintive flavour of the letter characterized many of the things written by Wells' supporters. They were profoundly divided: should they scold and condemn, or smile and encourage. *Anticipations* was the most structured and complete manual of eugenics ever to be written by a reputed author. Though it won applause in some circles, it was rejected by most of Wells' contemporaries as a pernicious and wretched book. Just a few years later even the applauders had changed their mind. Wells never did. As the Conservative Member of Parliament Victor Cazalet recorded in his diary on 14 December 1934, 'lunch with . . . H.G. Wells. We talked of Russia and dictatorship. Wells said if he were a dictator he would probably be very vicious.'

A photograph taken in the 1930s shows the Webbs sitting in their garden taking tea. The location is Passfield Corner; Passfield was the title Beatrice Webb took when she was ennobled, by the very establishment she and her husband had spent their lives attempting to emasculate. She sits with her spine rigid, one hand gracefully poised on her lap, the other reaching towards the table. Her haughtiness is, as always, firmly in place. Sidney holds his tea cup and looks on. He is a diminutive man with a full goatee beard and pince-nez. Serving them is a maid, in the starched white hat, pinafore and long black dress required of all staff of the period. It is a stylized portrait, a formal depiction of the royal couple of pre-war British socialism holding court. Neither Sidney nor Beatrice appears aware of the patent contradictions on display.

The Webbs chose their circle with precision and now, in 1902, it appeared that Herbert George Wells might qualify. Wells' public standing had expanded in leaps since the publication of *Anticipations* and his novel *Love and Mr Lewisham*, which appeared in 1900. The latter was the first of his books concerning the 'small men' of England. Its hero, George Edgar Lewisham, is an assistant master, barely able to contain his ambition and energy. He wears glasses unnecessarily, to give himself the appearance of age and sagacity; and attaches a schema outlining his career plans and hoped for success to his bedroom wall. The book is heavily autobiographical. It takes the young man to the Normal School of Science, socialist debates and relationships with two women. He chooses the prettier, the less cerebral, and sees his erstwhile dreams shattered by her pregnancy. Lewisham's story concludes with his pondering the now unattainable schema:

Then he compressed his lips and tore the yellow sheet in half, tearing very deliberately. He doubled the halves and tore again, doubled again very carefully and neatly until the Schema was torn into numberless little pieces. With it he seemed to be tearing his past self ... He found he was still holding the torn fragments. He stretched out his hands and dropped them into that new waste-paper basket Ethel had bought for him.

Two pieces fell outside the basket. He stooped, picked them up and put them carefully with their fellows.

The book's critical and commercial success, and its vivid portrayal of a young radical from a powerless social class, intrigued Sidney and Beatrice Webb. They had been founders, along with George Bernard Shaw, of the Fabian Society, that influential club of evolutionary socialists. Wells had already met Shaw through another Fabian father, Graham Wallas. Wells began to flirt with the Fabians in 1902, attending their meetings regularly the following year. He intended to take the movement by storm; the storm turned out to be a summer shower. His initial meeting with the Webbs was satisfactory, though he was more impressed with them than they with him. 'Wells is an interesting though somewhat unattractive personality,' Beatrice Webb noted in her diary, adding that Jane Wells 'is a pretty little person with a strong will, mediocre intelligence and somewhat small nature.'

Wells was able to show himself off to better effect when he rented a small flat in London, leaving Jane at home with their two young sons. Wells could now see his Fabian friends regularly, attending dinners and meetings with some of the most powerful and impressive men and women in the country. He gained an experience of power and the powerful that he had previously lacked. His membership of the Fabian Society was proposed by Bernard Shaw and Graham Wallas, and required unanimous approval from the executive and a period of probation – resembling, as the Fabians frequently did, an elitist London club. Wells was accepted by the beginning of 1903, and soon began to challenge for authority in the society. His first action was to deliver a paper, entitled 'The Question of Scientific Administration Areas in Relation to Municipal Undertakings'.[11]

The lecture argued the case presented in *Anticipations*, that communications were now so efficient and rapid – and would only improve – that the one viable form of government was a world state. All of this was delivered in Wells' high-pitched voice, lacking inflection and passion. Internationalism was not the philosophy of the Fabians, particularly when it was advocated infelicitously in a suburban accent. Wells took his rejection badly, as he always did, particularly when he was convinced that opposition was the result of ignorance and envy.[12] That whole first year in the society it seemed that Wells was on the losing side in Fabian arguments and on the 'outside' of the inner circle.

In 1904 he decided that he had had enough and opted to resign. Offers of resignation were common amongst early Fabians, as a tried and tested political manoeuvre. Akin to a disingenuous and half-hearted suicide attempt, this resignation was a plea for understanding and alliance from a man who felt isolated and misunderstood in the ranks of these full-time political dabblers.[13] Shaw and the Webbs attempted to placate Wells, insisting that he was valuable and valued. He withdrew his threat, but wrote to a friend of his chagrin, adding that 'I highly disapprove of the Fabian Society'.[14] He felt that he was not taken seriously by his comrades. To an extent this was true, for the Webbs had a suspicion of Wells which later grew into animosity. They always perceived him as an upstart on the lookout for his own personal gain. Shaw was a friend, but his loyalty and patience were often strained to the limit. The seemingly effortless success of Shaw within the society – which was in fact based on tireless work for the Fabians – irritated Wells, and he let it show. For his part, the Irishman was seldom one to pull his punches. He wrote:

Take all the sins he ascribes to his colleagues, the touchiness of Hyndman, the dogmatism of Quelch, Blatchford's preoccupation with his own method, Grayson's irresponsibility; add every other petulance of which a spoiled child or a successful operatic tenor is capable; multiply the total by ten; square the result; cube it; raise it to the millionth power and square it again; and you will still fall short of the truth about Wells – Yet the worse he behaved the more he was indulged; and the more he was indulged the worse he behaved.[15]

If Shaw believed this, it was certain that he influenced other Fabians to believe it as well. Wells' first year in the ranks of the thinking revolutionaries was not a happy one.

His difficulties with the Fabians were compounded by other problems. George Gissing had died in 1903. His death had been predicted for some time, but Wells felt the shock more profoundly than he had expected. He had seen Gissing, and to an extent their friendship, decay and die. He mourned this 'gaunt, dishevelled, unshaven, flushed, bright-eyed being', concluding his elegy with the words, 'So ended all that flimsy inordinate stir of grey matter that was George Gissing.'[16] He and Gissing had shared a mutual empathy and appreciation, but Gissing had also been a financial and emotional strain on Wells. The death left Wells an isolated if slightly less burdened young man.

He was finding it difficult to complete his novel *Kipps*; and *The Food of the Gods*, his tale of panaceas used without responsibility, was not as successful as anticipated when it appeared in 1904. It was almost as if Wells had given the public so much, so quickly, that they were no longer awe-struck by his scientific fantasies. *The Food of the Gods* is by no means a bad novel. It tells of the invention of a growth-stimulating drug. The results are, after a promising beginning, catastrophic. A breed of young giants develop and threaten to take over London. They reject terms which demand that they live apart from the rest of society and do not procreate. Says a giant child:

He would have us live out our lives one-by-one, until only one remains, and that one at last would die also, and they would cut down all the giant plants and weeds, kill all the giant under-life, burn out the traces of the food – make an end to us and the food for ever. Then the little pigmy world would be safe. They would go on – safe for ever, living their little pigmy lives, doing pigmy kindnesses and pigmy cruelties each to the other.

Wells later explained that the intention of the book was to expose the differences between 'localized' and 'de-localized' minds, particularly in the context of government and administration. This was certainly not perceived at the time.

Wells habitually reacted to negative criticism by returning the insult, not always at the offending party. This time he took the opportunity to lash out at the other Fabian members, demanding that they look again at their purpose and policies. He decided on a frontal attack. In January 1906 he read a paper entitled 'Faults of the Fabians' to the assembled society. The paper itself was a cogent blending of analysis and solution, and may have merited consideration if read in a more conciliatory manner, by a more conciliatory man. But Wells' delivery was fustian and dissonant, his poor oratory deteriorated still further as he became more excited, and by the end of the evening he had managed to provoke towards his personality, if not his policies, the unanimous hostility of the usually disparate Fabians. Criticism from a friend was perhaps permissible, thought the comrades, but an attack from this unfriendly quarter was beyond acceptance.

The contents of the paper were more sensible, and sensitive to the times, than Wells' opponents then realized. He had anticipated the popular and parliamentary success of the Labour Party, and advocated a larger, more substantial Fabian Society, more suited to the coming challenge. Finance, organization, structure and purpose must be reviewed, Wells argued. He also made personal criticisms, condemning the familiar atmosphere of the society and its addiction to nomenclature and jokes which only the initiated were meant to understand. He believed the Fabians to be elitist and incestuous; successful in spreading their ideas and influence inside the monied and powered classes, among leading civil servants, academics and intellectuals, but virtually impotent when it came to the broader labour and trade union movement. Wells was substantially correct but he refused to acknowledge that the Fabian Society never declared itself to be the spark for a mass movement. Though the Webbs may have played at parlour politics and revelled in the internecine squabbles of their comfortable club, they were sufficiently astute to be aware of the necessary limitations of their work. Shaw was even more conscious of the limited scope of Fabianism, and consequently was prepared to indulge its occasional lapses into animus and hubris.

Although the membership had no doubts as to what they thought of Wells himself, they were divided when it came to the quality of his actual proposals. Elements of the Fabian executive appreciated the need for change and were partial to aspects of Wells' paper. Others had made up their mind to reject the man's politics outright. According to Anthony West the old guard of the society

declined to admit that my father had become any sort of threat to them. They persisted in regarding him as a transient phenomenon, a self-advertising boomster who had come into their domain to see what publicity he could get for himself by ruffling a few feathers and kicking up a rumpus. Their feeling was that he had no principles and no serious intentions. Whether he succeeded or failed was all one, either way he would soon drop his game of the moment and move on.[17]

They were in part correct. Wells was given sufficient room to manoeuvre himself out of position. He worked behind the scenes to harness support for his call for change; he insulted members of the executive while their backs were turned, in an attempt to raise discontent amongst grass roots members; and he blatantly proposed to other members that it was he who should be given control of the society, forgoing the normal election process. His hortatory abilities and straightforward cheek rallied some to his cause. Most, however, were disappointed by his actions and moved to defend the established, comfortable order. Wells appeared to be campaigning not for Fabian reform, but for his own advancement. What right had he to demand so much so quickly?

Sidney and Beatrice Webb were by now determined to prevent any further promotion for their young opponent. Nevertheless, it would not be they who would dirty their hands in the political in-fighting which was about to reach its climax. Bernard Shaw was once again asked to deal with Wells.

Wells himself reacted curiously to the confrontation that was building. A letter he wrote to the novelist and biographer Edward Verrall Lucas showed that he was prepared at times to dismiss the whole affair with a wink. It also seemed to show Wells' bad faith: 'I have been up to my ears lately in 'stradordinary intrigues to upset the Fabian Society by making buttered slices for an old lady. Most amusing.'[18] Wells had turned the debate into a conflict between himself and the executive.

Shaw was well aware of Wells' duplicity. To satisfy his new demands, the entire committee would have to resign and Wells become, in the opinion of Shaw, an emperor. The campaign began in earnest, with Shaw insisting that whatever might happen in the coming months neither man would leave the society. This agreed upon, Shaw fired his broadsides, accusing Wells of unscrupulous and arrogant behaviour, of being impossible to work with, and with wasting the time and money of all concerned. Wells' Kentish hammer was no match for the Celtic rapier of Shaw. That he defeated Wells was nothing, reported Shaw, because it was 'like boxing with a novice who knocked himself out in every exchange'.[19] In the debates between the two men, and in the votes of support that were taken during the various discussions, Wells was humiliated. He received compensation in the form of election to Fabian committees; but his bid for power had been so ambitious in scope, and so embracing in its defeat, that real authority within the movement would for ever escape him. In his autobiography he recalled that 'no part of my career rankles so acutely in my memory with the conviction of bad judgement, gutsy impulse and real inexcusable vanity, as that storm in the Fabian tea-cup'.

During the Fabian wars Wells had published *A Modern Utopia*. The book, which came out in 1905, continued the development of his political ideas, although the language was less harsh and shrill than in *Anticipations*. It looked to a society divided into five strictly defined classes. At the top of the heap were the Samurai, exotically named extensions of Wells' romantic imagination. These were the rulers, the leaders, the masters. The Samurai would dispense justice and wisdom, and rule with an iron hand tempered by their immutable strength of character and correctness of thought. The Poietic class, 'possessing imaginations that range beyond the known and accepted', would take for their concern the creation of beauty. Practical needs would be treated by the Kinetics, 'very clever and capable people, but they do not do, and do not desire to do, new things'. These two subordinate classes would be respected for their contributions. Below them, however, came the Dull, and Wells is less tolerant of these creatures, though still somewhat ambivalent:

They are the stupid people, the incompetent people, the formal, imitative people, the people who, in any properly organized State, should, as a class, gravitate towards and below the minimum wage that qualifies for marriage. The laws of heredity are far too mysterious for such offspring as they do produce to be excluded from a fair chance in the world; but for themselves, they count neither for work nor direction in the State.

The Base were to stand at the bottom of the classes. They provoked no such ambiguity from Wells. They are, according to the brave new utopia, boastful and cruel, they lack frankness and any moral sense. They are 'an antagonism to the State organization'. Their precise fate was unsure, but their future was without doubt a limited one. In a chapter entitled, ominously, 'Failure In A Modern Utopia', Wells explained who would be defined as failures, and how they would be treated by the utopians. He asked: What would the phoenix-like state do with 'congenital invalids, its idiots and madmen, its drunkards and men of vicious mind, its cruel and furtive souls, its stupid people, too stupid to be of use to the community, its lumpish, unteachable and unimaginative people? And what will it do with the man who is "poor" all round, the rather spiritless, rather incompetent?'

His answer was that 'the species must be engaged in eliminating them'. Nature, believed Wells, would do the job by crushing, starving and overwhelming them. Nature, however, was not sufficiently able and would have to be helped by human endeavours. Society would have to resort to 'social surgery'. Freedoms would have to be curtailed, and as for the people who demonstrate an anti-social disposition – the definition of which would be decided by the Samurai – the authorities would 'seclude them from the great body of the population . . . in remote and solitary regions . . . they will be fenced in and forbidden to the common run of men'.

The vision grows more terrifying. Armed guards will patrol borders and ports, and boat-building will be illegal, because islands off the coast will be filled with undesirables. Malformed or ill children will be murdered at birth, and any sign of decadence or distraction from social tasks will be severely punished. Procreation is prohibited for all those who work below the required limit, or are labelled as dissidents, for the state must 'achieve the maximum elimination of its feeble and spiritless folk in every generation'. What would be done if an inferior race is found? 'A Modern Utopia is under the hard logic of life, and it would have to exterminate such a race as quickly as it could.' The proposals continue, from the absurd to the horrible: uniformity of clothes, marriages decreed and supervised by the state, government control of diet and recreation; a sickening homogeneity increases in a crazed and insatiable dash. No aspect, however small or meaningless, of human life is to be left in the hands of chance or the individual. In a grotesque form of Talmudic regulation, the routine from rising in the morning until resting at night is dictated and preordained. Wells' was a vision of the blackest pessimism.

4 The Man of Substance

In March 1905, even before he broke with the Fabians, Wells was made a member of the Reform Club. If any date and event represented a watershed in his life it was this. The Reform had been founded as a sanctuary and meeting place for Britain's nineteenth-century Liberals, and witnessed the hatching of more parliamentary coups and splinter groups than was altogether decent. It was firmly ensconced within the establishment: safe, comfortable, elegant and select. Wells had wanted to be elected for some time, a wish that represented what his son later described as Wells' 'self-conscious quest for visible respectability'.[1] Now, with his election to the Reform Club, the man who had been born in a dusty Bromley china shop had finally arrived.

When Wells effectively left the Fabian Society and its hectic politics for good at the end of 1906, it was to devote his enormous energies, at least in the short term, solely to writing. This was self-delusion on the grandest scale. Though Wells' literary output was, and always would be, almost boundless, his other urges were not to be denied. He desired, required, friendship: on a sexual level, with beautiful young women, and on a platonic level, with gifted and literate men.

Wells' friendship with Joseph Conrad had been dormant throughout the Fabian squabbles, and now came once again to life. It was Conrad who made most of the moves. He graciously requested permission to dedicate *The Secret Agent* to his friend, but Wells declined. He believed that his admirer was 'placed too high in the scale of literary achievement'.[2] He described Conrad as 'rather short and round-shouldered with his head as it were sunken into his body. He had a dark retreating face with a very carefully trimmed and pointed beard, a trouble-wrinkled forehead and very troubled dark eyes, and the gestures of his hands and arms were from the shoulders and very Oriental indeed.'[3] Wells often teased Conrad about his appearance in a stage whisper, indulging in some elaborate game that the Polish Conrad could not understand English. In reply Conrad merely smiled and held out his arms as if to plead indifference.

The relationship between the two men was never close. Wells could not come to terms with Conrad's dedication to the art of writing for writing's sake; for Wells his prose was a means to an end, to political influence, wealth, stature and celebrity. Nor could he empathize with Conrad's domestic happiness and contentment, which he saw as a sign of weakness and stifled ambition. While Wells was finding his feet socially, attending the theatre every week, enjoying the new wardrobe of clothes he had had made by his first London tailor, Conrad was increasingly closing the door on the temptations of the outside world.

Wells' friendship with G.K. Chesterton was also strained. Their ambivalent relationship took on a particular momentum in the years 1905 and 1906. Chesterton was some sixteen years away from converting to Roman Catholicism, but he had already laid his reputation as the literary champion of orthodox Christianity. His philosophy was as contrary to that of Wells as was his appearance. The tall, huge Chesterton, described by Bernard Shaw as the 'Man Mountain', appeared to tower over and engulf Wells, who was still slim and quite slight. 'He seemed to shrink from me,' wrote Chesterton to Maurice Baring, 'as though he were afraid of my touch.'[4] Antipathy did not come easily to Chesterton and although he and Wells engaged in time-consuming and often angry arguments, there was never any resentment on his part. Wells was disarmed by Chesterton's good nature, disturbed by his inability to pigeon-hole the man. On a summer's day in 1907, for example, Wells and Chesterton went to Oxford to attend a public lecture. Walking together after the address Wells began to harangue his friend about the 'bloody hands of Christianity'.[5] The diatribe lasted for over thirty-five minutes, without Chesterton making the slightest objection. At the end of it he turned to Wells, smiled and said, 'Yes, you do have a point.' Wells was always impressed by Chesterton, enjoyed his calling him the seldom if ever used Herbert instead of the more common HG or Wells. He saw in Chesterton a fellow contrarian.

Wells' friendship with American author Stephen Crane was built on an altogether different foundation. Wells and the author of *The Red Badge of Courage* stayed together at Brede House near Rye in Sussex, where they 'revelled until two or three every night and came down towards mid-day to breakfasts of eggs and bacon, sweet potatoes from America and beer'.[6] Wells chose to include a photograph of Crane in his autobiography. It shows a handsome man, with a full nose, large, dark, almost Italianate eyes and the drooping moustache of an American cowboy or civil war soldier. His expression is sombre, studious, almost accusative. 'He was a lean, blond, slow-speaking, perceptive, fragile, tuberculous being,' wrote Wells, 'too adventurous to be temperate with anything and impracticable to an extreme degree.'

Wells revelled in Crane's Americanisms and relished his tales of a country that always fascinated him. Crane was good for Wells, good as a literary influence with his terse, sinewy prose, good as a friend with his sense of commitment and loyalty. Wells later recalled one of the many harmless and endearing moments of friendship between the two men, an incident when they arm-wrestled and the winner was not the stronger man but he who could tell enough jokes to make his opponent laugh and break his grip. Wells the child was never very far beneath the adult veneer, and he was at his best when he allowed that aspect of his character to come to the surface.

Ford Madox Ford, unfortunately, never had this effect on Wells. If anything, Wells wore the mask of businessman and professional writer when he was with him, affectionate but never completely comfortable. Ford was remembered by Rebecca West as 'the author who is recognized only as he disappears round the corner'[7] and it is certainly the case that even today his influence far outweighs his profile. *The Good Soldier* and *Parade's End* are works of undoubted genius, lauded by writers as diverse as Ezra Pound, Graham Greene and Ernest Hemingway. Ford's tragedy in life was to be the feeding hand that was always bitten; rather than inspire loyalty, this gifted man seemed to provoke treachery among the young writers whom he patronized and sponsored.

The 'long blond with a drawling manner', as Wells described him, was intent on establishing a serious literary journal. The

English Review was conceived in early 1908 and was intended to reshape English letters, which Ford believed to be lacking the concern and colour of the French school and the seriousness of the German. It had, according to Ford, 'the definite design of giving imaginative literature a chance in England'. Joseph Conrad, the critic Edward Garnett and Ford's friend – and a powerful influence on several of his fictional characters – Arthur Marwood had agreed to support the concern, and Wells promised to provide half of the finance and co-edit with Ford. The overwhelming image of the initial meeting of the editors and backers of the magazine is of clouds of miasma-like smoke, half-empty glasses of Wells' favourite Irish single malt whiskey and discarded pages of paper lying on the floor. There was more dreamy optimism here than understanding of the authentic nature of maintaining a regular publication. By Christmas 1908 the magazine was metamorphosed into stinging and demanding reality. That reality was a little too much for Wells. He wrote to Ford, explaining that he was too broke to finance it, and added as a critical afterthought that Ford's financial skills were grossly insufficient. These were thin disguises. He had cold feet. In compensation he offered Ford the serial rights to his next novel, *Tono-Bungay*, and in return asked for one fifth of the magazine's profits.

The *English Review*, launched with the serialization of *Tono-Bungay*, still managed to lose money. The relationship between Wells and Ford was temporarily shattered over this. How could Ford not make a profit with such a book in his journal, Wells demanded? Ford replied that Wells had overestimated his public appeal. Wells, of course, did not react well to such criticism and whenever the two men met at parties or literary gatherings over the next year and a half, he retreated to another conversation or in one case, at a party in Taunton, ostentatiously walked out of the room. One of the few enduring links between them was Violet Hunt. She was a beautiful, vivacious, highly literate young woman who aspired to literary celebrity. Ford and Hunt had met briefly at a dinner party given by John Galsworthy, and the match was lit when the host suggested that Ford escort Hunt home. It took full flame when Wells, who had agreed to help Hunt's career, contrived their next meeting; he sent her along to Ford to contribute some work to the *English Review*. Ford and Hunt became long-term lovers. Ford and Wells engineered a form of rapprochement, cordial if not close. Wells confided to his friends that he never understood Ford, and at heart he did not really want to.

When *Tono-Bungay* was published as a book in 1909 it achieved a success more remarkable and lucrative than even Wells had predicted. The book was really a culmination of the early Wells, incorporating all of his literary and personal experience of the past five years as well as his difficult childhood. The story is narrated by George Ponderevo, the son of a housekeeper in a stately home on the Kent Downs. His father leaves the family when George is a child. The boy is attracted to the house's magnificent library, and inspired by some of the radical works it contains. First sent to school, he is later removed and apprenticed to a baker. He fights an atheistic war against the local chapel, gains entry into a college of science in London, and attends meetings of the Fabian Society, where he is profoundly disappointed at what he sees. He falls into a hasty love affair, marries, and is divorced. All this is transparently autobiographical.

The plot of the work, as it continues, is quintessentially Wellsian in its sense of imagination and originality. George's uncle, Edward Ponderevo, invents an ineffective, even harmful medicine which he calls Tono-Bungay, successfully promoting and selling it as a panacea. George becomes his factotum, and Edward makes a fortune. He conducts further dishonest transactions, but is eventually brought to ruin by an antagonistic press baron. This caricature of the state of Edwardian England is the crux of the book. The pride and triumph of Wells' country was, he believed, built upon corruption, theft and empty dreams; built, in fact, upon a chimera. George Ponderevo ends his narrative as an engineer working on the design of battleships. He watches a new destroyer, a metallic symbol of the era, passing down the Thames towards the North Sea, and muses on the metaphorical meaning of technology and the possibilities of science:

Sometimes I call this reality Science, sometimes I call it Truth. But it is something we draw by pain and effort out of the heart of life, that we disentangle and make clear. Other men serve it, I know, in art, in literature, in social invention, and see it in a thousand different figures, under a hundred names. I see it always as austerity, as beauty . . .

I do not know what it is, this something, except that it is supreme. It is a something, a quality, an element, one may find now in colours, now in forms, now in thoughts. It emerges from life with each year one lives and feels, and generation by generation and age by age, but the how and why of it are all beyond the compass of my mind.

That same year brought Wells a new romantic adventure. He was in love with Amber Reeves, 'the young woman who bore him a daughter on the last day of 1909, as fully as he was capable of loving anyone'. (This is Anthony West speaking – and not without irony.)[8] For her part, Amber Reeves was as well equipped as any woman to love Wells as an equal, on his own terms, and stand up to his severely indulgent and decidedly selfish view of romance. Born in 1887, she was an accomplished student at Newnham College, Cambridge, where she read Moral Sciences, and it was here that she first met Wells. Her parents, Magdalen Stuart and William Pember Reeves, were active Fabians and vociferous advocates of social change and sexual liberation. These ideas Amber digested and relished, going on to write feminist novels such as *The Reward of Virtue* and *A Lady and her Husband*, teaching at London's Morley College and standing twice for Parliament. When she met Wells she was still callow, and a little cautious. With her sensual eyes and aquiline nose she possessed an unorthodox but undeniable beauty, embellished by an infectious wit and sense of humour. Wells and Jane invited her to come to Spade House as a weekend guest, and it was not very long before she submitted first to Wells' advances, and then to his demand that they make the affair public. Jane decided that acceptance was the better part of valour. She assumed that the affair would evaporate without trace.

Wells was less sure of that. He had contemplated breaking his marriage for at least two years. Certain recurrent themes in his writings at the time are unmistakable, most noticeably in the novel *Ann Veronica*. Written through the first half of 1908, the work depicts a young woman who offers herself as her teacher's mistress. Wells justifies this action as an exploration of the new morality, arguing that only the contemporary generation can fully understand this need for sexual freedom. 'Life is rebellion or nothing,' exclaims Capes, the unfaithful husband in the novel who is Ann Veronica Stanley's biology demonstrator. He goes on to describe his actions as 'a great lark', something which 'turns life into a glorious adventure'. For her part, Ann Veronica is 'vehemently impatient' with the status quo, and 'wildly discontented' with the Victorian sensibilities and conventions of her father.

Amber Reeves' parents were no nineteenth-century authoritarians, and Wells was not the overwhelmed teacher Capes; but the novel's disregard and contempt for life-long marriage are real. Wells and Amber let these sentiments be their guide. The couple decided to elope to France and rent a house in Le Touquet on the coast of Normandy.

Once there, the first flush of love began to transform itself into the second thoughts of reality. Wells wanted a surrogate wife, someone who would care for his needs, supervise his home, comfort his worries. This was not what Amber wanted at all. More than this, Wells regularly returned to England, leaving his mistress with little to do and few people to talk with. When he was in London Wells began to appreciate the enormity of his actions. He had informed friends that he intended to sell Spade House, divorce Jane and set up house with Amber. Most of them saw this as outrageous and callous. They told Wells that he would be treated as an outcast in some circles. His first divorce had taken place when he was a young man, they argued, and people were prepared to forgive youthful folly; everybody knew and liked Jane and would not forgive his indifference towards her.

Wells took this to heart and refused to make any commitment at all. On his return to France the infatuation he had initially felt for Amber steadily declined. The couple began to argue. Amber shouted that she could neither live with Wells on this basis nor leave him. He responded that this was childish nonsense. Influenced by the advice and warnings of his friends, Wells told her that divorce was out of the question and she should consider marrying Rivers Blanco White, a young lawyer who had long been in love with her. By marrying this man, Wells continued, scandal would die down and the two of them could continue their relationship in secret. 'Amber virtually accused my father of acting as a pimp, and forcing her into prostitution just to avoid a difficult social situation,' explained Anthony West.[9]

The unhappy pair returned to Britain; Amber was now pregnant. They went to see the long-suffering Jane, who listened to their arguments, swallowed whatever pride she had left, and then declared that she refused to take sides. Amber was confused and frightened. She was in love with Wells but now felt very sorry for his wife. Vacillating and often in tears, she screamed at Wells that she had been a fool even to consider letting him divorce his wife; she could not live with herself, she explained, if he did this to the poor, pathetic woman. Wells shouted back at her and reiterated his friends' comments. He had changed his mind, he said, and was not about to throw over everything for a woman he now thought of as unstable and petulant. Both of them cried.

It was decided that indeed Amber would marry Blanco White. Wells agreed to rent a small cottage for the newly-weds in Woldingham, Surrey, an arrangement that outraged Amber's parents when they heard of it. Wells also made it clear that he wished to continue his relationship with Amber. This was certainly drama, sometimes played as farce, sometimes as tragedy, and occasionally – just occasionally – as downright histrionics.

Private gossip gave way to public notoriety. In October 1909 *Ann Veronica* was published by T. Fisher Unwin after Macmillan had rejected it on grounds of immorality. The similarities between novel and life were inescapable. Some critics, of course, had no desire to escape them. Although pundits as diverse, and unexpected, as G.K. Chesterton and George Bernard Shaw defended the book, others fired long-prepared cannon. The *Spectator*'s John St Loe Strachey, a champion of the National Social Purity Crusade, called it a 'pernicious book'; public libraries refused to place it on their shelves and Wells was ostracized at parties and literary gatherings. Sales were excellent.

'That book created a scandal at the time, though it seems mild enough reading to the young of to-day,' wrote Wells some twenty-five years later. 'It is rather badly constructed, there is an excessive use of soliloquy, but Ann Veronica came as near to being a living character as anyone in my earlier love stories. This was so because in some particulars she was drawn from life. And for that and other reasons she made a great fuss in the world.'[10] The 'fuss' was more than Wells could bear. Amber's parents were now relentless in their condemnation of him. He had abandoned membership of the Savile Club for fear of being snubbed, and now decided temporarily to vacate his beloved Reform Club. By the middle of 1910 Wells knew that he would either have to leave the country or leave Amber Reeves. There was really no choice any more. The affair ended.

It is difficult to understand Jane Wells' attitude throughout all of this. Even in the midst of her husband's rantings, when he threatened to divorce her, she continued her duties as secretary, factotum, housekeeper and hostess. Most friends of the couple saw her only in the last disguise. She appeared to be the perfect literary hostess, always with an understanding smile and a nod of encouragement. She agreed without protest when Wells asked her to leave Spade House and move with him to Church Row in Hampstead, so as to make his relationship with Amber Reeves a little more convenient. She herself seems to have remained sexually faithful to Wells. She still aspired to be a writer, and it is possible she found solace in that, or in her husband's literary successes. Perhaps we can best come to grips with her pathetic situation if we recall the way Wells wrote of her after her death. After a perfunctory and brief reference to his wife as a writer, he records the direction in which she turned her energies:

Jane ordered a house well and was an able 'shopper'; she helped people in difficulties and stood no nonsense from the plumber. Her medicine cupboard at home was prepared for all occasions. She had gone through a Red Cross course so as to be competent in domestic emergencies. She had a file of shop addresses where things needed could be bought. Her garden was a continually glowing success and she was a member of the Royal Horticultural Society and kept a garden book and a diary to check and improve her methods . . . She transacted and invested for her unhelpful uncertain husband, and she was wise and wary in his affairs.[11]

The Amber Reeves affair was not the first humiliation suffered by Jane and it certainly would not be the last. Wells lived a part-time existence with her in Hampstead, still seeing Amber Reeves when the fancy took him, until he finally lost interest in the young woman. He knew that whatever happened Jane would always be there waiting for his return. It is easier to condemn or to sympathize with Mrs Wells than it is to comprehend her.

In 1910, while Wells was still consoling himself over the loss of Amber Reeves, came the publication of *The History of Mr Polly*, by Thomas Nelson and Sons. Of all of Wells' 'little men', Alfred Polly is the most lasting, the most appealing and the most gratifying. Here Wells let his imagination soar, his abilities roar. Polly receives a shambolic, inadequate education, and by the time he becomes an apprentice draper he has invented his own arcane but picturesque vocabulary. 'Sesquippledan verboojuice' and 'Zelacious commerciality' are two of his favourites, which he uses in a delicious mixture of frustration and virtual malapropism. The reluctant draper is fired from his position following a fist fight. He falls for and marries a cousin, becomes a small shopkeeper, is desperately unhappy, and desires only to escape to his books, beer and bicycle. He tries to commit suicide, but even this last gasp goes humiliatingly wrong. In the blaze that he lights to end his life, however, he proves himself a hero by rescuing his neighbour's mother-in-law. All having failed, Polly simply opts out of his marriage and job, walks the road, and then finds work, and happiness, with a plump and homely inn landlady. Back at his former home he is presumed to be dead, and his wife settles down on the insurance money.

Polly is a tale of happy resolutions, of good endings. It is also flavoured with ambivalence; on the one hand the book bulges with humour and mockery, on the other it is clearly a reflection of Wells the discontent. Throughout his career, even with its galloping list of achievements, there was an almost tangible desire to return to a life he had only glimpsed and never really known, a life of more fundamental values and clarity of purpose. The novel's Uncle Jim encapsulates this in a conversation with Alfred Polly: 'Man comes into life to seek and find his sufficient beauty, to serve it, to win and increase it, to fight for it, to face anything and dare anything for it, counting death as nothing so long as the dying eyes still turn to it. And fear and dullness and indolence and appetite, which, indeed, are no more than fear's three crippled brothers, who make ambushes and creep by night, are against him, to delay him, to hold him off, to hamper him and beguile him and kill him in that quest.'

After reading the book H.L. Mencken wrote in *Smart Set* in July 1910: 'It seems to be pretty generally agreed by the critics, at least in the United States, that H.G. Wells has stepped into the long vacant boots of Charles Dickens, and for that notion, it must be confessed, there is no little excuse.' Yet Mencken was more critical of *Mr Polly* by the time he reached the last section of his review. He considered that the book 'is written with all of Mr Wells' customary facility and humour. The sheer fluency of the writing, in truth, is one of the book's faults. One feels that more careful polishing would have improved it – that it should have remained in the author's desk a year or so before going to the printer.'

Wells' enormous literary output during this period is even more remarkable when we consider how volatile his health was. He never fully recovered from his injuries as a child and young man, but he also suffered from a usually mild, though sometimes severe, depression. It is not uncommon for periods of blackness to follow great achievement and moments of virtual euphoria. Wells was a constant victim of 'downs' after a book was published. Female company, often without any sexual contact, was one way he found to relieve his suffering. Another was going to the theatre; around the time of the publication of *The History of Mr Polly* Wells attended matinées as well as evening performances, at times seeing the same production three or four times. In early 1911, if he is to be believed, he was at the theatre every day for two weeks, twice a day for half of the period.

Wells was always a driven man, seldom content with success or accomplishment. During these years his life was essentially one of endless work and publication, a treadmill of fine literary production which did not always appear to have any greater artistic purpose or ambition. He was not a man who believed in genre or stylistic form unless it was entirely subconscious and incidental; a means to an end. As he repeatedly told Jane, he had so many things to say and he was going to spend his life saying them. But although he was a man possessed, he did not lose his charisma and charm. He told J.B. Priestley the only partially humorous story of his imitating the whistling of a bird in the branches outside his bedroom window. 'It started to chirp and flap its wings and then settled on the branch nearest to me. It just stared. You see, I could charm the birds in the trees.'[12]

The New Machiavelli was published in 1911 and was a different proposition altogether. If we look at Wells' life before London and then after, *Polly* and *Machiavelli* clearly represent the two parts of the dichotomy. *The New Machiavelli* purported to concern broad social and political issues – which indeed to a large extent it did – but it also parodied noted political figures, and once again tackled matters of sexuality. As with *Ann Veronica*, the more conservative publishers were outraged, and three rejected the book. Their reaction was hardly surprising. The basis of the work is the contrived autobiography of an aspiring politician and editor named Richard Remington, who is brought down by personal animosity and his own provocative views. On his upward and downward path Remington takes a mistress, and the character of Isabel Rivers, who elopes with Remington to Europe and has his child, bore far too much resemblance to Amber Reeves for Edwardian sensibilities.

Then there were the characters of Oscar and Altiora Bailey, leaders of a liberal intellectual movement. They are brilliant and gifted, but also unscrupulous and small-minded. Altiora's 'soul was bony, and at the base of her was a vanity gaunt and greedy'. This was a pellucid depiction of the Webbs, and neither they nor other readers ever doubted it. There was equal certainty about former Prime Minister Arthur Balfour's portrayal as Evesham, Conservative leader and a curiously Laodicean politician. Evesham is admired but mistrusted. And so the list went on, including Graham Wallas, *Pall Mall Gazette* editor Harry Cust, and a large proportion of Wells' friends and enemies.

The book was eventually published through the good offices of Macmillan, by John Lane, who had earned a certain permissive cachet by publishing the avant-garde and iconoclastic *Yellow Book* in the 1890s. When it appeared there was less discussion of it, either negative or positive, than anticipated, and Wells was convinced that he had been humiliated first by pusillanimous publishers, then by dishonest critics. He was partly correct on the former, almost entirely wrong on the latter. R.A. Scott-James in the *Daily News*, for example, was entirely honest and accurate in his opinions. He admitted that 'No book of recent times has afforded so much gossip, excitement, scandal, and heart-burning as the serial which has been running in the *English Review* and is today published in book form', and concluded with: 'This book bristles with brilliant and even profound social philosophy, and it assails the nostrils with its meanness and its atmosphere of petty scandal. The fine and the paltry, the magnificently courageous and the insignificantly small, unite to make a book which will possibly become a notorious classic.'

Wells believed that his friends had let the gossips and the Cassandras batter his reputation, that *The New Machiavelli* was a serious work of literature which had been smothered by innuendo. He left London but returned after a week. Jane told him to be comforted by his sales, which were far from poor; he visited his club again and was heartened by the evident thaw in his reception.[13] It was from another quarter, however, that genuine distraction was to come.

Elizabeth von Arnim had been born Mary Annette Beauchamp in 1866, the same year as Wells, in New Zealand, and came via Australia and Europe to London in 1871. Her mother was a novelist, her cousin was Katherine Mansfield. In 1891 she married a Prussian count; her experiences on his Pomeranian estate are chronicled in her 1898 novel *Elizabeth and her German Garden*, a now-forgotten work which was a major success at the time. Her husband died in 1910, the same year her play *Priscilla Runs Away* was staged in London, making her an independently wealthy woman. She used some of the royalties to build a chalet in Switzerland. She had wanted to meet Wells as early as 1907 and she now wrote to him to praise *The New Machiavelli*. She could not have chosen a more appropriate book at a more appropriate time. 'You must forgive me for bothering you with my extreme joy over your wonderful *Machiavelli*,' she wrote. And continued, 'never did a man understand things as you do – the others all guess and theorize – you know – & the poetry of it, and the aching, desolating truth . . . '

Wells understandably found such praise irresistible. By this time Elizabeth had lost some of her earlier beauty, but had gained a sense of control and elegant balance which Hugh Walpole described as 'captivating and frightening'. Wells wrote to her, entreating her to come with him to Ireland. She refused. Wells wrote again, sent telegrams, pleaded with her. They never travelled to Ireland, but they did go to Italy for a romantic tryst. Wells then took the impetuous step of going to Switzerland to pursue her, and broke into a prolonged crying fit when Elizabeth terminated the affair, blaming among other things Wells' persistence, determination and what she contemptuously described as his 'excessively trying behaviour'. Nor was she willing to replace Jane as Wells' wife or prepared to play the role of mother for any other than her natural children. The pair remained friends, however, and the brief romance formed the basis for Elizabeth's 1914 novel *The Pastor's Wife*, one of over twenty books she wrote in a long and fertile career. When she died in 1941, Wells was genuinely heartbroken.

By 1911 Wells' finances, if not his love life, were secure and stable. He and Jane decided to search for a new home, perhaps outside the London maelstrom. Wells was stifled by the stone and steel of London, and even his Hampstead home with its proximity to the rolling green Heath was insufficient for the man who had grown up a country boy. Of all the counties now being swallowed up by London's inexorable growth, Essex, to the east, was fighting the most successful rearguard action. The west of the county was already accepting the metropolitan suburbs, but in the east it was as though the city did not exist. Wells looked at Dunmow, less than fifty miles from London, and liked what he saw. His friend R.D. Blumenfeld, the editor of the *Daily Express*, already lived in the area. Blumenfeld made inquiries for Wells and discovered that the local landowner, Lady Warwick, was prepared to rent out the Georgian Old Rectory at Little Easton. The house was surrounded by farmland and its owner was a slightly eccentric aristocrat with a penchant for socialism, authors and radical discussion. The lease was offered to Wells at 100 pounds per year, and the house, known as Easton Glebe, was ordered to be ready in early 1912.

The end of 1911 and beginning of 1912 was a period of quietude for Wells. The move to Essex represented something of a retreat, as did his next book, a novel entitled *Marriage*. This was very different from *The New Machiavelli* and *Anne Veronica*. It is a sanguine, somewhat reassuring tale about a couple who struggle through apparent incompatibility and eventually save their union in the tough environment of Labrador. The work was optimistic and inoffensive. There was an element of catharsis in the book for Wells. His leading character, Richard Trafford, a scientist, eventually abandons his career and his ambitions with the words:

I've grown – into something different. It isn't how atoms swing with one another, or why they build themselves up so and not so, that matters any more to me. I've got you and all the world in which we live, and a new set of riddles filling my mind, how thought swings about thought, how one man attracts his fellows, how the waves of motive and conviction sweep through a crowd and all the little drifting crystallizations of spirit with spirit and all the repulsions and eddies and difficulties that one can catch in that turbulent confusion. I want to do a new sort of work now altogether.

The Passionate Friends was certainly a new sort of work. It also brought Wells into greater and more intimate contact with a man he had known for some time, Henry James. Published in 1913, the book is narrated by Stephen Stratton, a young man of limited means deeply in love with Lady Mary Christian. She is fond of Stratton, but declines marriage because of his lack of status and wealth, and instead weds a businessman named Justin. Distraught, Stratton exiles himself to South Africa to fight the Boers. He returns as something of a hero, and also discovers that his father has inherited land and money. He meets Mary again, they conduct an affair, are found out; Stratton is threatened with ruin unless he desists. He does, goes abroad, and marries. An innocent reunion between Mary and Stratton, however, comes to the attention of Mary's husband. He divorces her and she commits suicide.

This bleak story is a morality tale based on Wells' reservations about marriage. The eponymous 'passionate friends' are married to other people; the implication is that passion cannot live in marriage. The book stresses repeatedly that women invariably suffer in an institution that can never be a partnership of equals. This is one of the sharpest examples of the dichotomy within Wells' character. We have no reason to disbelieve his intentions and beliefs in *The Passionate Friends*; he did not write it for financial gain or to gain facile popularity – indeed, the book won him few friends within literary circles, and Henry James – one of the people Wells hoped to impress with the work – thought it one of Wells' poorest products to date. Wells saw the evil in an exploitative marriage and realized that women often suffered terribly, but refused to reform his own standards or help liberate Jane Wells from what was often little better than privileged servitude.

It is difficult to relegate Wells to the ranks of the simple hypocrites. Here was a man capable of acts of generosity, certainly with the gift of literary genius and a fine, incisive mind. The most revealing answer to the Jekyll and Hyde H.G. Wells – ostensibly, in his fiction and much of his political writing, a supporter of female liberation; in his personal life, exploitative and often uncaring of women – is to be found in his autobiography. In a long, cathartic passage Wells wrote,

The old feminist movement of the early nineteenth century had undergone a sort of rejuvenation in the eighties and nineties . . . There was a growing demand on the part of women for economic and political independence, and at first it seemed to me that here at last advancing upon me was that great-hearted free companionship of noble women of which I had dreamed from my earliest years.

As the hosts of liberation came nearer and could be inspected more accurately I found reason to qualify these bright expectations. If women wanted to be free, the first thing was surely for them to have complete control of their persons, and how could that happen unless Free Love and Neo-Malthusianism replaced directed and obligatory love and involuntary child-bearing, in the forefront of their programme. ... These things and not any petty political enfranchisement, I reasoned, must surely constitute the real Magna Charta of Women, and I set myself to explain this with the same tactless simplicity and lucidity that had already caused such inconvenience to the politicians of the Labour Party.

But the leaders of the feminist revival were no more willing than were the socialists to realize where they were going. ... Confronted by the plain statement of the Free Citizen Woman as opposed to the Domesticated Woman their hearts failed them. It became increasingly evident that a large part of the woman's suffrage movement was animated less by the desire for freedom and fullness of life, than by a passionate jealousy and hatred of the relative liberties of men. ...

They wanted to remain generally where they were and what they were, but to have it conceded that they were infinitely brighter and better and finer than men, that potentially they were finer poets, musicians, artists, social organizers, scientific investigators and philosophers than men could ever be, that a man owed everything to his mother and nothing to his father and so forth and so on; that women therefore ought to be given unlimited control over the goods and actions of their lawful partners, be empowered to impose upon these gross creatures complete chastity, or otherwise, as the fancy might take them, and, instead of establishing a free and liberal equality, entirely reverse the ascendancy of the sexes. ...

That feminism had anything to do with sexual health and happiness was repudiated by these ladies with flushed indignation so soon as the suggestion was made plain to them. Their modesty was as great as their boldness. Sex – what was sex? Get thee behind me Satan! They were not thinking of it. They were good pure women rightly struggling for a Vote, and that was all they wanted. ... The new Feminist Movement had no more use for me therefore than the Labour Socialists. To both these organizations I was an enfant terrible and not to be talked about.

In other words Wells approached what he termed as 'the Woman Problem' in the same way that he approached every other political and social issue. He knew best, he thought, and if he was opposed it was because of personal reasons. Other people simply did not understand and had to be told. Wells only had sympathy with the feminist movement when it agreed with his type of feminism. *The Wife of Sir Isaac Harman* appeared in 1914 and also explored feminist ideas and aspiration. 'I tried to explain to myself and my readers the suppressions and resentments that might lead a gentle woman to smash a plate-glass window,' he wrote of the book. In fact the novel pursued similar themes to those in *The Passionate Friends*: a marriage entered into with good intentions, an unstable and possessive husband, a wronged wife. Lady Ellen Harman is the central character, a wretched woman dominated by her abusive partner. She is allowed no freedom or independent social life, but is helped by one Agatha Alimony, an aggressive feminist, and eventually manages to free herself. There follows a series of adventures and escapades, attempted good works and broken love affairs. Ellen Harman experiences an inner liberation near the close of the book, but then 'She came back into herself. Close to her a seated man stirred and sighed. She tried to get back her hold upon that revelation, but it had gone. Inexorably, opaque, impenetrable doors closed softly on her moment of vision.'

This book was not a particular success, and once again Henry James offered his opinion, that the volume was a badly formed and untidy work. James had been making comments like these for some time and it is probably to Wells' credit that he had responded only with patience and a quite touching willingness to learn from such criticism. He was willing to defer to the older man and more meticulous writer – but not for ever.

Henry James was twenty-three years older than Wells, a patrician American who desired to become a patrician Englishman. He was the apotheosis of the grand novelist, revelling in his craft, disdainful of those he considered to be populist or plebeian. Wells, different in most if not all these respects, fascinated him. Not long after Wells had published his first stories, James asked to be introduced to the young writer. On learning of this, Wells wrote James a letter that included his reservations about James' *The Turn of the Screw*. In December 1898 James replied graciously:

My Dear H.G. Wells,
  Your so liberal and graceful letter is, to my head, like coals of fire –

so repeatedly for all these weeks have I had feebly to suffer frustrations in the matter of trundling over the marsh to ask for your news and wish for your continued amendment. The shortening days, the deepening mud, have been at the bottom of this affair . . .

Of course I had, about my young woman, to take a very sharp line. The grotesque business I had to make her picture and the childish psychology I had to make her trace and present, were, for me at least, a very difficult job, in which absolute lucidity and logic, a singleness of effect were imperative. Therefore I had to rule out subjective complications of her own. . . . [14]

Wells responded to the letter three weeks later. He explained that he had continued to think about his criticism of James' book:

and latterly with increasing discomfort. Novel and disagreeable as the conviction is, I think that the other alternative is right. The story is not wrong – I was. My conversion was accompanied by the profound conviction of sin and culminated in the small hours . . . I've had a profitable time and I shan't make such comments on your work again. It isn't at all a lovely story but I treated it with a singularly vulgar lack of respect, and if you were a novelist, I should doubt of your forgiveness.[15]

The correspondence between the two men led to their meeting. They were a dissonant pair: Wells the lover, James the near celibate; Wells the indifferently untidy, James the scrupulously elegant; Wells the activist, James the apolitical artist. Wells would later describe James as 'a strange unnatural human being, a sensitive man lost in an immensely abundant brain, which had neither a scientific nor a philosophical training, but which was by education and natural aptitude alike, formal, formally aesthetic, conscientiously fastidious and delicate.' He went on, 'James regarded his fellow creatures with a face of distress and a remote effort at intercourse, like some victim of enchantment placed in the centre of an immense bladder.'[16]

Early on, however, Wells was less critical. The letters continued, and James initiated another meeting. He wrote to Jane: 'Mrs Wharton, staying with me briefly, had motored me over to Dover to see – and take – a friend (who has also been with me) off to Paris, and on our way back we just tried you on the chance – hoping yet a little fearing . . . '[17] James did eventually make it to Wells' home, but was not comfortable with what he found there. The two men were amicable in their correspondence, but inimical in person. Artistic disagreements were not, as has been thought in the past, the crux of their argument; at this point, James still genuinely admired Wells' work. It was their contrary personalities that were the problem.

Back-handed compliments began to be exchanged, long silence followed the sending of books and letters. On one occasion Wells witnessed James at his most exposed, in an act of gaucheness. G.K. Chesterton was staying in a nearby inn; its garden connected to that of James' house. James' brother William was eager to see the great man and climbed up a ladder to spy over the wall. James was furious, and the two men argued in loud American tones. Such was the contrived Englishness of James' accent that this was a rare lapse for him. Wells was at the door, and overheard everything. James was ashen-faced. This was more reason for keeping an uneasy distance. Yet the two men still shared an intellectual respect. James wrote about the hero of Wells' novel *Kipps* that 'he is not so much a masterpiece as a mere born gem – you having, I know not how, taken a header straight down into mysterious depths of observation and knowledge, I know not which and where, and come up again with this rounded pearl of the diver'.

For a time the two men managed to bury some of their personal differences beneath the hill of literary debate. But James was determined to wear the mantle of the master, which Wells would not tolerate for very long. They based their relations on distance, occasional flattery, prearranged as well as chance encounters at the Reform Club and a little mutual gossip and mockery. With the publication of *The New Machiavelli* in 1911 the conflict between them deepened. James saw it as his obligation to speak out against Wells' new novel and always took his obligation extremely seriously. He was not alone, but his severity was sharpened for Wells by the recollection of what at one time almost resembled friendship. James wrote in a letter from the United States:

There is, to my version, no authentic, and no really interesting and no beautiful report of things on the novelist's, the painter's part unless a particular detachment has opened, unless the great stewpot or crucible of the imagination ... has intervened and played its part – and this detachment, this chemical transmutation for the aesthetic, the representational, end is terribly wanting in autobiography brought, as the horrible phrase is, up to date. That's my main 'criticism' in the N.M. – and on the whole ground there would be a hundred things to say.

Wells replied with courteous, and generous, acceptance of some of James' criticisms, stating that 'as far as it is loving chastisement I think I wholly agree and kiss the rod. You put your sense of the turbid confusion, the strain and violence of my work so beautifully that almost they seem merits.'

The following year, 1912, saw a less subdued and gentlemanly clash of sensibilities. James wrote to Edmund Gosse that Wells' book *Marriage* was causing him 'extreme difficulty'. He continued: 'I am not so much struck by its hardness as with its weakness and looseness, the utter going by the board of any real self-respect of composition and expression.' James was aghast at the form, plot and development of the book, and its scant regard for conventional structure. The use of an aeroplane crashing into a party – at a time when the aeroplane was unknown to most people – appeared to him to be dishonest and unconvincing; equally unacceptable, he thought, was a contrived three-hour conversation between two people, the contents of which are ignored in the work, which results in a vital declaration of love. This was poor fiction, insisted James, and worse literature. Wells must not twist his protagonists into artificial devices, he continued, and have them explaining the plot and progress of the novel directly to the reader.

Wells had been patient long enough. He was forced to admit that the book could have been constructed in neater form, but refused to bow to James' condemnations. 'That would have taken more time than I could afford,' he wrote. He added, 'I do not mean by that I could have earned less money and been a more conscientious writer, though that consideration very probably came in, but I mean that I had very many things to say and that if I could say one of them in such a way as to get my point over to the reader I did not worry much about finish.' He pursued this point in greater depth and clarified it in a paper delivered to *The Times* Book Club in 1912, in direct response to Henry James' attacks. It was a statement of his own aesthetic, in which he insisted that the novel had no established structure any more than it should have an established content. He was a politician of the pen, he believed:

We are going to deal with political questions and religious questions and social questions. We cannot present people unless we have this free hand, this unrestricted field. What is the good of telling stories about people's lives if one may not deal freely with the religious beliefs and organizations that have controlled or failed to control them? What is the good of pretending to write about love, and the loyalties and treacheries and quarrels of men and women, if one must not glance at those varieties of physical temperament and organic quality, those deeply passionate needs and distresses from which half the storms of human life are brewed?

A great deal of good, responded James, who soon heard, as he was meant to, of Wells' paper.

An act of goodwill rebuffed further deepened the gulf between the two men. Edmund Gosse was trying to organize an Academic Committee of the Royal Society of Literature. Both Gosse and James had good intentions in proposing Wells for membership, which they thought would clear him of the stigma of his past scandals. Wells refused with rude alacrity. James, puzzled, wrote to him, complaining of his 'irresponsive and unsociable attitude'. He continued: 'On hearing of your election I felt a greater pleasure than anything in my connection with that had yet given me, and if you maintain your refusal I shall continue in pain and privation, to yearn for you . . . '

From this point on, James found little good to say of his erstwhile friend's work. In mid-March and early April 1914 James published two essays in *The Times Literary Supplement*, consisting of a distilled analysis of and attack upon what he called the new generation of writers. (In fact, their ages varied greatly.) He had some respect for some of them, reserved double-edged compliments for others, but was nearly unsparing of Wells:

What are we to say of Mr Wells who, a novelist very much as Lord Bacon was a philosopher, affects us as taking all knowledge for his province, and as inspiring in us to the very highest degree the confidence enjoyed by himself – enjoyed, we feel, with a breadth with which it has been given no one of his fellow craftsmen to enjoy anything. If confidence alone could lead [us] utterly captive we should . . . be huddled in a bunch at Mr Wells' heels.

Most of what James wrote of Wells was tinged with irony approaching contempt. Wells was deeply hurt, and deeply angered.

The war prevented him from devoting his energies to the quarrel with James, but he maintained a steady stream of condemnation whenever possible. To a very large extent the battle was unequal. James was by now into his seventies, and Wells was at the peak of his argumentative strength. In 1915 Wells published his experimental novel, *Boon*, and with it the rift between him and James became public and irreconcilable. Wells had written the book over a period of ten years, collecting thoughts here, images there. George Boon is a fictitious writer whose collected works are written under the pseudonym Reginald Bliss. Wells supplied the putative introduction but few doubted that Wells was the author of the entire work.

The contrived compilation is a heavily faulted work, a cathartic exercise for Wells, but lacking balance and with little artistic purpose. Wells provides an imaginary conversation between Henry James and the realist writer George Moore, part of a splenetic little chapter entitled 'Of Art, Of Literature, Of Mr Henry James'. The attack on James is inexorable. He is belittled, he is laughed at, he is lampooned. 'Meanwhile Mr James, being anxious not merely to state but also to ignore, laboured through the long cadences of his companion as an indefatigable steam-tug might labour endlessly against a rolling sea, elaborating his own particular point about the proposed conference,' Wells writes. He continues:

The only living human motives left in the novels of Henry James are a certain avidity and an entirely superficial curiosity. Even when relations are irregular or when sins are hinted at, you feel that these are merely attitudes taken up, gambits before the game of attainment and over-perception begins ... His people nose out suspicions, hint by hint, link by link. Have you ever known a living human being do that? ... If the novel is to follow life it must be various and discursive. Life is diversity and entertainment, not completeness and satisfaction ... [James] sets himself to pick the straws out of the hair of life before he paints her ... In practice James' selection becomes just omission and nothing more. He omits everything that demands digressive treatment or collateral statement.

He summed up the Jamesian approach in a blood-letting and merciless paragraph: 'It is leviathan retrieving pebbles. It is a magnificent but painful hippopotamus resolved at any cost, even at the cost of its dignity, upon picking up a pea which has got into a corner of its den. Most things, it insists, are beyond it, but it can, at any rate, modestly, and with an artistic singleness of mind, pick up that pea.'

To compound the attack, and to make sure that James was aware of it, Wells personally delivered the book to him at the Reform Club. The old man, his eyesight declining quite rapidly now, read the book through the evening, and was hurt to the core. He managed to retain his sense of etiquette and wrote to Wells the next day.

... I have more or less mastered your appreciation of H.J., which I have found very curious and interesting after a fashion – though it has naturally not filled me with a fond elation. It is difficult of course for a writer to put himself in the place of another writer who finds him extraordinarily futile and void, and who is moved to publish that to the world ...

... However, there are too many things to say, and I don't think your chapter is really enquiring enough to entitle you to expect all of them. The fine thing about the fictional form to me is that it opens such widely different windows of attention; but that is just why I like the window so to frame the play and the process.

Wells, perhaps taken aback by the senior writer's objectivity, replied in emollient tones, admitting that 'so kind and frank a letter' gave him great embarrassment. He went on to say: 'You may take it that my sparring and punching at you is very much due to the feeling that you were "coming over" me, and that if I was not very careful I should find myself giving way altogether to respect.' Wells' note was an apology of sorts, and he was careful to describe himself as a 'rebellious and resentful admirer'. This semi-humour was highly characteristic of Wells and his writing. Although he found making an apology and showing contrition extremely difficult, he was conscious of when he was in the wrong. Hence he tried to inject humour and laughter into his apologies, mocking himself as well as others. Unfortunately these attempts were often misunderstood and just as often made the situation even worse. In this case matters had gone too far; the argument was now in the public domain.

The critics were able to take sides in the conflict behind the façade of their reviews of *Boon*. One of the most influential, and partisan, was *The Times Literary Supplement*:

It is easier to forgive Bliss and Boon for being blind to the place of art in life and the work of beauty in the world, than for their attempts to be funny at the expense of great writers past and present. They believe all reputations, from Homer's onward, to be founded on 'booming' or some imagined 'need for great men'. Even in their gibes at the unsuccessful writers of the day they remind the reader of rude little boys who put out their tongues. When they attack the great, their sense of humour is still meaner.

The review hit its mark. Although he was never able to ignore his reviews or simply avoid them, Wells had developed a specific formula to cope with such criticism. His reaction consisted of two stages. The first was to lock himself away in his study for a full twenty-four hours without seeing or speaking to anybody. This usually took place in London, for he said that the sounds of the street reassured him that he was not completely alone. He would re-read all the favourable reviews of his past books, hundreds of which he kept in a dog-eared cardboard file. Although he almost knew these pieces off by heart he still savoured every word, reminding him that he was revered and respected. After ten or twelve hours of this he would drink several glasses of brandy – never any other alcohol – and then go to sleep, often on the floor by his desk. The second stage was a return to the world, a quite manic succession of visits and meals with friends and acquaintances until the initial depression and anger began to recede. It was an elaborate process; from all accounts it seldom worked.

Opinion within the literary community shifted towards Henry James. He was perceived as an eminent figure of a past generation who was being teased and taunted by an inferior spirit. Wells had misjudged badly. He told friends and enemies alike that the book had not been a serious work and that his attacks on James were merely the friendly arrows of a fond companion. These pleas were shown in their proper light by James' reply to Wells' letter. It was a highly appropriate and fitting testimony, and 'did put HG in his place'.[18] He began by rejecting Wells' justification and partial apology. He continued:

Nor do I feel it anywhere evident that my 'view of life and literature' or what you impute to me as such, is carrying everything before it and becoming a public menace – so unaware do I seem, on the contrary, that my products constitute an example in any measurable degree followed or . . . successfully pleaded: I can't but think that if this were the case I should find it somewhat attested in their circulation – which, alas, I have reached a very advanced age in the entirely defeated hope of. But I have no views of life and literature, I maintain, other than that our form of the latter in especial is admirable exactly by its range and variety, its plasticity and liberality, its fairly living on the sincere and shifting experience of the individual practitioner. That is why I have always so admired your so free and strong application of it, the particular rich receptacle of intelligences and impressions emptied out with an energy of its own, that your genius constitutes; and that is in particular why, in my letter of two or three days since, I pronounced it curious and interesting that you should find the case I constitute myself only ridiculous and vacuous to the extent of your having to proclaim your sense of it. . . . It is art that makes life, makes interest, makes importance, for our consideration and application of these things, and I know of no substitute whatever for the force and beauty of its process. If I were Boon I should say that any pretence of such a substitute is helpless and hopeless humbug; but I wouldn't be Boon for the world, and am only yours faithfully,

Henry James

Wells replied three days later, with, 'I don't clearly understand your concluding phrases – which shows no doubt how completely they define our difference.' This was the end of a battle which saw the defeat of both men. James was seventy-two years old and drained of physical and emotional strength. In December 1915 he suffered a stroke, as he himself said, in 'the most approved fashion'. He died at the end of February in the following year. G.K. Chesterton provided the most apposite obituary: 'The older civilization gave him the wonderful things he wanted: but the wonder was his own. His whole world is made out of sympathy; out of a whole network of sympathy.' Wells was very much alive. He was vibrant, successful, bursting with creative energy; but a little less respected, and a little less content.

Also, Wells was more than occupied with someone else, a woman he had first encountered when his novel *Marriage* was published. The book had been given a clever, sardonic and scathing review in the 19 September 1912 edition of the feminist journal *The Freewoman*. The critic had written:

Mr Wells' mannerisms are more infuriating than ever in *Marriage* . . . Mr Wells' habit of spluttering at his enemies. He splutters less in *Marriage* than in *The New Machiavelli*, but in the hospital atmosphere of the latter, where a soul-sick man drugged himself with the ether of sex, it seemed less offensive than in this purer, brighter air . . . I wonder about the women who never come across any man who was worth loving (and next time Mr Wells travels in the tube he might look round and consider how hopelessly unlovable most of his male fellow-passengers are), who are not responsive to the lure of Dutch clocks, and forget, as most people do, the colour of the dining-room wallpaper, who, being intelligent, can design a becoming dress in five minutes and need think no more about it. I wonder how they will spend the time. Bridge-parties, I suppose, and possibly State-facilitated euthanasia.

The author was a gifted young writer named Rebecca West. Wells was determined to learn more of the woman behind the review.

5 A Woman of Some Importance

In the section of Wells' autobiography that was published posthumously, and entitled by his son G.P. Wells *H.G. Wells in Love*, Wells writes that:

In all my life I think I have really loved only three women steadfastly; my first wife, my second wife and Moura Budberg. . . . I do not know if I loved Rebecca West, though I was certainly in love with her towards the latter part of our liaison. I had one great storm of intensely physical sexual passion and desire with Amber Reeves. Beyond that, all these women I have kissed, solicited, embraced and lived with, have never entered intimately and deeply into my emotional life. I have liked them, found them pretty, exciting, amusing, flattering to the secret rakish braggart in my composition. I was jealous of them as one is jealous in a partnership, and jealous about them as one is jealous in a competition – and my impression is that I got nothing better than I gave. I was loved as I loved.

Rebecca West was born in 1892 as Cicily Isabel Fairfield, and took the name Rebecca West from the heroine of Ibsen's *Rosmersholm*. She had played the part in a production of the play and first used the name in 1912, but she always explained it as merely a random choice of a *nom de plume* with no more profound significance; her family and early friends always referred to her as Cissie. She was an ambitious and gifted young woman, combining a vivacious and precocious self-confidence with a biting intelligence. Those who knew her as a girl never doubted that 'great things were in store', recalling that she had systematically copied out and learned extensive passages from Shakespeare, Browning, Yeats, Whitman and Newbolt.

She studied at the Academy of Dramatic Art for a year but was never really satisfied with the theatre, preferring dramatic criticism to dramatic participation. Her first love was, and always would be, journalism, and she threw herself into feminist writing with a passion and vengeance that were almost unparalleled. First on *The Freewoman*, then *The Clarion*, *The New Statesman*, *Daily News* and *The Star*, Rebecca West compounded her reputation as one of the leading young journalists in the country: fearless, provocative and, more surprisingly, invariably correct. In her reviewing and journalism (more so than in her later books) she evinced a pungent wit and a relentless, caustic ability to draw the blood of her victims. By the time she was nineteen years old she was in enormous demand in Fleet Street, this woman with piercing eyes, slightly protruding teeth, a seductive laugh and the ability to capture the attention of all of those around her.

It was at the age of nineteen that she reviewed Wells' *Marriage*, a review which 'aroused his curiosity and amused Jane Wells, with the result that she was invited to come and spend a weekend with them at Easton Glebe'.[1] There was an immediate attraction. Rebecca encountered a man in his mid-forties, with an infectious laugh, a dumpy body and a mind as quick as that of anyone then writing. She found him a gracious host, as he showed the young critic around the lawn, offering her the sandwiches which Jane had just made. For his part, Wells, who normally was unforgiving of negative criticism, was intrigued by the author of *The Freewoman* review. She had, he said, 'a mixture of maturity and infantilism about her. She had a fine broad brow and dark expressive troubled eyes; she had a big soft mouth and a small chin; she talked well and she evidently read voraciously – with an excellent memory. We argued and she stood up to my opinions very stoutly but very reasonably. I had never met anything quite like her before, and I doubt if there ever was anything like her before.'[2] Wells employed a Swiss governess at the time and she recorded Rebecca West's visit in her diary. 'She looks about twenty-two years of age, and is very vivacious. She writes in *The Freewoman* and has just reviewed Mr Wells's new novel *Marriage*.' Governess Meyer was not in the habit of chronicling mere social visits in her diary. It was obvious to everybody even at this early stage that Rebecca West would play an important part in Wells' life.

Wells and West exchanged some letters and Rebecca visited him in Hampstead, where he and Jane (in reality, Wells alone) still maintained their London home. It appears that at this point Rebecca was mostly the pursuer, Wells the quarry, a situation Wells relished very much indeed. Only one letter from the period survives, written by Wells in early 1913. Although it is soaked in ambivalence and euphemism, it reveals the existence of an expanding relationship:

You're a very compelling person. I suppose I shall have to do what you want me to do. But anyhow I mean to help you all I can in your great adventure. You consider me an entirely generous and sympathetic brother in all your arrangements. I'll help you all I can and I'll take the risk of its being known about and misunderstood and I trust you implicitly to do your best that it isn't known about. I post this in London. I've maintained my small boys today and I motor home this evening (Wednesday). Tomorrow I get up again about six p.m. Friday my wife comes home from Switzerland and we go to Little Easton.

Wells succumbed eventually to a romantic link and wrote that 'face to face with my book-shelves . . . we paused and suddenly kissed each other'. He also insisted that the affair must be on a purely temporary basis. He was a busy man, he explained somewhat contemptuously, a regular contributor to the socialist press, including the *New Witness* and *New Age*, and in the mainstream press, in Northcliffe's *Daily Mail*. As well as this he was a married man, he insisted, and appearances were everything. Initially Rebecca accepted this businesslike and mercenary attitude but she soon realized that what she was experiencing was no infatuation or a straightforward case of sexual desire; she was in love. The middle four months of 1913 were agonizing for her.

She need not have worried; there was something in Rebecca West which Wells could not resist. Their son Anthony later defined this as the qualities of youth and promise. 'She was the embodiment of that audience of younger people that had, only a few years before, seemed to be in the hollow of his hand.'[3] Their passion was tinged, enhanced, by argument and debate. She seldom retreated from a position, and he enjoyed that. Once, during a romantic walk along the Essex coast, the couple began to discuss birth control. Wells agreed that it was a vital part of any package of reforms. West was suspicious, demanding to know if such a measure would be for the benefit of men or the benefit of women. Both, replied Wells, surprised by his lover's vehemence. No no, said West, it is not a question of male pleasure and convenience but of female liberation. They fell silent. Then Wells began to defend himself, explaining that he had not been thinking of simple lust but of a woman's control of an often oppressive nature. You say that now, interrupted West, but only because I demanded an explanation. Wells nodded and smiled; you're right, he said, and I love you for it.

Such compromise, such a conciliatory attitude, was rare indeed in H.G. Wells. West later stated that 'H.G. when he wrote letters to me was a different person from the one who spoke to me. He was always much more reasonable when he was with me than when he wrote to me. I can hardly remember any actual scenes taking place between us, I can hardly bring to mind one occasion when we raised our voices to each other, but when he wrote to me he was possessed by this curious irrational frenzy.'[4]

West and Wells were happy. They argued and fought but this only heightened their mutual passion and desire for each other. 'I must say I like Wells,' wrote Rebecca. 'He hasn't made love to me and it's fun watching his quick mind splash about in the infinite.' The situation rapidly changed. In Wells' recently acquired flat in St James's Court, Westminster, the couple made love and a child was conceived. Wells claimed that he would usually have taken contraceptive precautions but his ardour and fear of interruption prevented this. Both partners always maintained that they were 'extremely unlucky'.

Rebecca's mother had been strongly opposed to the liaison from the beginning, and was incredulous when she heard that her daughter was pregnant by Wells. She screamed at her that she was a foolish child, and had given herself at a ridiculously low and sordid price to an older, unscrupulous man. For his part Wells was profoundly shocked, and guilt-stricken, explaining that 'It should not have happened, and since I was the experienced person, the blame was wholly mine.' He knew of Rebecca's literary ambitions, knew that they would be difficult to fulfil when she had a young child to care for. Rebecca later insisted that Wells had wanted her to be pregnant so as to secure the relationship between them, but this is probably not the case. Wells asked his mistress to consider an abortion, but she would have none of it. Wells tried to reassure himself that after the birth it would be business as usual, and made arrangements for Rebecca's pregnancy. He had her hidden in Hunstanton in Norfolk and later stated that he lived with her there 'as much as possible'. In fact he was out of the country for much of the time or travelling on speaking tours elsewhere in Britain. It was a humiliating and isolating experience for Rebecca West, and it says much about her courage and tenacity that she survived the time at all.

Jane Wells had known of the relationship and the pregnancy all along. She had been aware of her husband's infidelities from as early as his first affair and had decided to accept matters. Wells and Jane had

long since ceased to be lovers. . . . Wells also made it plain to Rebecca that she had no reason to feel guilty with regard to Jane. For many years it had been agreed that, though the Wells household would present a respectable front to the world, he was at liberty to lead his emotional life elsewhere. Though Jane took no overt notice of the affair, she was as completely informed about Rebecca as she had been in the past about Amber and 'Elizabeth'. One may suspect, indeed, that her chief initial response was relief at seeing her erratic husband quietly settled in a new pattern.[5]

As long as Wells told his wife of his activities, and as long as she approved of the women involved, they had agreed there was to be no opposition. What Jane demanded was that there be no threat to her marriage from the other woman. Rebecca, on the other hand, knew nothing of this arrangement. She was not aware that during his long absences Wells returned to Jane whenever possible and that he was intent on regarding his wife as his long-term companion. In letter after letter to Rebecca, Wells stressed his devotion and dedication to her and her alone.[6] Considering Rebecca West's intelligence, it is perhaps surprising that she trusted her lover for so long. She was determined not to play the role of 'the nagging wife' and hence gave Wells more room than he probably deserved, and certainly more freedom than was prudent. His protestations that he was terribly busy with writing and speaking appeared, however, to be genuine. Wells' output of journalism was vast during 1913 and 1914, and Rebecca West thought that no man could be so busy and still find the time to spend with another woman or to return to his wife and even, on one occasion, attend the gala night of a West End theatre opening.

Wells was terrified that the impending birth might become public knowledge. The Amber Reeves scandal had almost destroyed him and a second such escapade would surely close the gates on his future ambitions within the social world. With his accommodating lawyer E.S.P. Haynes he organized a plan of action and a series of hiding places for mother and baby. It was vital, he told friend Haynes, that there was no publicity about the event. The timing of the birth, then, could not have been more fortuitous and fortunate. Anthony West was born on 4 August 1914, the day Great Britain declared war on Germany. It was a difficult and more than usually painful birth. 'I cannot see that childbirth is creative at all,' said Rebecca, 'one is just an instrument.'

Few people were cognizant of the baby's existence. Those informed gossips who did learn of the event were busy discussing the early triumphs of the British Expeditionary Force rather than the recent triumphs of H.G. Wells. Wells informed a selected group of friends, adding that he was delighted to have a son. A friend asked him if he had a preference for boys; 'a daughter,' he replied, 'would probably be more of a problem.'[7] Problem or not, Wells did not spend very much time with the mother and child. When he did venture forth to Norfolk, he was invariably disappointed, and made sure that this was known to all present.

Rebecca had surrounded herself with a nurse, a maid and other household staff; she was taking the role of mother and housekeeper extremely seriously, and did not have much time for a visiting elder Romeo. The roles of mother and mistress of the house did not, however, come easily to Rebecca West. She seemed to have a knack for choosing the wrong servants and compounded the fault by trusting the least trustworthy of people. The servants fought, stole and gossiped. When Rebecca reprimanded them they questioned her authority, implied that as an unmarried mother she was in no position to criticize. She would panic, pace the floor in increasing anxiety, and would rub 'her left wrist and thumb so rapidly and so vigorously with her right hand that she sometimes broke the skin over the radius and the lower part of her thumb'.[8] So common was this ritual that many photographs of Rebecca West show her with extended cuffs, covering the self-inflicted wounds.[9] Wells' task when he visited was usually to pacify the mistress and placate the servants. He knew servants, after all. He had been raised by his mother in servants' quarters.

Wells moved Rebecca and Anthony to Quinbury in east

Hertfordshire, only ten miles from his home at Easton Glebe and thirty miles from London. Rebecca needed him, she implored, to be nearer to her and the child, and both had a right to greater and closer contact with him. Wells was well aware that he was taking something of a risk. It was not in fact the location of the village that was such a poor choice – Rebecca's friends were now within reach and this was good for everyone concerned – but its size and character. The villagers soon began to ask questions about their new neighbour, and some refused to believe her story about a busy journalist husband in London. The more travelled of the local farmers had heard of a married man with two children living elsewhere in the county. When a dishonest housekeeper was fired and sought revenge by telling all she knew of Rebecca and Wells to the local townspeople, matters became intolerable. There were more letters from Rebecca, and replies from Wells:

You know it's as clear as daylight to me that you are my love. Mentally, temperamentally, physically, I've never been so warm and close with anyone as with you. And we have been ragging it all to pieces and spoiling it with detailed bothers for which we are both indisposed and naturally not very capable. ... Let us for the rest of the time regard Quinbury as the joke it is – a joke a little against us but still a very amusing joke, and with much very beautiful too.

It was a joke that did not, unfortunately, appeal to Rebecca West's sense of humour. Wells insisted that she stop writing to her friends and asking them to travel from London to Quinbury. Only those who could be trusted implicitly such as Ford Madox Ford and Violet Hunt, Wells insisted, should now be invited to visit.

Wells tried in every way to make Rebecca stay, urging her to consider what an upheaval another move would be. But the isolation and the darkness had become too much for Rebecca and she insisted on leaving the village. More than this, she specified that she must return to London. Wells responded by placing a newspaper advertisement: 'Family of two with nurse and child (ten months) want apartment (4 or 5 rooms) in any good outer suburb, north or west London. Use of garden. Accommodation for small car desirable. From 3 to 5 guineas a week according to conveniences. Permanency. Apply office of the paper.' In the context of the circumstances the advert is rather ridiculous, and strangely clinical. Yet the goodwill it demonstrated on Wells' part pleased Rebecca.

As it transpired there was no need for such publicity as a theatrical acquaintance of Wells, William Foss, offered a house in Pinner, near enough to Rebecca West's friends and the heart of London to satisfy her. But the location was not to be permanent. During the following years Rebecca would spend time in Maidenhead, Whitby in Yorkshire, north-west London and Leigh in Essex.

Not surprisingly, in view of her wanderings, she complained that she seldom saw Wells; she began to describe him mockingly to her friends as a distant *éminence grise* or 'The Great Man'. She was seldom allowed to see him, she said, 'and when I do it is usually in a public hall or on some similarly intimate occasion . . . I am in the most miserable state. Every thing emotional that has kept me going through the worries and hardships of the last three or four years has suddenly failed me.' Wells denied that he avoided her, writing later that he did indeed spend all possible time with Rebecca, and complaining for his part that she bothered him with pleas to leave Jane and marry her. His reminiscences appear to show that such an outcome was not at all likely. The tone of Wells' comments about his mistress is a hybrid of a teacher's and father's, with little authentic passion finding its way into the writing. 'I pestered her for three years "Construct, construct," – until she turned upon me fiercely and called me a "nagging schoolmaster".'

By the end of 1915 Anthony West was described by his mother to anybody who inquired as a young nephew whom she was caring for. She had originally considered claiming that she was a war widow with a son but this absurdity was soon abandoned. Wells would visit as a family friend and philanthropist, and a special room was put aside for him. He was becoming increasingly tired of the situation, writing to Rebecca, 'You ought to write a straight letter as one man to another to your mother, pointing out that your one chance of social rehabilitation and becoming independent of me is for your family to help. . . . Represent me as a penitent.'[10]

This unsatisfactory relationship continued throughout 1916, with West complaining again and again about Wells' lack of attention. 'Do you realize you were away from me for a month and that I have only seen you twice since?' she wrote. The letter was all too typical. In early 1917 she moved to Southcliffe, Marine Parade, in Leigh-on-Sea, Essex. The setting was picturesque but dangerous;

the German air force had included Leigh, by the Thames Estuary, on its list of targets for special and frequently deadly attention. On one occasion Rebecca found her cat dead outside her front door, its body riddled with machine-gun bullets. Wells laughed the incident off, joking that the Kaiser would have to hit his feline target eight more times before he could properly claim a victory. Rebecca was more concerned and sent Anthony, just three years old, off to London for safe keeping. It was assumed, ironically, that the Germans could not and would not reach London on their bombing raids. Before very long, of course, the attacks on London were systematic and highly destructive, and Rebecca, along with most of those who lived in the capital or had loved ones there, was shocked and shaken.

Rebecca West may not have been the most attentive of mothers but she did possess a genuine maternal instinct. She screamed at Wells that he must find a safe haven for their son. Instead of feeling pleasure at this view of Rebecca the mother and protector of his child, Wells was worried, displeased at this different side to the woman, an angry, family-centred aspect he had not seen before and did not appreciate. By September 1917 they were in the midst of a full and acrimonious argument about the raids, Anthony and the appropriate response. Wells wrote to Rebecca in the middle of that month:

The raid night gave me a shock. My instinct is to alter or avoid disagreeable things if that can be done and to sit tight and jeer if it can't. You behaved like a different sort of animal altogether. I hated your going out in the passage and talking to whoever chanced to be there and going to the door. The next night when I was tired and jaded and trying to get away from it by playing a mechanical patience you set up loud and exasperating cries of 'Oh God oh God!' For which I detested you. These trivialities seem to have released my mind to look at a whole group of facts that I have refused to look at before. I thought, 'I'm just going on with this business. Do I love this woman at all?' I thought, 'I've made up a story about her and it isn't the true one. What is the true one?' As far as I can make it out it is this. I love your artistic vigour, your wit, your fat old voice, a real greatness and beauty that shines through you, much that you enjoy, and the perfect delightfulness of our embraces. Companionship and desire, that ought to keep two people together. But there is a shadow which has grown darker until it blackens out all that. So far as I can make it out it is this. I am constantly dismissing evil realizations from my mind. The world and everything may be damned but I won't believe it. The whole world may be against me, the world is wrong. That's my temperament, my habit of mind. You are – otherwise. You go out to get the fullest impression of any old black thing. Every disagreeable impression is welcome to your mind, it grows there. All the past four years which might have been a love-adventure in our memories, your peculiar genius has made into an utterly disagreeable story – which has become the basis for an entire hopelessness about anything yet to come. A silly woman with a taste for cinema drama like Mrs Morse [Rebecca's one-time housekeeper] has become the presiding genius of our lives – she and your mother. Mrs Morse has destroyed any joint life for us. . . . A Dickens character, she was. We never met but your mother's grizzling because we are not married drops like a corrosive liquid on any happiness there may still be in our meeting. Poor old witch she is to damn two lives like ours. But these poor people, and such people as your nurse, dominate you. I have no power against them. This is not an accusation. I wish it was, because that would mean there was a remedy. If I could wrangle with you and fight for a change there would be some hope in the situation. But this is the statement of an absolute and incurable incompatibility. It is your nature to darken your world and blacken every memory. So long as I love you you will darken mine. It hasn't been a conscious process, it has been just my natural subconscious expression that has worked out at last to a rejection of the idea that I am in love with you. . . . I'll stick by you in most essential things but I'm not going on pretending that you are my happiness maker, my pride, my hope, my necessity. 'Votion has been asung. The Panther and the Jaguar's natural habitat is up cheerful trees. I expect when I get well away I shall begin to dream again of that dear Panther I loved, who was to be of an incomparable courage, who was to be my love mate and happiness mate, who was to succeed gallantly, who was to continually increase the tale of our happy memories together, who was to make a great history with me. Until sundry landladies, cook-generals and nurses said No. But here is the reality.

The letter was aggressive, out of balance, fatuous and, simply, completely wrong. Wells was an extremely possessive man and grossly overreacted to the influence of Rebecca's various friends and guardians. He was also a volatile man and within two months of writing the strident letter that appeared to deliver a fatal blow to the relationship he was once again proclaiming his love. 'So long as you sticks to me,' he explained to Rebecca, 'I sticks to you.' Rebecca accepted Wells' retraction and contrition but never completely trusted him again. She told Martha Gelhorn many years later that 'He never stopped loving me you know, in spite of all his shouting and silliness. I stopped loving him though, I really did.'[11]

With the end of the war came celebration and euphoria, particularly for the anxious mother Rebecca West and the concerned advocate of a world state H.G. Wells. Rebecca's sense of well-being was cut short, however, by pneumonia. Wells never reacted well to other people's illnesses and he stayed away from her for as long as he could. When she recovered he took her to Dorset, where on Rebecca's insistence the couple visited Thomas Hardy. On her return Rebecca was determined at last to come out of hiding and soon found a new home in highly desirable Queen's Gate Terrace in South Kensington. There was more contact now between Rebecca and Wells but the two still maintained a screen of pretence when it came to their son.

In April 1920 the couple drove to South Cornwall in Wells' new and much prized motor car. While staying with their mutual friends G.B. Stern and her husband Geoffrey Holdsworth in their cottage, Rebecca fell into an open cistern in the garden late one night during a customary walk before going to bed. It was only a rapid rescue that prevented the accident from being fatal. As it was, Rebecca badly cut her arm, the wound promptly turned sceptic and before very long the infection spread to her face. She was rushed in a horse-drawn ambulance to a nursing home in Redruth where she spent six unhappy months. 'You poor dear,' wrote Wells the following month, 'I wish I could come down and say kind things. But I'm busy getting visas, medicines and things.' He was referring to his planned trips to the United States and the Soviet Union. He did not refer to the fact that he had met and fallen for the American political activist Margaret Sanger.

While in the Soviet Union Wells let neither his affection for Rebecca West nor his infatuation with Margaret Sanger prevent further romance. He had a brief affair with Moura von Benckendorff (later Budberg), the twenty-seven-year-old secretary of Maxim Gorky. The affair may have taken him further away from Rebecca and certainly put him in a belligerent mood when he returned to Britain. During his first meeting with Rebecca since his tour he had a violent argument with her about Anthony, and in the heat of the quarrel revealed that he had betrayed her in Russia and been unfaithful on other occasions as well. Rebecca was outraged and responded by saying that if promiscuity was good enough for Wells, it was good enough for her. Wells was quick to the defence.

'Please love me and be faithful to me,' he wrote. 'It is much bitterer and more humiliating for the male and I can't bear the thought of it. I love you and want to keep you anyhow, but I know that in spite of myself I shan't be able to endure your unfaithfulness. I am horribly afraid now of losing you. It will be a disaster for both of us. It will cut the heart out of my life. I don't think it will leave much in yours.'[12] This was the lowest point of the relationship so far, and with Rebecca in Italy and Wells about to embark on a lecture tour in the United States, reconciliation looked unlikely if not impossible. Wells wrote to his Panther in desperate, pathetic and occasionally humble tones:

I am almost unendurably lonely and miserable. I've got tired. I've done no end of work and good work. I've really changed British policy about Russia and when I sit in judgement on myself I smother myself with (w)reaths. The *Outline of History* is going to change History. I've done good things and big things. It doesn't matter a damn so far as my wretchedness is concerned. Righteous self-applause is not happiness. Russia excited me and kept me going. Now I'm down. I'm alone. I'm busy. I'm tired. I want a breast and a kind body, I want to be treated kindly and to feel safe and warm and near. I want love that I can touch and feel. And I don't deserve love. I've trampled on people. I've nagged at and bullied you. I've not kept faith: I've almost tried to lose you. You are probably the only person who can really give me love and make me love back. And because you've been ill I've treated you so's I've got no right to you any more. I don't believe I'll find you next April. If I don't find you then I hope I'll find Death. I can't go on being the dull slave of the Salvage of the World. I can't – in my present state anyhow – bank on religion. God has no thighs and no life. When one calls to him in the silence of the night he doesn't turn over and say, 'What is the trouble Dear?' I'm miserable and lonely and disgusted and flat. Have I ever got into your arms to cry? I would like to do that now. (Though I believe we should presently forget about the crying in our mooshal efforts to comfort each other.) Dear Panfer. I wonder how much this is just being cut off from you. I don't know, but of the unexampled misery of my mind there is no doubt whatever.

Rebecca had no illusions about the letter and realized that it was profoundly manipulative and largely contrived. She embarked on a holiday in Capri, to stay with Faith Compton Mackenzie and her husband, the novelist Compton Mackenzie. Wells was aware of the trip, and aware that Compton Mackenzie was an attractive, intelligent and successful man who was perhaps overly fond of

Rebecca. The last thing Wells could tolerate was other people's desires for 'his women'. It was something Rebecca intended to exploit to the full. Although the flirtation was never anything more than platonic fun it was sufficient for Rebecca's aims and provoked Wells into paroxysms of impotent anger. One of his standard reactions in such a situation was to pace around his study throwing a cricket ball at his desk chair in an effort to turn it around 360 degrees. Because this ambition required so many attempts Wells usually dented or ruined half-a-dozen valuable books and pictures before he succeeded.

Yet in this case his temper was completely misplaced. Apart from the innocuous nature of the Compton Mackenzie relationship Rebecca also had her hands full caring for her friend Faith, taken ill shortly after Rebecca arrived on Capri. She acted as nurse and factotum for as long as she could and then left the island in a state of near collapse and exhaustion. When the Panther and the Jaguar met again in 1921 they were a different couple, not the Wells and West who had met in a bucolic country garden, not the carefree children of the gods who had fallen in love so many years earlier. He was increasingly cynical and depressed, often tearful and unsure. Jane had recently had a hysterectomy and Wells to his credit felt very guilty, sometimes believing that he had caused the problem by putting his wife through so much emotional turmoil. Rebecca was worn down and had lost some of that invincible optimism that had so permeated her character in the past.

They tried to start again by travelling to Amalfi together and attempting to recapture some of the spark and sparkle of former days. They stayed at the Hotel Cappucini, tried hard to laugh at each other's jokes and respond to each other's moods and desires, but this became ever more difficult – the trip was not a success. When Wells returned to England Rebecca remained in Europe. He immediately began to write her flaming love letters in rapid succession.

I shall be so glad when you are back in London. I am beginning to miss you dreadfully. I didn't at first. I was busy with coming back and all sorts of things. Now that I have settled down, I begin to want someone about who is – you. Someone to go about with, to stroll in to and scold, to go out to lunch with, to take to a movie and all the little dear companionships one hardly notices while one has them. (And there are such things as beds.) We were tremendously together all that time . . .

And later:

I love you more than any other human being. You are my dearest companion. I love and admire you. If I did not love you I should still think you one of the wisest and sweetest of human beings. You've got all sorts of superficial faults and weaknesses but the stuff of you is the best stuff I've ever met inside a human skin. (And it is lovely to have you.) I want to be with you as much as I possibly can. I love your voice. I'm not really happy except when you are about. I am prouder of being your 'dear Jaguar' than anything else in the world.

By the middle of 1921 the couple had reunited but the lukewarm relationship was a pale imitation of what it had been in the past. They knew but were afraid to admit that they had settled down to the sort of suburban and enervated existence that they had so mocked when times were better. The excitement had gone out of this shattering affair but neither participant was quite prepared to examine the evidence and find the appropriate conclusion.

Their arguments took on a familiar pattern. For example, Wells had put on weight and Rebecca did not like it. After repeated warnings about his corpulence she finally let fly, and on one Sunday morning with the bells of the local Roman Catholic church beckoning people to worship, Rebecca began to shout. Did he enjoy being a fat man, she screamed, and how would he feel if she became flabby? Wells said nothing, turned bright red in the face and neck, and stormed out of the flat in Queen's Gate Terrace swearing he would not return. He was back within the hour with flowers and apologies. She was right, he said, he had begun to get fat. These arguments were never constructive, did not leave Wells and West closer or more in love with each other when they were resolved. The signs were clearly there to be read by everybody, apart that is from Rebecca West and H.G. Wells.

In October 1921 Wells travelled to the United States. He grew to love America but this trip pained and annoyed him. He wrote back to Rebecca complaining of American insularity and lack of imagination. 'Be a good panfer,' he wrote in one of his letters. 'Not to be kissed or flattered too much. You've got me and that's what you want.' Rebecca eventually met up with Wells in Gibraltar in January 1922 but the meeting was less than both of them expected. Rebecca had left Anthony behind in London extremely reluctantly and was in poor spirits when she arrived in Gibraltar. For his part Wells fell ill with a sore throat just as he arrived and immediately began to demand the best doctor that Gibraltar could offer. He began to lose his temper as his throat deteriorated and ordered Rebecca to contact the Admiral of the Fleet in Gibraltar and get the man's personal surgeon to look at his throat. Rebecca replied that she was not Wells' personal nurse and that not even a nurse should be screamed at in such a manner. Wells then rang the manager of the hotel and demanded the same service. The hotelier proved to be more obliging than the lover. In the end an old and retired medical man was found who was unimpressed with Wells' suffering and prescribed nothing more than an occasional gargle and mouth-wash. This was Wells at his worst, and Rebecca at her best. He moaned and complained about medical incompetence, how close he was to death and how cruel those around him were. Rebecca was still ill and run-down but she nursed Wells night and day, eating only sandwiches for her meals because he complained that the sound of knives and forks scratching on a plate would surely kill him.

In public Wells' treatment of Rebecca was even worse. He seemed intent on consciously and deliberately humiliating her, making her fetch and carry for him to such an extent that first their hotel's proprietor and then the Anglican chaplain offered to give her the money to return home to the safety and dignity of her mother. Rebecca still held on, hoping for a change if they moved their location. She suggested Granada, with its delicious mingling of Christian, Islamic and Jewish cultures and artistic heritages. Wells at first rejected the plan, arguing that 'Arab civilization in Spain was only a low form of civilization and not worthy of his consideration.' Rebecca shot back that Wells was a 'pompous schoolmaster'; reminded perhaps of his former days, Wells was deeply hurt and moved by the insult and changed his mind about Granada. From that beautiful city they travelled to Madrid and then on to Paris. In Paris Wells again launched into Rebecca, refusing to take her to see Anatole France because, as he explained in clinical tones, she was 'not good looking enough'.

After returning to England, in March, Wells wrote a letter of partial explanation and justification to Rebecca;

The old male Pusted [i.e. cat] has read her letter attentively and declines to plead guilty to an Enlarged Egotism. He objects to the Better Jaguar Movement.

The Better Panther Movement (nagging schoolmaster) was dropped before the Italian holiday. It had only one revival when Jaguar insisted upon having that book finished before the Spanish holiday. It is now dead altogether. Panther can be, do and act as she damn pleases. Jaguar proposes no further comments – only resistance or non-participation when he personally is involved. He thinks the Better Jaguar Movement had better follow the Better Panther Movement tout suite.

The old male Pusted does not care a damn about any Scandal except in so far as it distresses her imagination. That sort of Mook Scandals anyhow. He does not care how things strike people.

He went to Granada after all to please her. It pleased him but that he did not know beforehand.

He funked 48 hours on the train because she does not travel well and neither of them were in the mood for much mutual helpfulness. A Scandal about Madrid or Paris would not have hurt her; it would have smashed up his political influence (such as it is) upon the Franco British situation.

The above sort of argey-bargey is a bore.

The old male Pusted will henceforth treat the young female Pusted with a courtly politeness. He will, so help him, never ask her to fetch his coat downstairs or any such insulting service again. A barrier of respect shall be set up between them. If the projected Better Jaguar Movement goes on he will receive its intimations with attention but he does not propose to treat them as commands. And when he does not feel up to being improved by Panther and her Friends he will just have to keep away.[13]

Rebecca did not take the letter very seriously; she knew Wells too well and knew the shape and form of his empty defences. She outlined her grievances some years later, while Wells was still alive, in a private note: 'he treated me with the sharpest cruelty imaginable for those horrible years, that he humiliated me . . . that he overworked me and refused to allow me to rest when I was ill, that he has cheated me of all but one child, that his perpetual irascibility ruined my nerves, that he isolated me and drove away my friends.'[14]

It is difficult to understand just why Rebecca remained with Wells during this time. There was still an infatuation, that of a younger writer for an older and internationally respected novelist. When Wells praised Rebecca's work or flattered her abilities she was overjoyed, submerged in enough euphoria for her to forgive any number of transgressions. She also truly believed that she could change Wells, that he was capable of radical change and improvement. Then there was the financial aspect of the relationship and the care and education of young Anthony. Wells was never a parsimonious man and was munificently generous with both Rebecca and her son, so much so that Rebecca was genuinely nervous about losing such income. So in spite of her undeniable intelligence and her belief in feminism and the need for women to assert themselves in public as well as private life, Rebecca West remained in a damaging, perhaps even abusive relationship. Such an occurrence is far from unknown.

Rebecca's career was going particularly well and as an author and journalist she was in constantly greater demand. She was consequently part of an independent, young set of literary and artistic figures who did not include Wells in their number. Wells was thus twice threatened. His age excluded him from this group and shook his self-confidence; and his position as Rebecca's premier friend was now in question. He contemptuously dismissed some of these new allies as 'little friends' and advised Rebecca to look elsewhere for companionship. She laughed at his attacks and continued to meet with her companions in Porlock, Somerset, where Wells twice went to visit them. On the second occasion Rebecca later left a description, which would not be out of place in one of Wells' novels of whimsical lower-middle-class life in Southern England:

We drove all over Somerset and Devon one day. He refused to stop at any inn for lunch because they all looked wrong. When he settled on one it was too late and there was a row because they would not serve us. Finally we settled in for the night at a curious inn right in the middle of a barren moor, near a place which I think was called Box. This was kept by a man who was obviously going out of his mind and who lived there alone with his despairing daughter. I think this man had bought the inn on some gratuity he got at the end of a term in the colonial service. Anyway nobody was coming to the inn, which seemed natural enough as there was not a soul in sight, the nearest village was miles away. Someone else arrived, a commercial traveller, and H.G. and the landlord and the commercial traveller played some three-handed game of cards for a whole day, and the daughter and I sat in the kitchen and she wept and we did household chores together. Then H.G. took me back to Porlock and went off in a huff.

Wells' jealousy was by now out of control, and it combined with his increasing realization that the end of the affair was inevitable and imminent. He believed that Rebecca was romantically involved with some of her new friends, principally Hugh Hart. He wrote to Rebecca that

as I see it I was squeezed out . . . while you had Hart there and your sister had her lover. I don't know how far things went. I know you tolerate enormous familiarities from the Holdsworths. No doubt this is unjust and so forth. The thing that matters is the emotional estrangement. I detest Holdsworths. Either you clean up that corner and get rid of this irritating follower or you lose any intimacy with me. It's no good starting a tu quoque.

He compounded this attack by alleging that Rebecca's arts columns in the *New Statesman* were slanted towards her friends and that she was too easily influenced by those with whom she dined and played. In short, she had no sense of independent judgement or any ability for objective thought. Moreover, he eviscerated her recent novels, principally *The Judge*, which he described as 'an ill conceived sprawl of a book with a faked hero and a faked climax, an aimless waste of your powers'. This was gratuitous and harsh, motivated by spleen rather than balanced judgement. He had not finished there, however, and went on:

I've tried to let you down easily about *The Judge* but I feel that if we are to go on you've got to have exactly what I think of it. The book is too important in our lives. If we are to have suppressed opinions about it – or on your part about my books – the irritation of the suppression will destroy any sort of mental community. I've got no use for you at all as a humbugged pet woman. If I am going to have a female pet I could get any number of prettier and more amusing pets than you. With us it is either complete companionship or nothing.

Rebecca was outraged and accused Wells of double standards and crass hypocrisy. If she ever made even the most innocuous and constructive criticism of Wells' work, she said, he became angry and sullen and walked out of the house. How dare he now try to rationalize plain and simple cruelty? She continued that if this was how he genuinely felt about her and her work he should completely break the relationship.

Wells was surprised by the reaction and soon replied. 'I am very sorry if this storm has distressed you. I have been unhappy for four years. Except for the Pusted-Fido business you have given me no love and no help for a very long time. I wanted to see if you thought there was anything worth making a fight for between our minds. Manifestly you don't think there is. You let me go.' Ever volatile Wells was in a different frame of mind shortly after he wrote this letter, anxious to appear more conciliatory. He gave a potted history of the relationship and concluded:

We've had a love and friendship so dear and good that it wasn't good enough. We've been the dearest friends and lovers and we have afflicted and attacked and encumbered each other all the time. This last journey to Cornwall was full of such dear and delightful things. Whenever we have been free together and alone together I have been happy. Our spring holiday was perfect to me. Thetford, the sands beyond Hunstanton, much of Braughing, that deep flooded ditch there where we waded, Gladys in those days, the Leigh flats, the air raids we shared, Monkey Island, – and Claverton afternoons. And all the while we have been fighting against each other – discontents – contentions. Seeing it was so near perfect why didn't we and why don't we now make it perfect? Because it's just about that that we always quarrel. Our ways of work and a lot of our personal habits are incompatible, ungracious warrings. My memories of you run in two sets but the greatest set is truly you, my Panther, dignified and wise and dear.

He continued in this vein in a later note, arguing that Rebecca was

wise in setting about as you are doing to save the rest of your life from me. Your decision is my infinite loss but it will not be a fatal loss. I don't feel deeply. I curse and swear and spend sleepless nights wandering about the house or doing work and I drowse during the day. I shall get on with it all right and you have no obligation to me. 'Consolations' will come fast enough. And if I can be any sort of friend or companion to you I shall be glad. Do realize that though I can curse you, be unfaithful to you as I was in Russia, goad you and scold you, abuse your work, bring fantastically absurd (self tormenting) charges of unfaithfulness against you and so on and so on – you have the catalogue – nevertheless I love you intensely. You have the most wonderful brain I have ever met, the sweetest heart, the most loving and delightful humour, wit abounding, on ten thousand occasions you have been supremely beautiful to me.

Nevertheless I think you are wise to disentangle the rest of your life from mine.[15]

With the benefit of distance and lack of involvement the letter appears to be hackneyed, the standard paradoxical plea from someone who knows they have wronged their partner and can think of only one way to keep their relationship intact. Yet the ploy worked and again Rebecca gripped on to the lifeline of Wells' contrition and willingness to change. So committed was Rebecca that she even tolerated public degradation for the sake of the affair. In March 1923 an effort was made to prevent her entering the United States on grounds of 'immorality', a local zealot alleging that as an unwed mother and notorious mistress of a famous figure she was an unwanted guest in Christian America. Rebecca's lawyers in New York remedied the situation but her nerves were badly shaken by the publicity. On another occasion Rebecca was asked to take her son away from his school because of rumours and gossip concerning his legitimacy. The only way out of the situation was for Wells to leave Jane and marry Rebecca. It was never in reality something Wells would have done. When Rebecca asked him to reconsider his life with Jane and also cried to him about her treatment in New York and by Anthony's school, his reply was mocking and unsympathetic:

I don't think it fair for you to turn on me with this growing mania of yours about the injustice of my treatment of you in not murdering Jane. The thing goes on and on with you and I am tired to death of it. I do regret very bitterly that I ever met you but I have done what I could to make some sort of tolerable life for us. I can do no more than I have done. It's your business, in my idea, to disregard these fool scandals and go to America and succeed, as you certainly will do if you go, in spite of them. It's not your business, it's not playing the game, to lacerate me about it. For ten years I've shaped my life mainly to repair the carelessness of one moment. It has been no good and I am tired of it.

Rebecca did not back down and met with Wells at the Savoy Hotel for dinner to talk through their problems. During the meal she began to cry. Wells knew that such a public demonstration of emotion was untypical and believed in her sorrow and grief. But tears could not move him and he suggested again that they separate, with Rebecca being in full charge of Anthony and Wells paying all school fees and paying Rebecca 500 pounds a year until she was married. He then began to backtrack, again admitting that he had been amiss, perhaps even callous. He knew he was mercurial, he said, but that was the way he was and it did not alter his love for Rebecca. This time Rebecca was harder, more sceptical and less malleable. Wells had misjudged her; there was nothing for it, he would have to resort to his old trick.

You know you must face certain facts about me. It is a most important thing for you to understand how persistently I doubt the possibility of anyone loving me. I dislike myself as an inadequate instrument. I am maddened by my fluctuations of will and mood. I think I am ill looking. I am not amused at myself in any way. I cannot understand anyone loving me. I can understand you being intensely loved or my boys being loved. But not this hard, strained inconsistent thing with a sort of greatness and a voice and a life that jangles.

I want you to save the rest of your life from me, but do let me help you in every possible way to keep your life dignified and free. I will come to the flat when you return and we can surely come to an understanding on these matters. I rebel against you, I try to get rid of you, but I love and also I respect you. I'm not really a Jaguar or a Pusted or a Fido or any of the dear things I have loved to pretend to be. I am a man who has had the dearest most wonderful love and has requited it ill. But I do now want to help and sustain your life as well as I can. . . . And if the Jaguar you created vanishes there remains a man you don't understand who cares for you and worships you as well as insulting and raging and beating at you. He's done these things, insults and rage and so on, for the last time since you dismiss him but he will work with you if he can.

I don't know Panther. I haven't the face to ask you to try again. If we try again you will be you and I shall be I. We may have learnt a mutual consideration but it is foolish to make promises. We shall love and we shall jar. You say the love isn't worth the torment of the discord.

Leave it at that.

Rebecca was only prepared to meet Wells halfway, to write to him but not to meet him and certainly not to resume any sexual contact. The next time they met was when they dined with Sinclair Lewis and his wife, and Wells complained after the meeting that Lewis had made advances towards Rebecca. Wells had seen, he wrote to Rebecca, Lewis 'slobber his way up your arm'. Rebecca first laughed at this suggestion, then became angry at its implication. Then something happened which was too unpleasant and too far-reaching for Rebecca to forgive or for Wells to escape from.

Wells had begun a relationship with Hedwig Verena Gatternigg, partly because the woman amused him but also because he wanted to annoy and provoke Rebecca. When the young Austrian had outlived her usefulness Wells rejected her and refused to continue the affair, and the wretched, unstable woman attempted suicide in his flat. He explained to Rebecca, 'I was harsh and savage with her and smashed the door on her too hard so to speak, but I was tired and suffering nervously and she was unspeakably tiresome – you cannot imagine how tiresome. A gnawing incessant little rat she was, threatening all my peace with you and everything I cared for.'

Some of Wells' friends blamed Rebecca for what occurred, perversely concluding that she had forced Wells to treat Gatternigg in such a manner. The press also traced the story to Rebecca, literally banging on her front door for interviews and explanations. Rebecca escaped to the Hotel Klinger in Marienbad but Wells followed her there. It would do no good, she insisted, matters had gone too far now. They returned to Britain, only meeting in public and in larger groups of mutual friends. Rebecca embarked on an American tour and hardly wrote a letter to Wells. He panicked and tried to use Anthony as a weapon. 'I'm inclined to think I ought to adopt him,' he wrote. 'A boy ought to have a man in his life. I've told Gip about him and I shall tell Frank when a favourable occasion arises and I think they'll be good elders for him.'

Rebecca was frightened but not moved. There was worse to come, however. During a New York party one female guest loudly proclaimed that

we are all disappointed in you. You have put an end to a great illusion. We thought of you as an independent woman, but here you are, looking down in the mouth, because you relied on a man to give you all you wanted and now that you have to turn out and fend for yourself you are bellyaching about it. I believe Wells treated you too darn well, he gave you money and jewels and everything you wanted and if you live with a man on those terms you must expect to get turned out when he gets tired of you.

Rebecca blamed Wells directly for the incident, convinced that his version of their relationship was now accepted as the truth. The romance was well and truly at an end. She would not, she swore to Wells, resume a passion that had caused her so much anguish and inflicted so much damage on her reputation. It was over.

There was another meeting, quite by chance. Wells and West actually bumped into each other at a theatre in London and perhaps for the first and last time in their lives both of them were speechless. They gathered their wits and chatted but said nothing of importance and Wells did not even attempt to change Rebecca's mind. He wrote one last letter declaring his love, although he knew in his heart of hearts that there was no point. 'I've always been in love with you and I always shall be,' he wrote. 'Panther is my lost love and a black hole in my heart.' There was no reply.

The purest, most noble aspect of the affair was the occasional friendship between the two of them. Wells wrote lovingly of it in his memoirs:

But I cannot close this chapter on Rebecca without a word or two about the peculiar wit that made her companionship at its best the warmest, liveliest and most irreplaceable of fellowships. She filled our intimate world with fantasies and nicknames. She kept, for example, an imaginary public-house and she was the missus and I drove the gig. There were times when we almost materialized that gig. Or we were two melancholy but furry and eccentric animals, the Pussteads. Or she was a fantastic mixture of herself and Emma Goldman and Violet Hunt; she gave lectures upon refined subjects and had startling indelicate lapses, and in that shape was called, I forget now why, the 'Legendary Panther'. We would concoct long passages of a lecture or conversation by the Legendary Panther in which she struggled phrase after phrase, with unavailing snatches at circumlocutions and evasive allusions, towards the ultimate unavoidable shock. . . . She was a great invention.

Yet ultimately many people lost a great deal because of the much dramatized relationship between H.G. Wells and Rebecca West; West for certain, her son Anthony without any doubt, Rebecca's mother and of course Jane Wells. All losers, all defeated. Perhaps, in fact, the only person not to suffer very much and to continue his life in triumph was H.G. Wells himself.

6 Sniffing at the Heels of Reality

'I was taken by surprise by the Great War,' Wells wrote some years after the event. 'Yet I saw long ahead how it would happen, and wove fantastic stories about it. I let my imagination play about it, but at the bottom of my heart I could not feel and believe it would really be let happen.' He was not alone in this ambivalent point of view. The pattern for conflict had long been perceived: evolving empires on a direct crash course, internal strife within the European powers, vociferous minorities, military expansion and economic change. Yet few had thought that the world conflict would come along when and how it did, provoked by the half-bungled assassination of a Hapsburg heir in the Balkans.

Wells had, as he claimed, predicted an international collapse and a subsequent Armageddon. In both *The World Set Free* and *In the Days of the Comet* he had foreseen the coming crisis. The latter book, published in 1906, depicted a mass mobilization of the military, very much along the impressively organized lines of 1914. The arrival of a comet, however, provides a celestial halt to the posturings. In the former book, which appeared in 1914 but was written well before, he (in his own words) 'described the collapse of the social order through the use of "atomic bombs" in a war that began, prophetically and obviously enough, with a German invasion of France by way of Belgium'.[1] The book is more appreciated today than it was in 1914, when bellicose confidence was overwhelming. Anthony West has described how the work was

grotesquely untimely in the context of the events of 1914. In the summer and winter of the previous year, when he was writing it, he must have been one of the very few people in the world thinking seriously, or at all, about the horrors that atomic warfare might bring into it. As 1914 rolled on, and the threat that a civil war might spread out of Ulster and into England gave way to the certainty that there was going to be a great European conflict before the end of the summer, the sheer irrelevance of the subject became startling.

This is a harsh judgement, jaundiced by the slights which West received from his father. Wells' theme in the book was that humanity would be so terrified by the atomic bomb that warfare would be anathema – an early theory of nuclear deterrence. He also, however, had the invention of an atomic motor causing economic chaos, enormous unemployment and an international financial crash in 1956. A war follows, and atomic bombs are dropped on major urban centres. Wells clearly understood the potential, and reality, of nuclear capability quite brilliantly. This was proved by the case of the scientist Leo Szilard, who was one of the leading minds behind the Hiroshima bomb. He had been working within the field of nuclear physics for some time when he came across *The World Set Free*. Wells had promised a scientific breakthrough in 1933, the very year Szilard had come to grips with the intricacies of the nuclear chain reaction and pushed atomic research into another generation. He was moved, and terrified, by Wells' predictions of nuclear catastrophe. When he was about to reveal his findings, he found himself turning to *The World Set Free* for counsel. 'Knowing what this would mean,' he wrote, 'and I knew it because I had read H.G. Wells, I did not want this patent to become public. The only way to keep it from becoming public was to assign it to the Government. So I assigned it to the British Admiralty.'[2]

Wells also used the book to discuss and pursue his ideals of social engineering and the rule of the preordained few. When the nuclear war is over – Wells did not understand the long-term effects of radiation – a World Republic is founded, and with it a great central index of knowledge. 'The old tendencies of human nature', he wrote, 'suspicion, jealousy, particularism, and belligerency, were incompatible with the monstrous destructive power of the new appliances the inhuman logic of science had produced. The equilibrium could be restored only by civilization destroying itself down to a level at which modern apparatus could no longer be produced, or by human nature adapting itself in its institutions to the new conditions.' Here were the themes originally outlined in *Anticipations*, but in less strident terms: death, followed by resurrection, followed by obsessive organization.

When the predicted German invasion took place in August 1914, Wells, no longer part of the organized left in Britain, took little notice of the pacifist wing of the Fabian Society or of those in the wider labour movement imploring socialist leaders to put the fraternity of the working class before national pride and national war aims. Wells was convinced that the war need not be such a terrible thing, and that it could shake humanity into a new order. German expansionism and militarism, he was convinced, had to be smothered. He recorded in his autobiography:

People forget nowadays how the personal imperialism of the Hohenzollerns dominated the opening phase of the war. I shouted various newspaper articles of an extremely belligerent type. But my estimate of the moral and intellectual forces at large in the world, was out. I would not face the frightful truth. I anticipated an explosion of indignant common sense that would sweep not simply the Hohenzollerns but the whole of the current political system, the militant state and its symbols, out of existence, leaving the whole planet a confederated system of socialist republics.

He devoted his literary services to the war effort. Here was a patriotism which had not been detected before. In September 1914 he published *The War that Will End War*,* an ironic title, in that in the modern sense, this was in fact the war to start them. The compilation of articles and essays evinced an almost pathological hatred of Germany and all things German. Wells was not alone in such antipathy, but most of his bedfellows at the time were in the conservative camp, jingoistic and xenophobic politicians who were not his usual allies. His feelings towards the Germans – the people as well as the regime – alienated even some diehard British nationalists. In a rare moment of support for the Jewish people he claimed that the only good literature from Germany was written by Jews. He wrote that he would personally help loot Berlin after the victory; that German railway tickets should be stamped with 'Extra for Louvain Outrages – Two Marks'; that 'Never has any state in the world so clamoured for punishment . . . Every sword that is drawn against Germany now is a sword drawn for peace';

* Wells coined the phrase, though others later claimed authorship.

he called for an American blockade of the Germans, so as to starve them into submission. As when he was a boy in Kent, the glamour and glitter of war made his head swirl with images which belied reality.

Various friendships were twisted or broken by Wells' attitudes during the war, but no rupture received more publicity than that with George Bernard Shaw. Ever since the Fabian campaign Wells and Shaw had tiptoed along a thin, crooked line between strained friendship and downright contempt. They had walked well and successfully. Now Wells learnt that Shaw's attitude towards the war was that of informed cynic. Nobody was entirely correct, he believed, but he and his family happened to be resident in Britain and hence did not desire a German victory. He playfully compared the combatants to pirates. Late in 1914 Wells wrote an article in the *Daily Chronicle* on the subject of Scandinavia's role in Northern Europe, and referred to Shaw's muddle-headedness. This was the spark for the latest episode in the debate. Shaw soon replied:

There is a point at which Mr Wells' mind gives way. There are two symptoms. One of them is the now familiar and apparently inevitable English symptom of a kind of breakdown; a sudden and unprovoked attack on me. Mr Wells, without a word of warning, calls me muddle-headed. Muddle-headed! Me! Bernard Shaw! the man whose clarity England can often hardly bear! I ask you – ! Well no matter . . .

He went on to eviscerate Wells' argument about Swedish intentions and aspirations, and as in past disputes to make Wells appear as a callow amateur, this time badly versed in diplomacy.

Wells' reply was long and heartfelt. His letter claimed that Shaw was a mischief-maker, an attention-seeker, an eclectic gatherer of second-hand theories and opinions, an irresponsible and shallow man. He continued:

The first thing he does almost invariably in his controversies, if one may give his displays so dignified a name, is to create a serio-comic atmosphere, the Shavian atmosphere, by wild boasting about his mental clarity and facetious abuse of his antagonist. My mind he declares is 'giving way' and so on. At this the well trained Fabian spinster smiles almost maternally and prepares for the next phase of the 'intellectual treat'. This is a carefully untruthful statement of the antagonist's position.

I say 'carefully untruthful'; he does not err, he deliberately distorts. In this instance he declares that I think that Germany is holding out Finland as a bait to Sweden and so on. It is nothing to Mr Shaw that I did not suggest anything of the kind; the glib falsehood is necessary in this case and he utters it with as light a conscience as if, instead of offering rubbish as international politics, he was introducing a panacea at a fair.

This was an angry and hurt H.G. Wells. He had never fully recovered from his drubbing at the hands of Shaw and the Fabians. This was more than a dozen years later; Wells had achieved so much in his life, yet those same people still dared treat him with suspicion, even patronizing dismissal. For his part, Shaw was genuinely disturbed by Wells' political posturings. The difference was that the eternally self-confident Shaw could hide his feelings behind humour and contrived indifference; Wells was rarely, if ever, capable of such disguise. In this respect Wells was the more honest of the two men and certainly deserves some sympathy. He had not been brought up to play what Shaw saw as the 'great game' of witty insults and pithy attacks. Arnold Bennett was certain that he once saw Wells cry after a morning of quarrelling with Shaw, partly because he was sorry for himself but mostly because of sheer desperation and an inability to fight back with the same weapons. Wells' life-long protestations that he was at heart just a simple man were to a certain extent true.

The conflict deepened when Shaw published 'Common Sense About the War' in the *New Statesman*. The series of articles poured scorn on the allied effort, claimed that the war was merely an excuse for the British to take on their long-term imperial rivals, and urged the rank-and-file military to rebel and shoot its leaders. Wells hit back:

Mr Shaw is one of those perpetual children who live in a dream of make believe and the make believe of Mr Shaw is that he is a person of incredible wisdom and subtlety running the world ... an idiot-child screaming in a hospital, distorting, discrediting, confusing, and at the end, when it is all over, we shall have voluminous pamphlets and prefaces explaining how modestly and dexterously he settled the Prussian hegemony and rearranged Europe.[3]

The argument simmered throughout the war, but although Shaw came close to it, he never completely lost his temper with Wells and refused to forsake his former friend or join with others in condemning and ostracizing him. There were many within the anti-war movement who refused to speak to Wells ever again and took every opportunity they had to slander him and blacken his character. They could not forgive him for describing their resistance to the popular mood as a 'scream of extreme individualism'[4]; they would not forgive him for achieving so much acclaim by his actions during the war. Some of the Fabians and certain members of the Bloomsbury group were particularly venomous; writing some forty years after the events, Bertrand Russell still dipped his pen with malice:

Wells was assailed in the Press ... for his advocacy of free love. He replied somewhat heatedly that he had not advocated free love, but had merely prophesied possible effects of new ingredients in the atmosphere without saying whether he thought these effects good or bad. This seemed to me disingenuous, and I asked him, 'Why did you first advocate free love and then say you hadn't?' He replied that he had not yet saved enough money out of royalties to be able to live on the interest, and that he did not propose to advocate free love publicly until he had done so ... After this I did not see much of him until the First World War had ended. In spite of his previous attitude about war with Germany, he became exceedingly bellicose in 1914 ... [5]

The war represented a watershed in Wells' life. Not only had he altered his political positions, but he had also taken on a new attitude in his personal and social affairs. He seemed to age quickly in the early years of the war, taking on a haggard look not previously noticeable. In the past most of Wells' friends, and some of his enemies, remarked on his seemingly eternal youthfulness; his features and demeanour were often boyish, they remarked, in spite of regular bouts of physical pain and the onslaught of diabetes and stomach ulcers. He drew up a new will in 1914, and asked Robert Ross to be his literary executor. He and Jane placed their sons Gip and Frank, now thirteen and eleven years old, in Oundle boarding school, and settled into the now completed home, renamed Easton Glebe.

This was a relatively good period for the partnership of Wells and Jane, a time when they saw much of one another and appeared to relish the duties and obligations of master and mistress of a sizeable country home. At various stages in his life Wells felt an overwhelming need to play the roles of husband and father and to return to Jane and the family home. The new will and bouts of poor health certainly brought on such a phase. Wells' autobiography lovingly and proudly reproduces photographs of the building of the house and of the interior of the study. Easton Glebe was comfortable and informal, capacious and aesthetically pleasing. Twelve bedrooms meant that guests could be accommodated, and the house was rarely free of them. As if to deny the effects of advancing age Wells planned intricately organized games of hockey and volleyball, and a full-size tennis court was built for those less enthusiastic about team sports. He was determined and merciless when he played sport, particularly if his opponents were younger than him – there was something to prove. The Wells house was a gathering place, a meeting place, a recreational think-tank. Jane worked hard on the garden and in supervising the kitchen. For a while the household was a content, even happy one.

Arnold Bennett was a frequent visitor, a friend now of Jane as well as Wells. He recorded in his inimitable journals a stay with his friends in October 1915.

Left home at 10 a.m. and drove over slippery roads in a Scotch mist to Little Easton. I walked with Wells in the park at dusk. Stag rutting season. All the bucks were roaring like lions, and we were somewhat intimidated. Two of them made a show of fighting, but funked it. Before this, original ball games in the arranged barn, in front of which a farmyard and cesspool had been turned into a very slightly sunk garden with bathing tank in the middle.

Immense park, belonging to Lady Warwick, and practically wasted for useful purposes. And there must be hundreds such. 'It ought to be taxed out,' said H.G.

Lady Warwick was something of a patron. She had long been a friend of Wells, had supported him financially when times were particularly difficult and had also acted as his champion in polite society. She was at the centre of a political and artistic set which numbered Fabian writers, labour politicians and fashionable novelists among its members, and she relished their controversial views and heated exchanges. She was often at Easton Glebe and invariably brought some of her followers with her. The Wells house was in turn at the centre of a small literary community. Journalists R.D. Blumenfeld and J. Robertson Scott, editor of *The Countryman*, were neighbours, and author H. de Vere Stacpoole lived only a couple of miles away. The weekends sometimes expanded into three- and four-day sojourns, with alfresco suppers and readings, spontaneous lectures, endless ball games in the barn and amateur theatricals. Frank Swinnerton recalled:

They began, sedately enough, with partial unpacking and tea; but by Sunday night the entire house would be strewn with dozens of pairs of white shoes which had been used from store in every kind of outdoor game, with discarded costumes hunted out of great chests and closets for the exacter verisimilitude of charades, and with the general litter of a tempestuous assembly . . . And through it all was Mr Wells, leader in every activity from lawn tennis, hockey, quoits, and dancing to bridge and a frightful pastime known as Demon Patience; Mr Wells, full of hospitality and the high spirits always engendered in him by the society of young, active, laughing people.[6]

Wells at play was seldom very far from Wells at work. He published *Bealby: A Holiday* in 1915. It is a light, relatively unimportant book much in the tradition of Mr Polly, but lacking the wit and verve of that volume. Arthur Bealby is the teenage stepson of a gardener at a country home. He is an isolated, even persecuted character, unhappy with his work and his life. After a fight with the footman, in which Bealby stabs him with a toasting fork, and a farcical escape, a series of adventures begin. He is befriended by travelling actresses, taken up by a burglar tramp, chased by the police and eventually, by the most circuitous of routes, is taken back at Shonts, his country home.

Wells relied on some of his own childhood experiences for the book, and there are clearly some lovingly recalled aspects of his younger life on display. The *New York Times* thought the book 'as unpolitical as *Alice in Wonderland* and as innocent of economics as of astrology. A deliciously amusing comedy of action swift, violent, and fantastic.' The *New York Globe* was less flattering and more accurate when it described *Bealby* as 'Wells on a vacation, a vacation from the war'. But the volume was more a distraction than a holiday for its author, enabling him to ignore but not forget the war for a short while, and the demands of defending it in print.

A more worldly book was *The Research Magnificent*, which also appeared in 1915. Its central character is William Porphyry Benham, whose story is told by an ex-schoolfriend named White, who quotes from Benham's papers throughout the book in long and sometimes laborious chunks. A product of a broken marriage, Benham leads an early life characterized by atheism, resentment of authority and a cowardice he systematically attempts to overcome by outrageous and foolhardy tests of bravery. He is the son of a wealthy and possessive mother, who attempts to dictate his political and social views and instil in him her detestation of socialism and change. Benham becomes an advocate of a form of the inevitable elite, the natural aristocracy, the Wellsian samurai:

I know there is a better life than this muddle about us, a better life possible now ... If I had no other assurances, if I were blind to the glorious intimations of art, to the perpetually widening promise of science, to the mysterious beckonings of beauty in form and colour and the inaccessible mockery of the stars, I should still know this from the insurgent spirit within me. ... Now this better life is what I mean when I talk of Aristocracy. This idea of a life breaking away from the common life to something better, is the consuming idea in my mind.

Benham eventually resolves to tour the world and examine how each country is governed and organized, to ascertain whether democracies are more efficient than dictatorships or vice versa, and how widespread his 'natural aristocracy' really is; it is this which is the 'Research Magnificent'. His plans are partly aborted by a love affair and eventual marriage. (He and his wife invent the esoteric names of 'Leopard' and 'Cheetah' for themselves, with strong echoes of Wells' and Rebecca West's 'Panther' and 'Jaguar'.) His affection for his wife, however, is not as powerful as his need to travel; and it is on one of his travels that he is killed, during a fight about politics in South Africa. He leaves as his testament the following philosophy:

Man, I see, is an over-practical creature, too eager to get into action. He takes conclusions ready-made, or he makes them in a hurry. Life is so short that he thinks it better to err than wait. He has no patience, no faith in anything but himself. He thinks he is a being when in reality he is only a link in a being, and so he is more anxious to be complete than right.

The book's fantastic and unconvincing adventures were no match for the newspaper accounts of fighting in France and Belgium. Nor was the time right for a thoughtful, discursive work. Wells would in fact later lament that a book he considered among his more important had been published at such a time. It received relatively few reviews and was too often simply dismissed as being irrelevant. 'I may complain that *The Research Magnificent* is a book deserving to be remembered and yet seems to be largely forgotten,' Wells wrote in his autobiography. 'I liked it when I re-read it and I find it remarkably up to date with my present opinions. It was blotted out by the war. But Amanda is alive and Benham has his moments of vitality.' Yet there were islands of enthusiasm for the book, particularly in the United States. The *New York Times* thought that it 'challenges discussion at a hundred points. It abounds in stimulating ideas'; while the *New Republic* concluded that it was 'An Extraordinary ... a Wonderful Book'.

But Wells also had other matters to concern him. He was not surprised at the sepulchral stalemate on the Western Front, but he was angered and frustrated with it. Millions of men were dying to gain and then lose territory in roughly equal proportions, and neither generals nor politicians appeared to have the courage or the initiative to break the deadlock. Wells had long hoped for a strong and dynamic leader to put matters right in the field, and was disappointed time and time again.

In 1916 he was invited to tour the front lines, along with other influential writers. This was part of a government propaganda and morale campaign, and the authors involved were taken by the hand wherever they went. 'I was kept loafing about in Paris for some weeks or so, I had a talk with Papa Joffre and was presented solemnly with a set of coloured postcards of all the chief French generals, and very good postcards they made,' Wells wrote, with his tongue firmly in his cheek. 'I went through North Italy by Gorizia to the Carso, returned to France to the front near Soissons and then went at my own request to the British front about Arras, to compare the British and French organizations for aerial photography ... It was an interesting but rather pointless trip.'

Wells increasingly felt that his contribution to the war effort was 'pointless', and that he was an impotent figure in a time of international importance. He wrote with a greater pace and passion for the *Daily Mail*, *Daily News* and *Daily Chronicle*; he lambasted corrupt arms manufacturers, called for a greater and more intelligent use of women workers in wartime industry, argued that the generals had no original ideas for victory, no bold new concept or even foolhardy master-plan to end the war. He wrote furiously, both in quantity and in tone, to the letters pages of all the major newspapers, becoming a regular correspondent to *The Times*, *Manchester Guardian* and *Morning Post*. His letters were flavoured by a sense of his own neglect: how could the authorities not utilize a man who had predicted trench warfare? Why did they not employ his services and talents for the war effort in a constructive and useful way?[7]

The novel with which he was occupying himself, *Mr Britling Sees It Through*, was, therefore, as much a cathartic exercise and a clamorous plea as an act of literary creation. The book is a slice of autobiography, the most evident example since *The New Machiavelli*. Hugh Britling Senior is undoubtedly Wells himself, as Edith Britling is Jane. Mr Britling possessed

a naturally irritable mind; this gave him point and passion; and moreover he had a certain obstinate originality and a generous disposition. So that he was always lively, sometimes spacious, and never vile. He loved to write and talk. He talked about everything, he had ideas about everything; he could no more help having ideas about everything than a dog can resist smelling at your heels. He sniffed at the heels of reality. Lots of people found him interesting and stimulating, a few found him seriously exasperating. He had ideas in the utmost profusion about races and empires and social order and political institutions and gardens and automobiles and the future of India and China and aesthetics and America and the education of mankind in general . . .

It was a deft, if somewhat sanguine, sketch of the adult Wells, who himself 'sniffed at the heels of reality'. The autobiographical aspects of the character went further. Britling was a journalist and social commentator who has become an author who is an international celebrity. He lives in a small Essex village, a thinly disguised Easton referred to as Matching's Easy. Early in the book Britling drives a guest, a young American named Direck, in his much-prized car. He is an appalling driver, and directs his vehicle into a ditch. Wells had crashed several times, once giving himself quite severe injuries, requiring a period in bed and the nursing services of Rebecca West.

It is via Direck that we first perceive the Britlings at home. Wells uses the American character in a filmic way, focusing in with him on certain characters, brushing past others with a quite careless sweep. The Britling home, Dower House, is full to the edges and bustling with activity. Apart from Hugh and Edith there are Hugh Junior, Britling's son from his first marriage, two sons from his marriage to Edith, a German student-teacher named Herr Heinrich, and Britling's secretary, Teddy, with his wife, baby and sister-in-law.

Direck has come to England to persuade Britling to deliver a lecture to the Massachusetts Society for the Study of Contemporary Thought. His efforts are limited by his inability to interrupt the loquacious author, who holds forth on numerous Wellsian themes. He is also introduced to hockey, and bewilders his host by mastering the game almost immediately. Wells' autobiographical honesty went further. Britling has a mistress, a Mrs Harrowdean, who in some respects – she is courted by another man, she is concerned about Britling's public reputation and how it will affect their relationship – resembles Rebecca West. Britling decides to end the affair and to continue his marriage. But it is the war which is the central theme of the book. Its first effect is to smash the happy, eccentric family. The German tutor returns to his country to enlist in the army, while Teddy and Hugh Junior join the British forces. Britling is anxious and afraid, but in the end he agrees with his son's decision.

Britling's subsequent change of heart over the war is not so much one of increasing distaste as of declining enthusiasm. So it was too with Wells. The letters from son to father, even after official censorship, paint a terrible and depressing picture of failure and folly. He decides to write a pamphlet to express his outrage, entitled 'And Now War Ends', but abandons it as being too flaccid to convey his thoughts. The next months bring only chaos and suffering. Direck joins the Canadian army so as to be able to participate in the war, Teddy is reported missing, though he returns home with an arm amputated, Heinrich dies in the German cause, and young Hugh is killed. Britling writes to Heinrich's father, and while he is never less than critical of Germany and German policy, he now aspires to internationalism and a workable and lasting peace. The letter comprises the conclusion of the book, and the moral message Wells hoped to leave with his readers:

Let us pledge ourselves to service. Let us set ourselves with all our minds and with all our hearts to the perfecting and working out of the methods of democracy and the ending for ever of the kings and priestcrafts and the bands of adventurers, the traders and owners and forestallers who have betrayed mankind into this morass of hate and blood – in which our sons are lost – in which we founder still.

These sentiments, and the book itself, touched a chord in the British public. Readers wrote letters of condolence to Wells on the loss of his son, believing the entire work to be a disguised memoir. *Mr Britling Sees It Through* ran to thirteen editions within the first year of publication, and earned over 20,000 pounds in American royalties alone. In many ways it was the foremost popular novel of the First World War, but it was also a success in critical terms. Some, though by no means all, of the literary pundits who had previously dismissed Wells as a mass communicator rather than a serious author changed their minds. John Galsworthy, that erudite and severely objective critic, thought it 'generous' and 'big-hearted'; others thought it one of the most agile leaps of literary empathy in a decade.[8] *The Times* announced that 'For the first time we have a novel which touches the life of the last two years without impertinence. This is a really remarkable event, and Mr Wells' book is a proud achievement . . . a creation with which we have as yet seen in this country at least, nothing whatever to compare.' Nor in the United States, it would appear, because the *Chicago Tribune* thought it 'not only Mr Wells' best book, but the best book so far published concerning the war'.

Wells himself wrote later that: 'The story of Mr Britling's son and Mr Britling's grey matter could be repeated with ten thousand variations . . . I think I have contrived in that book to give not only the astonishment and the sense of tragic disillusionment in a civilized mind as the cruel facts of war rose steadily to dominate everything else in life, but also the passionate desire to find some immediate reassurance amidst that whirlwind of disaster.' *Britling* was written before some of the worst tales of trench warfare had arrived in Britain, but by the time it appeared, horror and atrocity stories were common. Publication of the book coincided with a popular clamour for movement and by the beginning of 1917 Wells' profile was very high indeed. It seemed only a matter of time before the government or the government's friends employed him in some capacity.

The year 1917 witnessed the realization of another Wellsian anticipation, one he had written and spoken of with some glee. The pathos of hundreds of thousands of Russian soldiers lacking rifles, yet still marching to face the enemy, had finally taken its toll. In March, the first of that year's Russian revolutions brought the liberal Kerensky to tenuous power. Wells wrote to Maxim Gorky, congratulating him and the Russian people, and sending his fraternal support for 'this struggle to liberate mankind . . . and to establish international goodwill on the basis of international justice and respect'. Inspired by the Russian example, Wells envisaged radical change in Britain. It is true that there had been mutinies within the French army, and a tiny revolt within British and Commonwealth forces in France, but neither the conditions nor the experience of the British people at home could have precipitated a revolution. Nevertheless, Wells wrote to *The Times*, calling for a republican society; but was forced to withdraw his comment when public opinion turned, quite energetically and vociferously, against him.[9]

There was more support for Wells' call for an international organization which could conciliate between countries, a sort of world referee. Wells had been an advocate of the League of Free Nations for several years, recently demonstrated in his writings, *Elements of Reconstruction* and *What Is Coming: A Forecast of Things after the War*; later on he would publish the propaganda-like *In the Fourth Year: Anticipations of a World Peace*, and then *British Nationalism and the League of Nations*. In 1915 a League of Nations society had been formed by Leonard Woolf and some of his allies from the Bloomsbury group and their fellow travellers. Here Wells was on firmer ground. There was a general feeling abroad that something, though few people knew exactly what, had to be done to prevent another European war from exploding. This conflict had been a failure on almost every front. Rather than save small nations, it had destroyed them; and far from being over by Christmas, it was still roaring after three such seasons. Wells again began a letters campaign in the daily press, and sat on a committee of the League of Free Nations Association, but few were willing to listen to well-meaning committee reports while Zeppelins were dropping high-explosive bombs in the middle of London.

That year was the worst year of the war yet for the British, both at the front and at home. In the closing months of 1917 and the early period of 1918 Prime Minister David Lloyd George radically restructured his cabinet. He invited various figures from outside the House of Commons to join it, figures beyond the normal governmental pale. Max Aitken's appointment as Minister of

Information was something of a surprise, but Lord Rothermere as first Minister of Air and Lord Northcliffe as Director of Enemy Propaganda stunned the political establishment. It was in reality a sound move, perhaps even an inspired one. The old military and political leaders had failed miserably. The three new men were press barons and, as such, powerful, ambitious and, some might argue, monomaniacal men. If their efforts could be secured to winning the war, great things were possible.

Northcliffe wasted little time in summoning Wells to see him. He offered him the position of head of the Committee for Propaganda in Enemy Country. But the two figures were too similar to get along with one another. Both possessed undoubted abilities and energies, both aspired to greatness. But Wells was the revolutionary to Northcliffe's reactionary; and though Wells was hot-tempered and splenetic, Northcliffe could be downright unstable. They also approached their new positions from radically different points of view. Wells now proclaimed that the war was against injustice, and the Germans were merely the current and transitory enemy. Not so Northcliffe. Defeat of Germany was his only aim. His plan was to bombard the German people and military with war propaganda, convincing them that they could not win, and that if they did not surrender defeat would be a terrible thing. Wells favoured a far more subtle and conciliatory approach. Outline the Allied peace proposals, he argued, and make the Germans understand that the end of the war need not mean humiliation and occupation. 'The harder Northcliffe blew, the tighter the Germans would buckle their field-grey coats. Wells wanted to shine a few rays of sunlight on them, and get them to remove their own coats.'[10]

Wells assembled his own committee of dignitaries to present a 'minority report' to Northcliffe and then to the Foreign Office. But the well-meaning committee failed on two counts. First of all it recommended that a security council be established, composed of the leading handful of world powers. As we have seen since the foundation of the United Nations, such a body, with the authority of individual veto, has effectively obstructed any progress within the United Nations. Second, Wells and his people were far too sanguine about the honesty of their own and other people's politicians. Not only had surreptitious agreements and treaties been made before and during the war, but the government had no intention of seriously analysing the recommendations of 'a group of artists and radicals'.[11] Wells had worked hard on the committee's report, sometimes existing on five hours' sleep a night, working until dawn on more than one occasion. He was disappointed and embittered by his treatment by the authorities; by authority.

'I had no illusions about the fundamental wisdom of the British and French Foreign Offices,' he wrote in his autobiography:

They were, I realized, in the hands of men of limited outlooks and small motives, whose chief control was their servitude to tradition. They had far less grasp of the world situation than an average intelligent man. ... This memorandum was sent, with a covering letter from Lord Northcliffe, to Lord Balfour for the endorsement of the Foreign Office. We had all been kept in the dark as to the cramping secret engagements which had been made by our diplomatists, and we had no suspicion that our broad and reasonable proposals were already impossible. ... It is terrifying to think that these vast powers, the Foreign Offices of the world, are being run to a very large extent by little undeveloped brains ... that they are immensely protected from criticism and under no real control from educated opinion. And what they do affects and endangers hundreds of millions of lives.

Wells was also angry at the anti-German hysteria which Northcliffe was promoting in his newspapers; as a convert from that position he had no time for those who refused to follow his example. The *Evening News* was the worst, with its constant use of atrocity stories from the early days of 1914. Wells wrote to Northcliffe, urging him to reconsider, reminding him that the intention of the propaganda department was to win the war, not libel the Germans. Northcliffe's replies to Wells were increasingly sharp. He wrote, 'I entirely agree with the policy adopted by my newspapers, which I do not propose to discuss with anyone. I have not wandered about Prussia for two years without learning something, and if you will wait you will find that I will unearth much sinister and active Prussianism in England.' Wells had had enough. Petty firings of men of vague German ancestry, late-night interruptions of Wells' schedule by an agitated Northcliffe and the sheer wrongness of the committee and the propaganda campaign led him to resign.

Wells' energy at this time was staggering. Friend and colleague Jerome K. Jerome, editor of *The Idler* and author of *Three Men in a Boat*, recalled a visit, and in spite of Jerome's inveterate

H. G. Wells' parents, Joseph and Sarah.

H. G. Wells with his elder brother Fred *c.* 1869.

H. G. Wells aged ten.

Above: Uppark, where the fourteen-year-old Wells made his first forays into journalism, producing and editing *The Uppark Alarmist,* while his mother worked as manager of the house staff.

Left: H. G. Wells as a student at the Normal School of Science, South Kensington, which Wells attended from 1894 until 1897, when he failed his final geology exam.

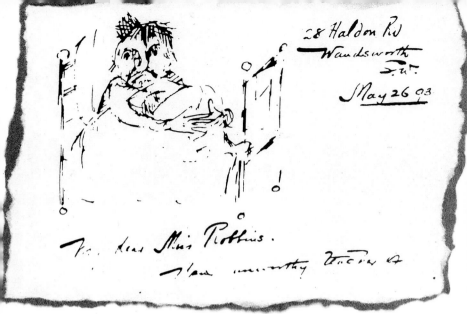

The Invalid Teacher, drawn on a letter that Wells wrote to Amy Catherine Robbins on 26 May 1893 while suffering from one of his countless bouts of ill health. Wells married Catherine in 1895; when he decided he did not like her Christian name he changed it to Jane.

Isabel Wells, H. G. Wells' first wife. The marriage lasted only three years, ending in an acrimonious divorce in 1894.

HG and Jane Wells setting off from Woking, Surrey, for a cycling trip, 1895.

Above: Spade House, which cost Wells £3,000 – at that time a small fortune – to build.

Right: Rebecca West, the mother of Wells' son Anthony.

HG and Jane Wells in the nursery of Spade House with their sons George Philip (Gip) and Frank Richard.

Left: Beatrice and Sidney Webb, co-founders of the Fabian Society. Wells immortalized them in *The New Machiavelli* (1911) as Oscar and Altiora Bailey, brilliant but unscrupulous and small-minded leaders of a liberal intellectual movement.

Below left: George Bernard Shaw, with whom Wells had a turbulent relationship. Wells is said to have wept with frustration and self-pity after one particularly bitter argument with Shaw.

Below: Henry James, whose initial admiration for H. G. Wells' work gave way to voracious criticism.

A set of caricatures of Wells which appeared in *The Sketch* in 1912 at the same time that Wells' articles on labour unrest were causing a furore.

H. G. Wells on the western front in 1916. He had been invited to tour the front lines, along with other influential writers, as part of a government propaganda campaign.

George Bernard Shaw, Hilaire Belloc and G. K. Chesterton in 1927. Belloc publicly humiliated Wells in a series of notorious debates.

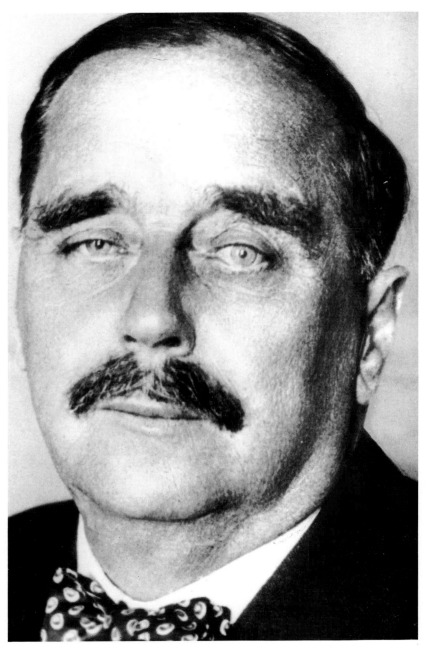

H. G. Wells aged about fifty.

penchant for hyperbole, the picture is an accurate one of Wells in his prime.

He writes a new book while most people are reading his last; throws off a history of the world while the average schoolboy is learning his dates; and invents a new religion in less time than it must have taken his god-parents to teach him his prayers. He has a table by his bedside; and if the spirit moves him will get up in the middle of the night, make himself a cup of coffee, write a chapter or so, and then go to sleep again. During intervals between his more serious work, he will contest a Parliamentary election or conduct a conference for educational reform. How Wells carries all his electricity without wearing out the casing and causing a short circuit in his brain is a scientific mystery. . . . To 'rest' in the neighbourhood of Wells is like curling yourself up and trying to go to sleep in the centre of a cyclone. When he wasn't explaining the Universe, he was teaching me new games – complicated things that he had invented himself, and under stress of which my brain would reel. There are steepish hills on the South Downs. We went up them at four miles an hour, talking all the time. On the Sunday evening a hurricane was raging with a driving sleet. Wells was sure a walk would do us good – wake us up. 'We'll all have a blow,' said Wells.[12]

Regard for Wells, however, was far from universal. Historian and author A.L. Rowse was from a younger generation than that of Jerome, perhaps a more sceptical one. He has written: 'Let us dismiss him first. . . . He was singularly unimpressive on the platform: a dumpy, bright-eyed chirpy little man, with an unregulated wispy moustache, and a pipsqueak of a voice. It was obvious that he was no gentleman, and no proletarian either . . . he was unmistakably lower-middle-class.' Rowse goes on to refer to a meeting, initiated by Wells, at the Reform Club, and how neither man was willing to listen to the other. Rowse remembered 'plump, pink, well-manicured little hands', and how Wells sent him inscribed copies of his books, which Rowse in turn sold. 'In later years,' he writes, 'I have occasionally felt – or thought that I ought to feel – sorry. After all, he had been kind to me, and he was a man of genius.'[13]

Wells' output during the second half of the war was, as usual, and as Jerome had described, copious beyond the abilities of normal men. In September 1917 Cassell and Company published *The Soul of a Bishop*, subtitled *A Novel (with Just a Little Love in It) about Conscience and Religion and the Real Troubles of Life.* Bishop Edward Scrope of Princhester is a well-meaning, closeted cleric whose appointment to an industrial northern diocese imposes a terrible strain on him. He is shocked by the new. His difficulties with his bishopric are compounded by anguish at the outbreak of the First World War and insidious doubts about his faith. All of this causes insomnia, and in an effort to find some sleep he consults his doctor. The medically prescribed drug to ease Scrope's mind actually causes hallucinations, and he has a vision of an angel of God. He reveals his inner thoughts to the being:

'Slowly through four years I have been awakening to the need of God. Body and Soul I am sick for the want of God and the knowledge of God. I did not know what was the matter with me, why my life had become so disordered and confused that my very appetites and habits are all astray. But I am perishing for God as a waterless man upon a raft perishes for drink, and there is nothing but madness if I touch the seas about me. Not only in my thoughts and in my nerves and bones and arteries I have need of God.'

The visiting angel explains that the punctilios of religious worship and the differences between various forms of religion are mere pedantries; there is one God, and all that He requires is a basic belief in His majesty. Scrope tells a fellow bishop, Likeman, about his vision, and about his subsequent decision to leave the Church and spread the new good news. He is dissuaded for the time being. He takes the sleeping potion again, the angel returns, and takes him around the world in a Scrooge-like fashion, to listen to other people's conversations. He hears discussions of familiar Wellsian themes – a common device in Wells' novels of the period – of the possibilities of science, the desire to prevent war, the need for some sort of world state.

Scrope can no longer trim his views. He publicly rejects established Christianity, particularly the Trinity, and resigns from his position and from his Church. When he attempts to get hold of more of his drug, he is told that the doctor has been killed, and no record of the drug's composition exists. More than this, other people, he is informed, have hallucinated under the prescription. The book loses its drive after this revelation, with Scrope making the best of what he is left with, and trying his utmost to bring about further visions without the aid of stimulants.

The volume was a critique, an attack, upon organized religion. The influence of his mother's evangelicalism was still very strong on Wells. He was not a believer but, in his own words 'a victim'.[14] Religion always fascinated him, even if it repelled him. He certainly experienced some form of religious conversion during the First World War. It was not unusual, and millions searched for some sort of explanation, justification, rationalization, for the holocaust that had taken place in France and Belgium. Wells attempted to modify the stern, Calvinistic faith which his mother had taught him. He was not very successful, and his sojourn in the supernatural passed as quickly as it had started. He was embarrassed by it in his later years, writing that 'I cannot disentangle now, perhaps at no time could I have disentangled, what was simple and direct in this theocratic phase in my life, from what was – politic. I do not know how far I was being perfectly straightforward in this phase, how far I was – as the vulgar have it – "codding myself", and how far I was trying to make my New Republicanism acceptable in a different guise to that multitude which could not, it seemed, dispense with kingship.'[15]

In *God The Invisible King*, also published in 1917, he had written on the Trinity, this time referring to the conversations he had had with the philosopher William James, brother of Henry James. He attributed most of the errors of contemporary Christianity to the Council of Nicaea, and their codification of the Trinity. Publication of the book precipitated a lunch interview with the Archbishop of Canterbury, on the Archbishop's suggestion. It also provoked a combination of incredulity, from those who thought Wells was temporarily unstable, and copious praise and acclamation, from those who were hopeful of a lasting conversion. Today the book reads like a time-piece, a slice of intellectual debate among atheists and religious searchers, preserved in literary aspic. It devotes chapters to 'The Religion of Atheists', 'Heresies; Or The Things That God Is Not' and 'Modern Ideas Of Sin And Damnation'. Wells summed up his theology in the Preface: 'This book sets out as forcibly and exactly as possible the religious belief of the writer. That belief is not orthodox Christianity; it is not, indeed, Christianity at all; its core nevertheless is a profound belief in a personal and intimate God.' Those who anticipated a pious or prayerful Wells were to be disappointed. He wrote later:

They [the religious] are straining back to the instinctive faith of 'little children', that ultimately everything is all right. They are frightened people who want to be told that they need not brace up to the grimaces before them. With all the will in the world I could not bring myself to present my God as that sort of God. I could invent a heartening God but not a palliating God. At his best my deity was far less like the Heavenly Father of a devout Catholic or a devout Moslem or Jew than he was like a personification of, let us say, the Five Year Plan . . . As he is presented in *God The Invisible King* he is no better than an inspiring but extremely preoccupied comrade, a thoroughly hard leader.

Wells' last important novel of the war years was *Joan and Peter*, published in 1918. The book covers the late-Victorian and Edwardian age, from 1893 to 1918, and principally concerns the cousins Joan and Peter Stubland and their uncle, Oswald Sydenham. Peter Stubland is the central character, and it is his and his cousin's early experiences which form the first section of the book. His parents die when he is a boy, and he and Joan are brought up by two aunts. They attend a progressive school, where they are content and happy: this enables Wells to discuss his views on education and the need for change in the school system. Again Wells includes an attack on the established Church, depicting Peter's forced baptism and Joan's fears that her cousin is about to be drowned like a discarded kitten.

The story unfolds when Uncle Oswald takes over the children's education. He is a Victoria Cross winner who lost half of his face during an enemy bombardment, a sailor, a diplomat and an eccentric. Oswald takes Peter to visit Russia, where he sees St Basil's Cathedral, 'that barbaric caricature'. By the middle of the book the story wanders, at times seemingly aimlessly. At the outbreak of the First World War both Peter and Oswald volunteer for service; both are wounded, the former several times, to a ludicrous and unbelievable extent. After the war Joan and Peter are married, and Oswald lives out his final few years calling for a World Republic and looking to the League of Nations as the only hope for humanity. He places the responsibility of change and salvation on the shoulders of Joan and Peter and their peers, instructing them to:

Listen when the old men tell you facts, for very often they know. Listen when they reason, they will teach you many twists and turns. But when they dogmatize, when they still want to rule unquestioned, and, above all, when they say 'impossible', even when they say 'wait — be dilatory and discreet', push them aside. Their minds squat crippled beside dead traditions. . . . That England of the Victorian old men, and its empire and its honours and its court of precedences, it is all a dead body now, it has died as the war has gone on, and it has to be buried out of the way lest it corrupt you and all the world.

The book is contrived, overlong and often indulgent. Its didactic strains alienated many of its readers, and its high cost due to the wartime paper shortage and subsequent rise in book prices made its sales even more disappointing. Wells defended it throughout his life, considering it one of his more serious and poignant works. 'To me it seems a far finer piece of work than *Mr Britling Sees It Through*,' he wrote, and added almost pathetically: 'Joan I like as a character; A.A. Milne has said nice things about her.' Very few critics agreed with him, though Virginia Woolf in an unsigned review in *The Times Literary Supplement* did write that 'Mr Wells's ideas put on flesh and blood so instinctively and admirably we are able to come up close to them and look them in the face; and the result of seeing them near at hand is, as our suspicions assured us that it would be, curiously disappointing.' Other projects were being prepared, however; projects which would open new doors, close old ones, and add an entirely new dimension to the life of H.G. Wells. He was appealing to the generation that was about to come into its own to take on their shoulders responsibility for the salvation of humanity. He was enlisting them in the cause that he himself had taken up with increasing urgency as the Great War drew to a close.

7 History and Mr Belloc

'A camel is not a horse designed by a committee; a committee is a camel designed by a horse,' Wells once told J.B. Priestley,[1] and he might well have been thinking of his own experience in the League of Nations Union. He had been committed to the idea of the League of Nations for some time but this commitment involved enough sitting on committees to tire even the most devoted and long-suffering of camel lovers. Wells could not see the point of, or the progress being made in, interminable meetings to discuss the pedantries of this proposed organization. He wrote, disapprovingly, in his autobiography:

There were at that time several small organizations promoting the League of Nations idea. I took part in a successful attempt to consolidate these into one League of Nations Union, which would not merely spread but develop the idea. I put the stress upon the development. It was conspicuously evident that, so far, the idea was lacking in detail and definition; it was like a bag into which everything might still be put and there were a number of things that I felt were very undesirable as occupants of that bag and others that were vitally important.

As time progressed Wells realized that the 'vitally important' contents of the bag had little power, and were always in a minority. He confided in Arnold Bennett, explaining that he saw his ideal being drowned in a sea of bureaucracy. Bennett refused to sympathize with him and mocked his commitment to the League. Wells was a writer, Bennett argued, and had no place anyway sitting on committees. If he wanted to achieve something, he must do it through his writing.[2] In fact Wells had already arrived at a similar conclusion. His desire for a world state and

151

a new order was not shared by most of the people he worked with in the League of Nations groups, many of whom saw no further than a pragmatic and maintainable peace in Europe.[3] He told his friend Gilbert Murray that 'I'm naturally a solitary worker. Team work for me is like using a razor to carve marble . . . For some time I've thought of writing an *Outline of History* as a sort of experiment.'

Wells had been fascinated by the notion of 'Salvation by History' for several years. He believed that the history of 'his people', those he thought of as 'the common people who are by no means common',[4] had not yet been properly recorded or written, and certainly not in a form that was acceptable to those very people. As a student he had given three lectures to the college debating society on the lessons of history, and had written more for the varsity newspaper.[5] At the South Kensington Debating Society he had spoken on the 'Past and Present of the Human Race', and much of his early writing, particularly *The Time Machine*, analysed contemporary man as a product of history who was still being moulded and shaped by historical forces.

When the Versailles Peace Conference to end the war showed itself to be merely a game of power politics, with individual politicians speaking for entire nations and the world just as divided as it had been four poisonous years earlier, Wells finally abandoned his work for the League of Nations. He was disillusioned, and felt cheated by the British delegation, particularly by the social democratic leaders who participated at Versailles. 'I began to talk more and more decisively of the need for "general history" and to express opinions such as I embodied finally in a pamphlet "History is One" (1919) . . . a history of mankind which should show plainly to the general intelligence, how inevitable, if civilization was to continue, was the growth of political, social and economic organizations into a world federation.'

Already by the middle of 1918 Wells had written a proposal for a book of world history, which he sent to Macmillan's at the end of October. They were less interested in the idea than Wells had hoped but were still prepared to publish the book. Wells was perceptive enough, and honest enough, to admit that he could not write such a book by himself and would need a small team of experts to 'blue pencil howlers and to note serious omissions'. He assembled a committee of academics, historians and friends. They included

Philip Guedalla, the Sephardic Jewish essayist and biographer of the Duke of Wellington; Sir Ray Lankester, the scientist and director of the Natural History Museum; Sir Henry Johnstone, the civil servant and explorer with experience in Africa and Asia; J.F. Horrabin, an artist and illustrator; and Gilbert Murray, Wells' friend and a noted classical scholar. Other important collaborators were Ernest Barker, an Oxford political scientist; Arnold Bennett; Henry Seidel Canby from Yale University; and Jane Wells, who acted as secretary, factotum and very important research assistant. Wells also picked the brains of other authorities in particular fields, writing, for example, to Sir Denison Ross after he had been overwhelmed by the intricacies of Chinese history: 'I wish I could tap your knowledge in the matter by half an hour's talk. Could I see you? If so, I should be very glad.'

How much of the final version of *The Outline of History*, then, was Wells' work, and how much the product of a brilliant group of philosophers, authors and teachers, is open to question. There is no doubt that parts of the book were written in Wells' absence. Those who composed the Wells think-tank were certainly far more than gifted amanuenses. The lawyer and literary enthusiast Reginald L. Hine wrote in his autobiography of an encounter he had with Wells during the writing of the book:[6]

Many a time have I listened to H.G. Wells, but only once did I speak to him. It was at the Quaker College of Woodbrooke, near Birmingham, where, for some years in the summer vacations, F.S. Marvin was accustomed to arrange lectures on history. One afternoon I was basking in the sun when Wells came up the drive, and, the warden not being present, I went to welcome him. As his baggage was being handed to the porter, I noticed a pile of papers laying at the bottom of the car. 'What about these,' I queried, 'shall we take them too?'

'Perhaps we'd better,' he replied, 'it happens to be all I've written so far for my *Outline of History*. To-day I've motored from Stonehenge, and you may care to know that I polished that off in forty minutes.'

'Good heavens!' I gasped, 'a place that has been puzzling antiquaries for a thousand years!'

'Very likely,' he rejoined, 'but anyhow I've settled it to my satisfaction,' and then, catching sight of my horrified expression, 'I've left a couple of experts behind,' he added quickly, 'they have a fussy kind of knowledge that looks well in a footnote.'

Secretly I was glad, an hour later, when his lecture proved a fiasco. 'I'm sorry,' he apologized, as he gathered up his notes and broke up the meeting, 'but I've never been at home in these formal addresses. If you like to meet me at tea, or forgather with me on the veranda after tea, I'll promise to be more effective.'

Wells had no historical training; more importantly, he knew he had no historical training. Jane worked long and hard for him, spending hours distilling passages from the *Encyclopaedia Britannica*, Winwood Reade's *The Martyrdom of Man*, Holt's *World History* and Robinson's *Mediaeval and Modern Times*. Wells devoted himself to the project but also devoted other people to the project. His team of helpers contributed much more than a date here, a reference there; they were each paid 100 guineas for their troubles, a sum which represented either enormous generosity, or enormous gratitude. Anthony West wrote that 'my father was sometimes content to rush ahead, when he should have been looking back to check, check and check again. The *Outline* was his project, but the result was a collective achievement. I think Jane was as influential as anyone.'[7]

The aspects of the book which deal with ancient civilization, for example, were worked on by several people. Gilbert Murray edited all of the work on the Greeks and most of the other ancients, checked the material as it was written, and added information which friends from the academic world sent to him. Ray Lankester shaped the areas which dealt with the non-Hellenistic ancient world. Professor Eileen Power, Dr Charles Singer, Professor J.L. Myers, Mr Cramner Byng and Mr S.N. Fu, among others, also contributed to the *Outline*. Philip Guedalla, who was a major influence on the book, wrote of Wells that

his real merit as a prophet is not so much his evocation of the world in 1960 as an incomparably clear vision of the world in 1923 . . . that clear vision, which enables Mr Wells to depict men and women and wars and cities and bishops and Chinamen and shop assistants, to see the drive of a tendency across the plains of America and the little fields of Europe, and the slow drift of mankind down the broad stream of history, is his peculiar possession.[8]

Wells was the catalyst, the chairman, the conductor; he provided the impetus, detected the flow and formed the conclusions. It was impossible, in fact, for him to do more. *The Outline of History* took only one year to write, but various new editions, amendments and changes occupied Wells and his team until 1923. In that year

The Short History of the World was written, largely from the original *Outline*, for the use of students and advanced school pupils. Between March 1918 and the winter of 1923, Wells also wrote the bulk of the novel *Joan and Peter*, the pamphlets 'British Nationalism and the League', 'The Idea of a League of Nations', 'The Way to a League of Nations', 'The New Teaching of History', 'The World, Its Debts, and Rich Men', and all of the novels *Men Like Gods, The Secret Places of the Heart, The Undying Fire* and two collections of articles which required editing, extending and introducing.[9] There were limits even to Wells' energy and stamina. The man who wrote about time travel was not capable of including more than twenty-four hours in a day.

However much assistance Wells got from his collaborators, the arguments of *The Outline of History* and its structure are undoubtedly Wellsian. In his autobiography he spent a surprisingly brief time on this so important work. He described it as 'an essay on the growth of association since the dawn of animal communities. Its beginning was carried right back before the appearance of viviparous types of life, to those reptiles which shelter their eggs and protect their offspring, and it came on in one story of expanding relationship to the aeroplane-radio-linked human world of to-day.' The essay, he went on, 'grew beyond expectation, but that stress upon continually more effective communications, upon the gathering co-ordination of lives, is still . . . the gist of it all.'

In fact it said a great deal more. This 'magnificent intellectual achievement', in the words of Arnold Toynbee, detected trends, circles and movements in world history. Wells saw history as confirming his predictions and hopes for the future. In each and every age, the book argued, an elite or ruling cabal has come to power; just as, Wells argued, in the future the Samurai of *Anticipations* and *A Modern Utopia* would inevitably take over the reins of office.[10] A parallel was drawn between the biological and the political; just as species take form, prosper and then die, so with political ideas, social systems and ruling classes. *The Outline of History* perceived inevitable movements, and Wells' influence is unmistakable in the Social Darwinism and scientific comparisons which pervade the text. 'The rest of the history of mankind', Wells wrote, 'is very largely the history of those three ideas of science, of a universal righteousness, and of a human commonweal, spreading out from the minds of the rare and exceptional persons and peoples in which they first originated, into the general consciousness of the race, and giving first a new colour, then a new spirit, and then a new direction to human affairs.'

He believed that the study of history for its own sake was indulgent and unnecessary. History is a tool, a device, a ladder half finished; by climbing from its bottom rung we may see quite clearly which direction it is taking, and hence be guided and supported for the rest of the climb. The influences of Hegel and Marx, whom he read but, according to Anthony West, 'never really understood, at least in the way they intended to be understood,'[11] are plainly discernible. He questioned the validity of Christianity, believing that it had historical but no theological importance, played down (unlike Marx) the role of Europe, and particularly Britain, in the world's history, and emphasized the importance of the communal. He considered that there could be no 'social order, no security, no peace, or happiness, no righteous leadership or kingship, unless men lose themselves in something greater than themselves'.

The response to the book was greater, and better, than either Wells, his publishers or his co-authors had anticipated. 'Edition after edition was sold on both sides of the Atlantic,' Wells wrote in 1934. 'It made a new and wider reputation for me and earned me a considerable sum of money.' He recorded that over two million copies had been sold since 1919, that it had been translated into most languages except Italian ('it is proscribed in Italy because it detracts, they say, from the supreme grandeur of Mussolini's Rome') and it was continuing to sell widely. Wells attributed this to 'the ordinary man [who] had been stimulated by the war to a real curiosity about the human past; he wanted to be told the story of the planet and of the race, plainly and credibly, and since the "historians" would not or could not do it, he turned to my book.'[12]

It was historians, of course, who had actually written, or at least provided the meat for the book. Fellow historians H.A.L. Fisher and Carl Becker were equally enthusiastic, and Arnold Bennett considered the 750,000 words of the history 'the most useful thing of the kind ever done, and it is jolly well done'. At the height of its popularity the *Outline* outsold every other work written by a living author. Even Beatrice Webb, as scathing and bitter as ever, gave qualified praise to Wells' accomplishments. In her diary for 29 November 1920 she wrote:

A trifle to note. We are reconciled to H.G. Wells. He sent me his *History* with an inscription; I wrote a friendly acknowledgement; which he bettered in reply. And after he returned from Russia I asked him and his wife to dinner to meet Haldane and Krassin, Cole and the Shaws. He came: Mrs Wells was otherwise engaged. He is fat and prosperous and immensely self-congratulatory; towards us he was affable; but suspicion lurked in his eye and I doubt whether he is really friendly. Nor do I desire any renewal of friendship. But I am too near to the end of life to care to keep up a vendetta with any human being. Also I have never ceased to respect his work, and his *History* is a gallant achievement.

Praise was also international. One of the greatest supporters of Wells and his view of history was Kemal Ataturk. The Turkish leader was so delighted with the *Outline* that he attempted to read it in one sitting, keeping himself awake over a forty-hour stretch with copious amounts of black coffee and regular hot baths. He ordered the book to be translated into Turkish and be published by the government press. A little over a year later came a book commissioned by Ataturk entitled *Outline of Turkish History*. Wells became one of Ataturk's greatest heroes and was quoted by the founder of the new Turkey until the day he died. Whether Wells should have been proud of such adoration from this particular man is of course open to question.

Walter Lippman thought the book 'a wonderful thing to have conceived', Robert Blatchford wondered if Wells realized how much he had accomplished: 'In my opinion such a work will have a revolutionary impact on education and will change and expand man's view of life and the universe.' E.M. Forster was critical but still impressed. In the *Atheneum* in July 1920 he wrote of the first volume of the history:

It's no good humming and hawing; at least it is, but before the operation begins the following sentence must be penned: A great book. The writer tries to outline the history of the world, from the epoch of igneous gas to the establishment of Christianity; he succeeds, and it is the first duty of a reviewer to emphasize his success. Whatever he may do in his second volume he has achieved a masterpiece in his first, and one desires to offer him not only praise but thanks. Unconvincing as a Samurai or a bishop, he has surely come through as a historian. A great book; a possession for ever, for the ever of one's tiny life.

One person was so enchanted with the book that she claimed it as her own. A Canadian author and schoolteacher named

Florence Deeks alleged that Wells had stolen her work, which she had entitled *The Web of History*. Her case was that she had submitted a manuscript to Macmillan of Canada, who in turn sent it to London for further consideration by British editors. They had eventually turned it down, but Wells had somehow got hold of the proposal, renamed it, and paraded it as his own work. The Toronto woman was determined to pursue her point. She consulted several historians who had either worked with Wells on the *Outline*, or been aware of its progress. They all considered her claims to be absurd. But Deeks had supporters in Canada, and she was a vociferous and energetic woman. She filed a suit against Wells in 1928 in the Canadian courts, but they rejected her case. Deeks then appealed to the Privy Council in London. Wells tried to remain above the fracas, refusing to reply to her claims and dismissing his attacker as a lunatic. He was eventually exonerated, but the incident cost him over 3,000 pounds and besmirched his reputation in Canada for decades.

A far more considered and considerable threat came from another quarter. Of all of the opponents of the *Outline*, the most gifted and outspoken was Hilaire Belloc. This stocky, square, brutal, brilliant Roman Catholic writer with his bristling side-burns and passionate manner was the most successful and damaging enemy Wells ever had. He was inexorable, he was merciless, and he was committed to destroying the triumph of Wells. The battle between these two men brought Wells to his knees, and in the remaining twenty years of his life he never fully recovered.

Hilaire Belloc was born in 1870 in La Celle St Cloud near Paris, during one of the fiercest thunderstorms the area had ever seen. As a result, he was known as 'Old Thunder' in his family. Seldom has there been such an appropriate sobriquet. He was educated in England, at the Oratory School in Birmingham under Cardinal Newman, and later at Balliol College, Oxford. At Oxford he became notorious as a debater. Basil Joseph Mathews wrote a first-hand account of the young Belloc's argument:

It was one of those rare nights in the Oxford Union when new men are discovered. Simon had denounced the Turk in Thessaly, and Smith had held up the Oriental to admiration. Men whispered to each other of the future Gladstone and Dizzy whom Oxford was to give to the nation. No one would be fool enough to speak after such brilliant rhetoric . . .

Suddenly a young man rose and walked to the table. He was broad of shoulder and trod the floor confidently. A chin that was almost grim in its young strength was surmounted by a large squarely-built face. Over his forehead and absurdly experienced eyes, dark hair fell stiffly. As he rose, men started up and began to leave the house; at his first sentence they paused and looked at him – and sat down again. By the end of his third sentence, with a few waves of his powerful hands, and a touch of unconscious magnetism and conscious strength, the speeches of J.A. Simon and F.E. Smith were as though they had never been. For twenty minutes the new orator, Mr Hilaire Belloc, who was soon to sit in the seat of Gladstone, Lord Salisbury, Milner, Curzon and Asquith, as President of the Union, held his audience breathless.[13]

Author and Catholic activist Gregory McDonald knew Belloc and described him as 'the most ruthless, effective and unforgiving writer of polemic, and sustainer of argument and debate, whom I have ever encountered. He was a combination of bulldog and bloodhound: once he got his teeth into you, he never let go; and once he had your scent, he never gave up.'[14] Philip Guedalla, who had worked on *The Outline of History* with Wells, was by no means a friend of Belloc's. The two men had argued vehemently about religion and politics, and had gone so far as to exchange personal insults. Even so, Guedalla wrote of Belloc:

It is instructive enough to watch him reduce a problem to its most elementary terms, state its axioms with elaborate lucidity, define his words, slaughter imaginary objectors, and announce his conclusions with a slow, unanswerable dignity that would leave his auditors far too exhausted to make an answer, even if there were one. It is fun to watch him bowl the Professors over, scatter the politicians (dealing particular destruction among the enemies of religion and light refreshment), and defy with his ringing challenge the few remaining infidels. . . . but best of all, in one judgement, is to hear him play with a strange, lingering skill the incomparable instrument of English prose. He draws from those stiff keys . . . the full melody of which they are capable. His irony is sometimes a trifle jagged; and perhaps his solemn fun is a thought too solemn . . . and there are other moments when he is just a trifle boisterous for the modern palate.[15]

Another acquaintance said, quite simply, that trying to argue with Hilaire Belloc was like trying to break into a hailstorm (a comment that has, ironically, in the past been erroneously attributed to Wells).[16] Anecdotes about his rude behaviour are legion, as are stories of his wit and verbal skill. His attitude to conflict was best summed up in a song he wrote: 'Noël, Noël, Noël, Noël; May all my enemies go to hell.' His friend and biographer J.B. Morton, however, wrote in more defensive terms that 'Belloc dominated not by insensitive loudness, but by the force of his character. He talked with authority, and his presence suggested authority.'

Belloc wrote 156 books and pamphlets during his long and opinionated career, was elected as a Member of Parliament, served in the French artillery, and spearheaded, with G.K. Chesterton, Catholic letters and literature for almost half a century. He was capable of inspiring love and hate in almost equal proportions. He was a man of prodigious energy, once setting a still unbeaten record by walking from Oxford to London in eleven and a half hours. He could be vulgar, even disgusting; he would stuff pieces of bacon, bread and cheese into his cape pockets, where they would mingle with pamphlets, newspapers and unfinished articles. He could also be charming, seductive and, most of all, a winning and convincing genius. It was such a man who now took on H.G. Wells in intellectual combat. It was not really an equal fight.

Belloc and Wells had met occasionally at the Reform Club and even visited each other in their homes. They were never intimate, but they were certainly on friendly terms. Belloc became more splenetic, and much less open to differences of opinion, after his wife died in 1914. He never recovered from the loss, wrote on black-edged notepaper, and made the sign of the cross over his dead wife's room whenever he passed it. The Belloc of 1910 may have been more forgiving than the Belloc of 1920. In 1922, for example, the *Daily News* had asked G.K. Chesterton and Hilaire Belloc what they thought of Wells as a possible Member of Parliament. Chesterton wished him luck, but thought he would be better off continuing as a writer. Belloc, who detested the British parliamentary system and thought it run by conspirators and rogues, wrote: 'Of the effect of election upon Mr Wells' style I am not competent to pronounce. But in morals, temperament, instruction, and type of oratory, I know him to be admirably suited for the House of Commons.'[17]

Belloc disagreed with almost everything Wells wrote about the history of mankind. For Belloc, Catholic Christianity, the Roman Empire, European civilization, French culture and the fallacies of evolution were essential to any history book; they were, in fact, the basis of any study of history. As soon as the first editions of *The Outline of History* began to appear in 1920 Belloc rushed to his pen and began the duel.

His platform was not, as has previously been believed, the Catholic weekly newspaper, *The Universe*, but the *London Mercury* and the *Dublin Review*. In the pages of these journals he lambasted Wells for being inaccurate, for writing 'howlers', and for being wrong, wrong, wrong.

He still in his heart of hearts thinks 'alcohol' naughty and dreads to play cards. . . . He doesn't understand poetry – he has a vague suspicion that it is immoral. He associates gloom with truth. There are myriads of him about. Things are going at such a pace that he may quite soon be rid of his curse, shake himself, and wake up a happy man . . . So much for the book. It will have a prodigious vogue in its own world and an early grave.

Yet Belloc still expressed admiration for his opponent. 'When I think of its author I find a different mood,' he wrote. 'Never shall I forget the days when as a very young man I eagerly awaited month after month each new instalment of *The Time Machine* . . . He is lucid, sparing, direct, effective, a true maker.'[18] When, however, Belloc continued his attacks in *The Universe*, his tone was very different.

Yet even now the dispute could have been extinguished. Although *The Universe* was avidly and faithfully read by many Roman Catholics, it was almost unknown in the secular world, and if Wells had left Belloc's diatribes well alone the argument would have gone no further. He did not; because he could not. Wells was a thin-skinned man at the best of times, and Belloc's broadsides, delivered every two weeks, were too much to tolerate. He was foolish to take up the cudgels. Apart from the other many differences between the two men, there was one further distinction which was pointed out to Wells by Arnold Bennett, and which he should have paid heed to: Wells was not fond of acrimony and controversial dispute, Belloc virtually lived for it.

Wells considered the articles in *The Universe* to be 'grossly personal and provocative'[19], and he wrote to the paper's editor offering him six full articles covering the dispute, free of charge. Wells was a very hot property, and any newspaper in Europe would have jumped at the chance of such an opportunity. Not *The Universe*.

Wells was stunned, and wrote again to the editor: 'May I point out to you that Mr Belloc has been attacking my reputation as a thinker, a writer, an impartial historian and an educated person for four and twenty fortnights in *The Universe*? He has misquoted; he has mis-stated. Will your Catholic public tolerate no reply?'

These attacks, which were subsequently issued in a slightly edited book form under the title *A Companion to Mr Wells's Outline of History*, were severe, strident, even vicious. But they were also permeated with factual record and considered, urbane criticism of Wells' points of view. Belloc began with a prolonged attack on 'Mr Wells and the Creation of the World (Man)', and followed up with 'Mr Wells and the Fall of Man', 'Mr Wells and God', 'Mr Wells and the Incarnation', 'Mr Wells on Priesthood', and so on. Belloc adopted a haughty, pedagogic stance, a mixture of contempt and concern. In the introduction to the book of articles, he wrote:

My object in these pages is to follow Mr Wells's *Outline of History*; to point out the principal old-fashioned popular errors, which its author has repeated, and to state the opposing truths with their supporting evidence and reasoning.

It if be asked why I should devote such labour to such a book, I answer that, though ephemeral, the work has had a wide circulation, and is therefore of some momentary effect worth checking, while it is also representative of its type: a sort of newspaper literature commanding wide circulation which repeats as facts for general acceptation theories once respectable and now exploded. To check erroneous statement is always worth while.

Wells' first defect, Belloc continued, 'is that his book is Provincial . . . a schoolboy ought to know better than to write this . . . I am appalled to discover that he knows nothing of all the modern work against Darwinism.' Not only has he 'not kept abreast of the modern scientific and historical work . . . not followed the general thought of Europe and America in matters of physical science', but 'in history proper, he was never taught to appreciate the part played by Latin and Greek culture, and never even introduced to the history of the early Church. And this is the more remarkable as he assures us that he has a wide knowledge of modern languages, in which he reads French like English, and can handle German, Spanish, Italian, and even Portuguese.' After offering this ironical criticism – Belloc knew, as did Wells' friends, that he did not understand all of these languages – Belloc landed his attempt at the knock-out punch. 'With all this Mr Wells suffers from the very grievous fault of being ignorant that he is ignorant. He has the strange cocksureness of the man who only knows the old conventional textbook of his schooldays and mistakes it for universal knowledge.'

Wells fumed. He assembled a group of his friends at his house and asked for their advice.[20] Arnold Bennett suggested that Wells consciously ignore Belloc, because response was exactly what Belloc wanted. Wells went so far as to ask G.K. Chesterton, the larger and gentler part of the mythological 'Chesterbelloc', for advice.[21] Chesterton replied that as a friend of Belloc's, he was a poor commentator, but added that 'Hilary is not an enemy whom I would choose; but do I have the choice?' Wells certainly underestimated Belloc's ferocity and his willingness to take matters to the limit. He wrote:

Accustomed as I am to see Mr Belloc dodging about in my London club ... and even occasionally appearing at a dinner party, compactly stout, rather breathless and always insistently garrulous, I am more than a little amazed at his opening. He has suddenly become aloof from me. A great gulf of manners yawns between us. 'Hullo Belloc!' is frozen on my lips. ... He advances upon me in his Introduction with a gravity of utterance, a dignity of gesture, rare in God-fearing, sober men.[22]

Wells, not willing to let Belloc's invective go unanswered, chose among other platforms the book *Mr Belloc Objects to The Outline of History*, published by Watts in 1926.

The crux of the argument was about religion, faith and the Catholic Church. Belloc perceived Wells as the consummate Protestant, urban, modernist thinker. He detested his anti-Catholicism – and Wells was without any doubt an anti-Catholic, both on philosophical grounds and to a large extent on personal grounds, mostly due to the Evangelical teaching he received from his mother – and took it personally. 'He [Wells] tells us rather pathetically that he must know all about the Catholic Church, because he now winters on the Riviera. ... He inherits the old prejudice – flourishing strongly in the best No-Popery days – that for some unexplained reason a Catholic is opposed to that most interesting intellectual activity, the pursuit of physical knowledge.'[23]

Wells refused to believe that such passionate resistance was motivated only by religious conviction. 'I realized long ago,' he wrote, 'that his apparent arrogance is largely the self-protection of a fundamentally fearful man. He is a stout fellow in a funk. He is the sort of man who talks loud and fast for fear of hearing the other side. There is a frightened thing at the heart of all this burly insolence.'

Wells was fighting back, but he was not hitting in the right places. Belloc was immune to taunts of cowardice or intolerance; the former charge was too ridiculous to consider; the latter was a point of pride. Wells looked for a different battle-ground, but was already being outmanoeuvred by the master strategist Belloc. Combat would take place on the issue of evolution and the birth of man. Belloc rested his case heavily on St Thomas Aquinas, but flavoured his philosophical defence on the Christian theory of Creation with humour and aggression.

The old-fashioned Bible Christian thought that the Hen appeared mature in a twinkling, out of the air, like the mango tree of the Indian jugglers. His newly enlightened son has discovered that it comes from an egg. Mr Wells . . . appears in the role of the newly enlightened, and is most earnest to convince his erring and belated fellows that life can have come into existence as a 'natural' process: an idea which he conceives as repugnant to 'religious' minds. It is astonishing that either of these two back-waters of culture should survive: the back-water of the Bible Christian enlightened by elementary 'science', which gets rid of a Creator, and the back-water of the not yet enlightened Bible Christian, who can't think of creation except as the sudden appearance of familiar objects out of surrounding space. We may wonder with amusement what Mr Wells would make of such a Catholic sentence as 'God made this oak'. I suppose he would think it a confusion of acorns with God. He should read St Thomas.

He went on to discuss the fallacies contained in the notion of the family tree, explaining that Wells evidently 'doesn't know that Vailleton of Montpellier has knocked the last nail into the coffin of that facile and superficial Victorian short-cut. He has probably never heard of Vailleton and when he does he will suspect him for a foreigner. That is what I mean by being provincial and not abreast of one's time.'

Wells wasted no time in replying, and took on Belloc at his own game. He had, he confessed, heard of Vailleton the biologist; but he had heard of another Vailleton, a highly respected nineteenth-century embryologist, now in old age, whose theory, far from being new, was old hat a decade ago. Could Belloc, Wells asked with heavy sarcasm, have confused his sources or mistaken his references? It may be possible, Wells continued, because in France some students had 'run away with the idea that embryos consciously repeat their phylogeny . . . It is not an idea I have ever entertained . . . its only interest here is that it gives Mr Belloc a chance of showing how rudely he can set out his inaccuracies.'

This was brave stuff, but the strain was beginning to tell on Wells. He felt isolated; partly because some of this battle was taking place on foreign territory, on Belloc's territory, in and around the Catholic press; partly because his friends thought he was adopting the wrong policy, and refused to give him the appropriate support. He took the astounding, and politically unwise, step of writing to Belloc and asking for a truce.[24] This only spurred the Catholic champion on to further attack.

Belloc replied to Wells' comments about the naming of his scientist. He had, he confessed, made a mistake, and confused the names of Vialleton with Vailleton. But Belloc was not one to dwell on his own errors. Only a man as small-minded as Wells, he emphasized, would labour this point for over a page, and exploit a simple typographical error. Wells was still running away from the central argument. Wells was 'ignorant', his actions 'inexcusable', Belloc continued. Wells did not understand the notion of evolution, Belloc claimed, so how could he possible argue in its defence.

Then Wells made a clumsy mistake. He challenged Belloc to find contradictions within the *Outline*; he was confident that there were none. Belloc came up with a crippling response. He quoted Wells as saying on page 55 of his book that palaeolithic man did not 'know of the bow'. Belloc wrote that he was stunned that 'a person pretending to teach popular prehistorical science in 1925 should tell us of the cave painters that it was "doubtful if they knew of the bow" . . . because here before me, in Mr Wells' own book, were reproductions of these cave paintings, with the bow and the arrow appearing all over them.'

Wells had had enough. He packed his bags and went on holiday to the south of France where he could recuperate from his humiliation, and relax with his favourite sparkling wines and local pâté.[25] It was ironic that Belloc was half-French and much more at ease in France than Wells could ever be, a thought that certainly crossed Wells' mind. He was increasingly short-tempered and truculent, and at pains to win this battle once and for all. He cut short his retreat to the continent and returned to England. Belloc was still writing away, and speaking up and down the country of the errors in Wells' thinking. Wells decided to draw first blood this time. He used as his target part of an article by Belloc in which he had contemptuously rejected a piece of evolutionary argument. The Darwinists, Belloc argued, believed that one ancient wingless reptile gradually became a bird, its armour transformed into feathers, its legs into wings. 'By the very nature of the theory', Belloc wrote, this was ridiculous. 'Compare the "get away" chances of a lizard at one end of the process or a sparrow at the other, with some poor beast that had to try to scurry off on half-wings or to fly with half-legs.' Natural selection was a fraud; predestined purpose was the only logical and tenable explanation of the evolution of the world since the Creation.

Wells dissected the argument. Mr Belloc, he said, had shown himself to be an innocent in the world of science. He appeared to have no idea whatsoever that 'Mesozoic reptiles most closely resembling birds were creatures walking on their hind legs, with a bony structure of the loins and a backbone already suggestive of the avian anatomy. Nor is he aware that in the lowliest of living birds the fore-limbs are mere flappers, that the feathers are simpler in structure than any other birds' feathers, and that the general development of a bird's feathers points plainly to the elongation of a scale.' Further, 'the transition from a quilled to a feathered dinosaur presents . . . no imaginative difficulties, and the earliest birds ran and did not fly.' Wells described the Hesperornis, the Archaeopteryx, and used them to support his case. Here was valid and well-researched argument, but it did not achieve the desired effect. Readers were alienated by such exclusive pedantries, and Belloc publicly laughed at Wells' strenuous efforts to prove his point.[26]

It was not even his point, Belloc retorted, but the reiteration of an older scientific theory. Professor Wolff had laid the foundations of the attack on evolution a generation ago, and Korchinsky had extended it, Belloc wrote; yet Wells had clearly not heard of these seminal works and their vitally important authors. Wolff believed in a 'gradual development of the adaptation between one muscle-cell and one nerve-ending, through selection among an infinity of chance-made variations; but that such shall take place coincidentally in time and character in hundreds of thousands of cases in one organism is inconceivable'.

He continued that, 'between the foot of the land animal and the flapper of the whale, between the powerfully defensive and aggressive great ape, and the weak, more intelligent man, there must be [a stage] where the organism was at a positive disadvantage, and that consideration blows Darwinian Natural Selection to pieces'. Korchinsky 'calls selection through the struggle for existence a factor inimical to evolution'.[27] Belloc concluded with: 'hosts of men great and small, of high authority like these Professors or of no authority like myself, have been repeating that obvious bit of common sense for something like a lifetime, though it would seem that for some extraordinary reason Mr Wells has never heard of it . . . Great Heavens! . . . the abysmal lack of acquaintance Mr Wells shows with the thought of his time . . . I think I have said enough to expose Mr Wells's pretence of reading in modern biology. The bubble is pricked and has burst.'

Wells was furious; and shaken. He tore into his friends, his secretary, his researchers and his wife. Why had he not been warned that Belloc would keep presenting arguments, keep making Wells look rather ridiculous, keep winning the support of those following the debate? Most of his friends, if not all, told him that they had indeed warned of the dangers of confronting Belloc head-on. He again wrote to G.K. Chesterton, asking him if he would act as an umpire or mediator, and explaining that the time and energy demanded by this argument were pushing him towards collapse.[28] Chesterton replied within the week; and such punctuality was rare for him. He explained that he had spoken to Belloc, but no compromise was possible. Belloc would only accept contrition and apology from Wells. Wells once again had no alternative but to fight.

He claimed that Belloc had not even read the *Outline*, and that he had 'got the whole business upside down'. The idea of the survival of the fittest was a weak and populist one, and not really a part of genuine evolutionary thinking. 'Yet Mr Belloc insists upon writing of "the Fittest" as a sort of conspicuously competitive prize boy, a favourable "sport", who has to meet his female equivalent and breed a new variety.' Wells then committed a fundamental error. He lunged at Belloc by denying not an opinion or a theory, but a fact. He implied that some of the academic and scientific authorities whom Belloc quoted in his support were at best minor figures, unknown in serious circles; at worst, pure fabrications on Belloc's part. He repeated the point, in print and in lectures, and demanded that Belloc defend himself.

Belloc was only too pleased to do so; this was what he had been waiting for for weeks. He delivered a speech in Plymouth in which he described in some detail each person whom he had quoted, their qualifications and their beliefs. He also publicly referred to Wells as a fraud.[29] He then reiterated his defence in writing:

Mr Wells was foolish enough to write a hurried pamphlet in which he made the strange affirmation that my arguments against Natural Selection were of my own invention and that I cited no modern critics of Darwinism because no such critics existed: the intellectual movement of which I spoke was a figment of my brain, and I could quote no authorities supporting it.

From this it was clear, though astonishing, that Mr Wells had undertaken to write popular stuff about Evolution without so much as a casual acquaintance with the advance of biology in our generation.

I therefore append here the names of some few among the many authorities upon biological science who have exposed the error of Natural Selection.

He was not prepared to let Wells off the hook. He mocked him tirelessly with his appendage of names: 'a short list, drawn up at random ... some forty odd names such as a man of quite ordinary general education like myself with only a general interest in such matters can jot down from memory'.[30] Here was Dwight, Professor of Anatomy at Harvard University; Morgan, Professor of Experimental Zoology at the University of Columbia; Rosa, Professor at the University of Padua; leading scholars from universities in Bologna, Paris, Vienna, Leipzig, Amsterdam and Tubingen; names and more names; arrows and arrows. Wells could not fail but be pierced to the core.

By now Wells was at the end of his resistance. He was fighting not for victory but for survival. He summoned up whatever strength and will he had left and let fly at his indefatigable opponent. But this time the shot was peppered with compromise, even submission. He argued that it was impossible for anyone genuinely to win the argument, because by its very nature it was inexact, and no theory could ever be definitive:

Now if he will think what would happen today under such circumstances, he will realize that the fauna and flora of the stratum first considered will drift away, and that another fauna and flora will come in with the new conditions. Fresh things will come to feed and wade and drown in the waters, and old types will no longer frequent them. The fossil remains of one stratum are very rarely directly successive to those below it or directly ancestral to those above it.

Belloc claimed victory. He boasted that he had written over 100,000 words of criticism of Wells' history book, but Wells could only respond with half a dozen counter-attacks or defences. He gathered a group of friends at the home of G.K. Chesterton, and later in the week repeated the party at a pub in Essex Street, near Fleet Street. Chesterton provided four Stiltons, an entire roast pig and a dozen bottles of champagne. Belloc brought three dozen bottles of wine from his own cellar, personally chosen on a recent trip to France.[31]

Shortly after these bibulous celebrations Belloc met Wells at the Reform Club. The traditional account of this meeting, which is almost certainly untrue, depicts Belloc walking through the smoking-room of the club and seeing Wells bent double, searching underneath his armchair for a lost box of matches. Belloc is supposed to have asked, 'Still looking for Neanderthal Man, HG?' Wells allegedly replied, 'No — Woman.' What in fact occurred is strongly implied in a letter from Chesterton to Belloc,[32] following one from Belloc which described the incident and which, unfortunately, no longer exists. In his letter, Chesterton congratulates his friend on his reaction to meeting Wells by chance at the club, but adds that the time has come for reconciliation. It appears that Belloc ignored Wells, in as aggressive a way as possible. Wells made the first approach, and extended his hand to Belloc, who in turn refused the handshake with the words, 'best to save your palm for the evolutionary struggle, Wells. Do they still take Neanderthal men as members here?' Wells then scolded Belloc, and suggested that they declare the argument a tie. Belloc disagreed, laughed, and said that the definition of the word had obviously changed 'during the outline of history'.

Wells retreated to Essex to recuperate. Friends who visited him thought that something had been lost during the Belloc wars, or perhaps it was simply age taking its toll.[33] Either way, the man who walked away from the debate was not the same determined invincible battler who had begun it.

Writing in 1958 after both Wells and Belloc had died, Evelyn Waugh looked back on the notorious debate between the two men. In his biography of Ronald Knox, published the following year, Waugh wrote:

The decade opened with the dissemination of H.G. Wells' *Outline of History*. It is doubtful whether the author had planned it primarily as an attack on the Christian religion. He was the creature of his age and upbringing, and assumed that his ignorance and prejudice would be in sympathy with his readers. He was disconcerted when, on the reissue of his book in more alluring form in 1925 and 1926, Hilaire Belloc tackled him in earnest and trounced him in a full series of articles syndicated through most of the English-speaking world. He was even more disconcerted when he found that editors were not interested in the controversy. He was obliged to print his reply as a pamphlet, 'Mr Belloc Objects' (which provoked 'Mr Belloc Still Objects', another pamphlet). This refusal of the popular press to give him a hearing at the height of his fame, on what in his youth had been a question of vital general interest, was striking evidence of a new trend. Fleet Street had decided that the truth or falsehood of theological assertions was no longer relevant; there remained, however, a vague residual curiosity in the common man about his ultimate destiny.

Waugh may have been speaking with the jaundiced gift of hindsight but he was largely correct in his analysis of the situation. Not only had Wells lost his fight with Belloc but the fight itself was under attack. Wells was forced to ask himself whether the entire affair had been worth the monumental effort.

8 Debates and Farewells

Wells had written the bulk of three novels during the composition of *The Outline of History* and the early stages of the Belloc debate. The first was *The Undying Fire*, a twentieth-century version of the Book of Job; its central character is Job Huss, the headmaster of a public school. He is a champion of radical ideas in the field of education and has devoted the best part of his life to implementing them at Woldingstanton public school in Norfolk. Huss 'had been the first English schoolmaster to liberate the modern side from the entanglement of its lower forms with the classical masters; it was the only school in England where Spanish and Russian were honestly taught; his science laboratories were the best school laboratories in Great Britain and perhaps in the world, and his new methods in the teaching of history and politics brought a steady stream of foreign inquirers.' But this perfect place is suddenly split asunder by catastrophe. 'There had been an epidemic of measles in which, through the inexplicable negligence of a trusted nurse, two boys had died. On the afternoon of the second of these deaths an assistant master was killed by an explosion in the chemical laboratory. Then on the very last night of the term came the School House fire, in which two of the younger boys were burned to death.'

Wells was not content to leave his character without a school. Huss develops cancer, loses his savings in a rash investment and is informed that his son is lost, probably dead, in the trenches. He is visited by four 'Job's Comforters': school governors Burrows and Dad, Mr Farr, who is in charge of the school's technical department, and his doctor, Barrack. The visitors argue with Huss, proclaiming their belief that he was a dreamer; he should have devoted far less time to the study of world history, they propose, and tailored the school curriculum so as to prepare the students for careers in business or trade. This is the setting for a debate between a belief in education and a belief in training – between idealism and pragmatism. Huss has all the best tunes:

The end and substance of all real education is to teach men and women of the Battle of God, to teach them of the beginning of life upon this lonely little planet amidst the endless stars, and how those beginnings have unfolded; to show them how man has arisen through the long ages from amidst the beasts, and the nature of the struggle God wages through him, and to draw all men together out of themselves into one common life and effort with God. The nature of God's struggle is the essence of our dispute. It is a struggle, with a hope of victory but with no assurance.

Huss is operated on to halt the spread of his cancer and while under the anaesthetic experiences a vision of himself as the Biblical Job. He is tempted by God and Satan, and is told finally that everything depends on his own courage. In reality, matters resolve themselves; he is cured, comes into a legacy, fellow teachers support him in his successful attempt to regain his position as headmaster and he discovers that his son did not in fact die in the war. The book was read with more interest a decade after its publication than it was at the time, when it was perceived as a preparation for *The Outline of History* and reviews were relatively few and quite unflattering. Certainly the underlying themes contained in *The Outline of History* – progress, education and history – are also discussed in *The Undying Fire*.

The Secret Places of the Heart was published in 1922 by Cassell and Company, and was another of Wells' 'discussion' novels. Its hero is Sir Richmond Hardy, an arms dealer and public figure with influence in the world of politics and business. A workaholic whose membership of the Fuel Commission brings him to the verge of a nervous breakdown, he is obsessed with persuading the other commission members to support his point of view, which is that only by an international commitment to the saving and rationing of energy can the world guarantee its future. Hardy is conscious of his own poor physical state, however, and seeks the medical advice of nerve specialist Dr Martineau. The advice given is that the two men should take a holiday together, a tour of the West Country of England. The vacation provides Wells with an opportunity to explain, and try to justify, some of his own actions. Hardy reveals to Martineau that he has had extramarital affairs and also has illegitimate children. His wife, he explains, is eternally tolerant, always understanding and intellectually gifted; he is not completely sure why he is so promiscuous and unfaithful. It is while contemplating this that he falls for another young woman and energetically pursues her. Yet he feels guilty, not only because he is betraying his wife, but also because he is hurting his other mistresses. The holiday ends and Hardy returns to his zealous work for the Fuel Commission. The extent and intensity of the work eventually kill him.

This was Wells entering another stage of his life and reflecting on his deeds and misdeeds. The book was undoubtedly influenced, even shaped, by his relationship with Rebecca West — 'She found my hero's obsession with fuel a personal offence. It was perhaps a personal offence.'[1] — and his growing ambivalence towards sexual adventure.

His next book was far more confident and certain, and of a completely different genre. Wells had returned to his Utopian phase with a new enthusiasm and announced that he had fresh and exciting things to say. *Men Like Gods* was published in 1923, also by Cassell and Company. The hero this time is a very different person from Sir Richmond Hardy. Alfred Barnstaple is a radical journalist, disillusioned by the failure and empty promises of Woodrow Wilson and the League of Nations. He is driving near Slough one day when he is suddenly transported into a paradise by the experiments of some Utopian scientists. Wells is not at his best here, and the supernatural projection he describes has none of the grace and style of his earlier scientific romances.

Barnstaple is completely won over by what he sees in this new society, which is in essence the same terrifyingly authoritarian regime depicted, and promised, in *A Modern Utopia*. Here, however, the Samurai have developed and expanded to such an extent, and homogeneity has been so rigidly enforced and genetically controlled, that everybody is a member of the ruling elite. 'Nearly all the greater evils of human life had been conquered; war, pestilence and malaise, famine and poverty had been swept out of human existence. The dreams of artists, of perfected and lovely bodies and of a world transfigured to harmony and beauty had been realized: the spirits of order and organization ruled triumphant.'

Although this is a fictional discussion of Wells' utopian dream, it is still highly classified and elaborate; Wells had planned and organized it in his mind down to the smallest detail. It is, in its way, just as repellent and horrific as *Anticipations* and *A Modern Utopia*. Alfred Barnstaple, of course, does not think so. He cannot understand the qualms and reservations of the other Earth dwellers who have been projected into Utopia. They consist of the Conservative leader, Cecil Burleigh, and the Secretary of State for War, Rupert Catskill, who are easily identifiable caricatures of former Prime Minister and Foreign Secretary Arthur Balfour and Winston Churchill. Lord Barralonga, a property developer, is also in the party, as is Father Amerton, representing Christianity, and others who speak for journalism, the arts and other trades and professions with which Wells had particular quarrels. They are also all more or less spokesmen for various aspects of Wells' own age, an age which he juxtaposes with his Utopia, to the obvious disadvantage of the former. The visitors from Earth are poorly drawn, often crass, and seldom convincing. Of greater importance are Wells' passing references to the establishment of law and order; of, for example, the threats made to the orthodox Christian Father Amerton of 'corrective treatment' if he persists in criticizing the Utopians' atheism and lack of theology or belief.

Amerton is not the only critic of this perfect society. Yet he and all of his supporters are given the flimsiest of arguments and the most flaccid of defences against the Utopian philosophy. Wells was in no mood to make this a fair battle. The resisters are unbending and often flippant, and even when they do sympathize at all with the new order – as in the case of Lady Stella – it is on the most cosmetic and fatuous of levels. Burleigh's chauffeur, Penk, is described as gross and lascivious, and when he makes a pass at a Utopian woman she merely lays him to the ground with a blow of her hand. Here is effortless superiority from a physical as well as a moral and intellectual point of view.

One man who refuses to accept all of this is Catskill, who leads a revolt against the Utopians. This is futile and ultimately disastrous, and the Samurai 'quarantine' the area in which the uprising takes place, leading to the death of some of the fighters. Barnstaple remains a devotee of the new world, and eventually returns to Earth with a new optimism for the future. 'Some day here and everywhere, Life of which you and I are but anticipatory atoms and eddies, Life will awaken indeed, one and whole and marvellous, like a child awakening to conscious life. It will open its drowsy eyes and stretch itself and smile, looking the mystery of God in the face as one meets the morning sun.'

There were many critics who did not share Wells' hopes for the future. Aldous Huxley wrote his satirical novel and eternal caveat, *Brave New World*, as a direct rebuttal of *Men Like Gods*. Ironically, Huxley was the grandson of Thomas Henry Huxley, Wells' great hero and mentor, and hence this criticism cut to the bone. Published in 1932, Huxley's book features a world state in the seventh century AF (After Ford). Humanity is divided into scientifically decided classes, children are hatched in incubators and raised by the state to fulfil specific needs. Huxley introduces a 'savage' from New Mexico, who is appalled, bewildered and terrified by what he sees. It is during his arguments with the World Controller that we witness Huxley's pleas for personal liberty, and the inevitable conflict between individual freedom and the Wellsian idea of the future state. Huxley envisaged a state that was so powerful that even sensual and erotic gratification will be centrally provided and controlled. ' "Take hold of those metal knobs on the arms of the chair," whispered Lenina, "otherwise you won't get any feely effects" ... the stereotypic lips came together again, and once more the facial erogenous zones of the six thousand spectators in the Alhambra tingled with almost intolerable galvanic pleasure.'

But Wells had already seen the future in the Soviet Union, and he thought that it just might work. He had been relatively well informed about Russia and the Russians since 1915, more so than most of his contemporary authors in Western Europe. Hence he prided himself on not having an overly romantic or sanguine view of this enigmatic country and its band of dedicated revolutionaries; but this in fact was, at this stage, precisely the image he did possess. His former friend Henry Arthur Jones had already attacked Wells in a book entitled *Patriotism and Popular Education*, and now described him as irresponsible and mischievous for supporting the Bolshevik regime. Wells had argued and written that Britain and the Western allies should not adopt a policy of aggression towards the new regime in Russia, even after the Bolsheviks had unceremoniously abandoned the Allied cause and left the war. He thought that taking up arms against the inchoate Communist government would be not only immoral but also unwise – and in the latter he was to be proved correct. He had experienced the revolution vicariously, through the eyes of Maxim Gorky, who was a brilliant but not an objective or even perceptive observer of the Bolshevik takeover of the country. He did implore Wells, however, to come and see what was happening in Russia, and Wells agreed, at the same time making his position clear by urging his sons to learn the Russian language rather than study classics.

Yet the trip to the new Communist nation did not go as well as Wells or Gorky had hoped. Although Wells' meetings with Zinoviev and Pavlov were successful, when it came to Lenin there was only friction. This much heralded conversation ended with the Bolshevik leader dismissing Wells with 'Ugh! What a narrow petty bourgeois! Ugh! What a Philistine!' Wells later considered Lenin's attack, and Trotsky's subsequent defence of it, in his autobiography:

He, and Trotsky also, were of the same vital social stratum; they had indeed both started life from a far more advantageous level than I had; but the discolouration of their stream of thought by Marxist pretences and sentimentalities, has blinded them to their own essential quality. My conversation with Lenin turned entirely on the 'liquidation' of the peasant and the urban toiler – by large-scale agriculture and power machinery. Lenin was just as much for that as I was, we were talking about the same thing in the same spirit; but we said the same thing as though it was a different thing because our minds were tuned in different keys.

It may or may not have been the personal conflict with Lenin and Trotsky which altered Wells' view on the early Soviet Union, but by the early 1920s he had clearly lost some of his affection for the country. He now described Marx's *Das Kapital* as 'a monument of pretentious pedantry' and although he spoke on behalf of the Russian people and Russian aspirations, he was at best a lukewarm supporter of Lenin's Bolshevism. This was a position that George Bernard Shaw, for one, could not understand. The two men had of course already clashed over the Fabians and the Great War, an argument that had never been fully resolved. Shaw was still eager to fight, Wells less so. The latter's writings about the Soviet Union such as *Russia in the Shadows* were relatively objective and even-handed but unacceptable to Shaw. One passage in particular threw Shaw into his beloved boxing ring. Wells wrote:

In Russia I must confess my passive objection to Marx has changed to a very active hostility. Wherever we went we encountered busts, portraits, statues of Marx. About two-thirds of the face of Marx is beard, a vast solemn woolly uneventful beard that must have made all normal exercise impossible. It is not the sort of beard that happens to a man, it is a beard cultivated, cherished and thrust patriarchally upon the world . . . A gnawing desire grew upon me to see Karl Marx shaved. Some day, if I am spared, I will take up shears and a razor . . .

The heavily and proudly bearded Shaw wrongly interpreted this as a thinly disguised personal attack, or at least claimed to some of his friends that he did. Mutual friends of the two men, many of whom worked for or edited some of the most successful and popular newspapers in the country, heard about the fermenting argument and the story was soon doing the rounds of Fleet Street. One paper headed by an alleged friend of Shaw and Wells sent a journalist to see Shaw to discover what was really going on. During the interview the reporter asked what Shaw thought of Wells' comments on Marx and Marxism. Shaw, who had already rehearsed an answer to this predictable question, took down a copy of Wells' *Russia in the Shadows* from his bookshelves — the volume was conveniently placed at eye-level. He pulled himself up to his full stature, adopted his oratorical pose and in his best, melodic, mocking tones read: 'When I was a boy of fourteen I was a complete Marxist long before I had heard the name of Marx. I had been cut off abruptly from education, caught in a detestable shop and I was being broken into a life of mean and dreary toil. I was worked too hard and for such long hours that all thought of self-improvement seemed hopeless. I would have set fire to that place if I had not been convinced it was over-insured.' Shaw pointed out how personal the passage was, how Wells could not possibly have fully understood Marx as a teenager even if he had read him, let alone if he had never even heard of him. Quite clearly, he continued, a man could only make such a comment if he did not understand what he was talking about. It also showed, concluded Shaw, the 'flux of his mind'.

Wells was shocked at Shaw's seemingly unprovoked attack and asked friends whether it had really happened and, if so, why he had been so vitriolic. Although Wells was a man of deep hatreds he could also be touchingly trusting and even quite naive. Throughout his life he searched for close friendships and for allies, figures J.B. Priestley thought of as 'artificial brothers, new fathers, people who would never let him down, chums who would leave the room rather than listen to criticism of their friend. He didn't understand that criticism could be a sign of friendship and not a sign of betrayal.' When Wells was certain – or certain, at least, in his mind and on his terms – of his enemies, however, he was a different figure. The argument with Shaw continued into the mid-1920s and remained unfinished. Wells had never wanted to take on Shaw on the question of Marxism anyway and searched for an alternative field of battle.

The search was considered and time-consuming; Wells knew that preparation before the fight was essential with Shaw. If it was to be to Wells' advantage it would have to concern science and would have to be a subject that would provoke Shaw, and perhaps tip him from his usual sense of balance and control, even make Shaw angry enough to lose his temper in public and cause him to make mistakes. Wells considered various options and finally settled on the question of vivisection, something that he thought the vegetarian Shaw would find difficult to resist. He let fly in the summer of 1927 in the pages of the *Sunday Express*:

It is a clumsy and misleading name for experimentation on animals for the sake of the knowledge to be gained thereby. It is clumsy and misleading because it means, literally, 'cutting up alive', and trails with it to most uninstructed minds a suggestion of highly sensitive creatures, bound and helpless, being slowly anatamized to death. This is an idea naturally repulsive to gentle and kindly spirits, and it puts an imputation of extreme cruelty on vivisection which warps the discussion from the outset.

Shaw was not to be outdone. In *Shaw on Vivisection* he wrote:

We have it at last from Mr Wells. The vivisector experiments because he wants to know. On the question whether it is right to hurt any living creature for the sake of knowledge, his answer is that knowledge is so supremely important that for its sake there is nothing it is not right to do. Thus we learn from Mr Wells that the vivisector is distinguished from the ordinary run of limited scoundrels by being an infinite scoundrel. The common scoundrel who does not care what pain he (or she) inflicts as long as he can get money by it, can be satiated. With public opinion and a stiff criminal code against him he can be brought to a point at which he does not consider another five pound note worth the risk of garrotting or sandbagging or swindling anybody to get it. But the vivisector scoundrel has no limits at all except that of his ... own mental capacity for devising them.

Wells was not at all disturbed by this line of argument. He actually celebrated Shaw's picking up of the gauntlet by dining with friends in Soho and making sure that the press were informed of the gathering. He ordered a 16-ounce steak and told the waiter in his loudest voice that vegetables would not be necessary. This was courageous bravado in the face of such an enemy. It was also difficult because Wells did not enjoy beef and usually dined on fish or white meat, but he was prepared to sacrifice diet for the sake of the argument.[2] He then wrote his reply.

The medical profession massively supports vivisection and its testimony is that the knowledge derived from vivisection has made possible the successful treatment of many cases of human suffering ... So far as we can measure one pain against another, or the pain of this creature against the pain of that, vivisection has diminished the pain of the world very considerably. But Shaw will hear nothing of this.

Sides were now forming and each camp urged its spokesman to continue the fight. But Wells began to lose some of his enthusiasm. His diabetes was causing him more concern now and draining his energy. He also suffered from regular stomach aches, sometimes acutely painful and leading to vomiting and long periods of exhaustion. His ulcers and his prodigious work rate had begun to take their toll. Jane was also increasingly ill, her health having deteriorated rapidly and noticeably during the last two years. Some friends commented that the only time they ever saw Wells genuinely afraid was when Jane took to her sick-bed. Yet he refused to give in, not when he thought that the argument with his old Irish foe was going in his favour. He rested while Shaw launched another attack. When it came, as always, it was eloquent and effective:

When a man says to Society 'May I torture my sister or her baby in pursuit of knowledge?' Society replies 'No'. If he pleads 'What! Not even if I have a chance of finding out how to cure cancer by doing it?' Society still says 'Not even then'. If the scientist, making the best of his disappointment, goes on to ask may he torture a dog, the stupid and callous people who do not realize that a dog is a fellow creature, and sometimes a good friend, may say 'Yes'. But even those who say 'You may torture a dog' never say 'you may torture my dog' and nobody says 'Yes! because in the pursuit of knowledge you may do as you please.' Just as even the stupidest people would say 'If you cannot attain to knowledge without boiling your mother you must do without knowledge' so the wisest people say 'If you cannot attain knowledge without torturing a dog you must be literally a damned fool, incapable of putting knowledge to use.

Shaw's argument was applauded by his friend, and enemy, G.K. Chesterton, who was a keen observer of this latest debate. He refused to give his public backing to either of the champions but did comment that Shaw was a man who understood and Wells was a man who argued.[3] In 1928 Pavlov's *Conditioned Reflexes, an Investigation of the Psychological Activity of the Cerebral Cortex* appeared in English. Shaw of course was highly critical of the book, Wells of course was highly enamoured of it. He wrote that if he were standing on a pier, saw Shaw and Pavlov in the waves, on the point of drowning, and could find only one lifebuoy, he would have no doubt who he would throw it to. It would not be to George Bernard Shaw.

The personal element did not worry Shaw very much. Hesketh Pearson, who knew both Wells and Shaw, and wrote a biography of the latter, recounted Shaw's personal opinion of Wells in his memoirs. The passage throws light on the conflict between the two writers.

Bernard Shaw called Wells a spoilt child because everything had been made too easy for him and success had come too quickly. ... The slightest rebuff or criticism or disapproval would banish his sense of humour and goad him to exhibitions of baffled fury that resembled those of a pampered child when denied some gratification ... 'No one could be angry with Wells for long,' Shaw told me. 'He frankly admits that his temper is hysterical. I remember meeting him the day after the appearance of an outrageous article which he had written on me. Really, I'd have been entitled to punch his head. But he was looking small and uneasy, and I just shook hands with him. Another time, when he was very angry with me, he wrote to me that everyone believed me to be homosexual and that he, Wells, had always denied it, but in future he wouldn't.' Shaw and Wells were about as unlike each other as were Chesterton and Belloc, but they were the chief thought-influences of their age. Wells was a lesser Dickens, small and tubby and easily offended; Shaw was a greater Voltaire, tall and lean and impervious to insult.

He was indeed impervious to insult and laughed at the image of a lifebuoy floating off to Pavlov and not to him. Of the rescued swimmer's book he wrote, 'I am apparently the only person who has ever read it right through from end to end. All the rest gave in before they came to the nonsense and the tortures.' Shortly after this claim, Wells met Shaw at the Reform Club and immediately took issue with his comments about the book he so applauded. 'You, Shaw, are the one who did not read Pavlov. You misread him,' said Wells. 'Did you or did you not say that Pavlov's dogs liked him?' asked Shaw. Wells replied that sometimes they liked him. 'While he was cutting half their brains out, piercing their cheeks to study their salivation?' replied Shaw. Wells stated that during the experiments the animals were incapable of feeling because they were deeply anaesthetized. 'And during the experiments Pavlov made the shattering discovery of such concern to international welfare that a dog's mouth watered when he heard the dinner bell.' No, no, replied Wells, 'Put in its biological perspective an epoch-making discovery which you will never understand.' Shaw again: 'If the fellow had come to me I could have given him the same information in less than thirty seconds without tormenting a single dog.' Wells retorted that Shaw didn't know 'the Behaviourist position – you don't understand that the mind is a system of reflexes held together by a body – that it is not an originally unified assembly whose factors have lost touch with each other.'

And then the argument came to a sudden and silent halt. On 6 October 1927 Wells' wife Amy Catherine, known as Jane, died. She had been diagnosed as suffering from cancer earlier in the year and it was soon evident that it would be fatal. Wells had refused to believe the worst and had spoken, both to Jane and to his friends, about his wife as though she would survive the cancer and lead a long and healthy life. Wells was actually told of his wife's cancer while he was in Europe by his son Frank. He immediately made plans to return to England and wrote to Jane: 'My dear, I love you much more than I have ever loved anyone else in the world and I am coming back to take care of you now and to do all I can to make you happy.'

With Jane's death so near Wells began to question his treatment of his wife, his promiscuity and devotion to other women. He was terrified of being alone and also terrified of the pangs of guilt; in spite of what he pretended to himself, he was capable of such feelings. He sat with Jane in their garden, where she had sat so many times before, sometimes because she wanted to be there, often because her husband was with another woman and there was nowhere else to go. Friends visited them for a while, until Jane decided that this did not help her and she wanted to be left alone. There was relatively little pain but much regret and crying. Wells was once seen on his knees by Jane's side pleading with her. When she died he remained very still and very quiet. He then sat down in an old favourite chair and looked into the gaping fireplace. Nobody approached him.

The funeral was a secular one, a cremation without pageant or too many speeches; those who did speak praised this brave woman. Shaw advised that Wells and his two sons actually watch the coffin entering the flames – it would be better for them in the long run, he said. Wells later wrote:

What is more difficult to tell is our slow discovery of the profoundest temperamental differences between us and of the problems these differences created for us. Fundamental to my wife's nature was a passion for happiness and lovely things. She was before everything else gentle and sweet. She worshipped beauty. For her, beauty was something very definite, a precious jewel to be discovered and treasured. For me beauty is incidental, so surely a part of things that one need not be directly concerned about it. I am a far less stable creature than she was, with a driving quality that holds my instabilities together. I have more drive than strength, and little patience; I am hasty and incompetent about much of the detailed business of life because I put too large a proportion of my available will and energy into issues that dominate me ... We had to work out our common problems very largely by the light nature had given us. And I am appalled to reflect how much of the patience, courage and sacrifice of our compromises came from her. Never once do I remember her romancing a situation into false issues. We had two important things in our favour, first that we had a common detestation not only of falsehood but of falsity, and secondly, that we had the sincerest affection and respect for each other. There again the feat was hers. It was an easy thing for me to keep my faith in her sense of fair play and her perfect generosity. She never told a lie. To the end

I would have taken her word against all other witnesses in the world. But she managed to sustain her belief that I was worth living for, and that was a harder task, while I made my way through a tangle of moods and impulses that were quite outside her instinctive sympathy. She stuck to me so sturdily that in the end I stuck to myself. I do not know what I should have been without her. She stabilized my life. She gave it a home and dignity. She preserved its continuity.

It was probably the only possible tribute to this woman who had known of every affair and every transgression, who had experienced so many humiliations and so much pain, and who throughout it all had remained loyal and faithful to the man she had promised fidelity to so many years earlier.

Wells had not neglected his fiction during his arguments with Shaw and the illness and death of his wife. The best of his half-a-dozen novels between 1925 and 1930 was *The World of William Clissold*, published in 1926. This was the longest work of fiction Wells ever wrote, the first edition of the book appearing in a three-volume set. It was also given the honour of being parodied, in a book entitled *The World of Billiam Wissold*, by H.A.M. Thomson. The eponymous hero of Wells' book is a successful businessman and mineralogy expert who writes his autobiography, still unfinished at the time of his death. His early life is troubled and mysterious, his beloved father having died in hidden circumstances. William and his brother Dickon study together at the Royal College of Science and spend their nights, and some of their days, deep in discussion and argument. This was a device that Wells had used before and would again, enabling him to expand on his political and social theories within the framework of the novel.

The two brothers represent opposing points of view, Dickon the seeker of fame and fortune, and William dedicated to pure and untainted research. Once again Wells dipped his pen deeply into his own experiences as a young man and depicted William Clissold neglecting his work because of his infatuation with a woman. But in this book the main character is the victim of the romantic encounter, deserted by his wife who is pregnant by another man. Clissold take up with another woman, Sirrie Evans, and like the young Wells sees his career steadily improve. He travels the world, makes important discoveries and is eventually made a Fellow of the Royal Society. During the First World War

Clissold performs valuable work with the Ministry of Munitions, rejects a knighthood offered to him for his services and forms an extremely low opinion of the British establishment – he began his adult life as a socialist and a republican, and his experiences with those in authority in the military and the government only confirm his views. He has two further romantic affairs and dies with his last love in a tragic car accident. The book ends with an editorial from Clissold's brother: 'So it was my brother never completed his manuscript, and his dream of a vast conspiracy in London and America and throughout the world, to bring order into the dangerous chaos of human affairs, remains an unfinished scheme, a suggestion, a plan waiting to be worked out.'

The conspiracy he referred to was another manifestation of Wells' platonic elite, his cabal of the chosen or appointed ones to govern the world for the world's own sake and interest. Wells dismissed much of *The World of William Clissold* as 'rambling' but was proud of what he saw as the meat of the novel, the extension of those same ideas he had written of in *Anticipations*:

It is absurd to think of creative revolution unless it has power in its hands, and manifestly the chief seats of creative power in the world are on the one hand modern industry associated with science and on the other world finance. The people who have control in these affairs can change the conditions of human life constructively and to the extent of their control. No other people can so change them ... It is only through a conscious, frank and world-wide cooperation of the man of science, the scientific worker, the man accustomed to the direction of productive industry, the man able to control the arterial supply of credit, the man who can control newspapers and politicians, that the great system of changes they have almost inadvertently got going can be brought to any hopeful order of development.

The book is far too long and could have been heavily edited with no serious damage being caused to the underlying themes, plots and character portrayals. Yet there is within its pages Wells' last expression of what he perceived as optimism and hopefulness. There are also convincing and enjoyable portraits of Bernard Shaw, Karl Marx and Lord Northcliffe, and valuable insights into Wells' increasingly cynical attitude towards love between the sexes. Sex and physical contact, he told friends, were what romance was really about – there was not very much to it other than that. Mary Colum in the *Saturday Review of Literature* wrote: 'The World of William Clissold, let me state at once, is likely to remain news for some time, though it contains nothing that is really new, though its value as literature is almost nil, but it is remarkable because it is an emporium of most of the things that Wells has been teaching and preaching and writing since he began. The book, in other words, is important because it is a Wells book, and Wells is important because of his enormous influence, not on the best minds, but on a large number of the intelligent minds of his time.' A long-time reader of Wells was H.L. Mencken, who wrote in the *American Mercury* that 'There is here a profoundly enterprising, competent and original mind, and I believe that it will put its marks upon the thought of the next generation. I have, in my time, damned Wells as much as most. I formally damn him again. But I see no way for the human race to escape him.'

The years between 1927 and 1930 were as busy as ever for Wells, involving European travel and the usual amount of public debate and controversy. In 1930 two important books were published. The first, *The Autocracy of Mr Parham: His Remarkable Adventures in this Changing World*, was published by Heinemann and the second, *The Science of Life: A Summary of Contemporary Knowledge about Life and its Possibilities*, by Amalgamated Press.

The former, a novel, was described by Wells just four years after its appearance as 'a rather boisterous caricature not of the personality but of the imaginations of a modern British imperialist of the university type. ... It amuses me still but few people share my liking.' The timing of the book was unfortunate; Wells' description and prediction of an authoritarian British political figure was tame and uninteresting to those readers who could see fascist leader Oswald Mosley taking his followers' salutes on the newsreels and in the newspapers every day of the week. Wells' vision of the rise of British fascism was at times accurate and at times ridiculous. The actions of his 'Lord Paramount', such as dismissing the House of Commons, speaking directly to 'the people' and forging a new empire, are believable and consistent with later fascist aspirations; the long-term support for this movement from capitalism, strange and exotic alliances between disparate European powers and a naval battle between Britain and the United States are simplistic fantasies. Wells also chose the wrong target in the book, caricaturing Winston Churchill as his potential dictator when he was in fact one of the British Union of Fascists' most vociferous opponents and a man who understood the nature of fascism better than most of his contemporaries. Wells was provoked by Churchill's aggression towards the Soviet Union and Mr Parham is himself obsessed with containing and destroying Russian Communism. The book had its moments:

The Great War of 1914–18 had not only been the greatest war in history, it had also been the greatest argument about war that had ever stormed through the human mind. The Fourteen Points of President Wilson, the vague, unjustifiable promises of Crewe House to a repentant Germany, had been more effective than any battle. And now this great war the Lord Paramount had launched was taking on the same quality of an immense and uncontrollable argument.

In the long run man will be lost or saved by argument, for collective human acts are little more than arguments in partial realization.

And now that strange mixture of forward-reaching imagination, hardy enterprise, exalted aims, and apparently inseparable cynicism which makes the American character a wonder and perplexity for the rest of mankind was to become the central reality of the Lord Paramount's mind.

Wells saw his novels as important but saw his educational writing – notably *The Outline of History* – as vital. It was in this spirit that he undertook *The Science of Life*. Wells began working on the project in 1928 and asked his son, G.P. Wells, and Julian Huxley, the grandson of his old teacher and formative influence Thomas Huxley, to work with him on the book. In addition to these two men, a group of assistants and researchers were used, whom Wells would assemble in his study and even at the dining-room table to supervise their progress. He recorded in his autobiography that 'we worked very harmoniously throughout' but Julian Huxley confided to friends that he often resented Wells' heavy-handed approach and lamented the fact that Wells treated him, a full Professor at King's College, London, in the same manner as he treated his son.

In spite of the difficulties the book was completed and Wells was pleased with it. He had intended it to be a textbook of 'everything that an educated man – to be an educated man – ought to know about biological science'. It was published in Britain and in the United States, then translated into French. Though never as successful as *The Outline of History* it did satisfy an ambition that had nagged Wells for over forty years.

The poor reviews of *The Autocracy of Mr Parham* and the amount of work and energy expended on *The Science of Life*, however, sent Wells into one of his regular periods of frustration and depression. This was made all the worse because old friends were dying, old faces were no longer to be seen at Wells' favourite clubs and restaurants. The hardest loss was that of Arnold Bennett, who died in March 1931 from typhoid contracted while he was in France. Bennett represented the last real link with the early days of Wells' career and literary life, the old struggles and the groping for success and fame. What was worse was that Bennett had criticized Wells for his reaction to Jane's death, condemning him for gathering so many people around him for reasons of distraction and not simply mourning his wife with solitary dignity. This gave a sour note to the final months of their relationship and Wells never quite got over that. He remembered his friend thus:

After his first visit to Sandgate, we never lost touch with each other. We never quarrelled, we never let our very lively resolve to 'get on' betray our mutual generosity; we were continually interested in one another and continually comparing ourselves with each other. He thought me an odd card; I thought him an odd card. I became more and more involved in the social and political issues . . . I made all sorts of contacts outside literary circles, I broadened and spread myself; and maybe I spread myself thin; while he retracted and concentrated. The boundaries of my personality became less definite and his more and more firmly drawn. I have told already how I put my banking account under the control of my wife, did not know of my own investments, allowed matters of furnishing, house-building, invitations and so forth to go right out of my control. I have never had any household in which my role has not been essentially that of the paying guest. But Bennett's control of the particulars of his life remained always (the word was one of his favourite ones) meticulous. He loved the direction of organization; the thing breaks out in his Imperial Palace. His home at Thorpe le Soken, his home in Cadogan Square were beautifully managed – by himself. His clothes were carefully studied. At the Reform Club we used to note with all respect the accordance of shirt and tie and sock and handkerchief, and draw him out upon the advisability of sending our laundry to Paris. I would ask him where to buy a watch or a hat. 'Do you mind,' he would say to me, 'if I just arrange that tie of yours.'

The difference between Bennett and myself, particularly in our latter developments, is perhaps interesting from a psychological point of view, though I do not know how to put it in psychological language. We contrasted more and more in our contact with the external world as our work unfolded. He developed his relation to the external world and I developed the relation of the external world to myself. He increased in precision and his generalizations weakened; I lost precision and my generalizations grew wider and stronger.

In September Isabel, Wells' first wife, died. All of the feelings of guilt and regret that had been with him since he had left the woman now flooded back. He had told himself that there would be ample time to make amends, and to do something for her, perhaps even show appropriate contrition. Now it was too late. Wells was sixty-four years old and looking backwards rather than forwards.

9 The Shape of Things

In 1932 came one of Wells' weakest novels, *The Bulpington of Blup*, the story of Theodore Bulpington and the fantasy world in which he lives. The Blup of the title is Bulpington's imaginary kingdom and he, of course, is the imaginary king. Wells thought of the book as a 'very direct caricature study of the irresponsible disconnected aesthetic mentality' but in fact it was a hurried, deeply flawed piece of writing that lost its way for long passages and desperately needed the services of a skilled and courageous editor. Most of Wells' time was spent on another piece of writing and on another idea altogether. It would take fruition the following year.

In 1933 Hutchinson and Company published the last great book by H.G. Wells. It was entitled *The Shape of Things to Come: The Ultimate Revolution*. But it almost did not see publication. The poet Alfred Noyes recalled in his memoirs *Two Worlds for Memory* how he met Wells on the Isle of Wight and that

the author of *The War of the Worlds* alighted from the plane with a vivacity which suddenly vanished when he discovered that his luggage had been left behind – but he had no sooner made this discovery when a great thought entered his mind. 'This is very serious,' he ejaculated in his shrill little voice, which had a queer resemblance to the cry of a bat at twilight. 'This is very serious. The whole of my manuscript, *The Shape of Things to Come*, was in my bag. I have no other copy. If I lose it I shall have lost a year's work.' He appeared to be really agitated, and in my innocence I took him seriously.

Unable to get any information at the airfield, they returned to Noyes' home where Noyes thought Wells could make all the necessary inquiries on the telephone. To Noyes' surprise, however, Wells 'asked for writing materials and began to outline a kind of publicity campaign, the initial move being a nation-wide search for a manuscript lost at an airport. In fact, it would be hard to think of a theme more inspiring to the composer of headlines: "Priceless Wells MSS Lost in the Air" . . . Wells even wrote down 'the first moves in that prospective campaign . . . 1) Associated Press 2) Lord Beaverbrook 3) Scotland Yard'.

Noyes, in innocence, really thought that the loss was very serious to Wells, and enlisted his neighbour's help, for his guest 'had what appeared to be the beginning of a nervous breakdown'. His neighbour, a director of the airline, soon discovered that Wells' luggage had mistakenly gone to Newcastle with an old lady who was also named Wells. He arranged for its prompt return by a 'racing plane'.

I returned to Wells with the good news, and if looks could have killed I would have been a dead man. Apparently I had ruined everything. And worse was to follow: Later in the evening I had a call from my friend in the air service, telling me they had found Mr Wells' bag at Newcastle; it was too big to be put into the 'racing plane', but, knowing how anxious he was, they had taken the liberty of unpacking it and were bringing back all the contents at once. The bag would follow the next day. Then came the devastating climax! 'I think Mr Wells ought to be told immediately that we found his pajamas but there was no sign of any manuscript whatsoever.'

It was not an easy message to convey to the already infuriated novelist, softened though it might be by the obvious implication that here indeed was a case for Scotland Yard. But he dropped the subject completely.

For that night, however, I provided him with pajamas, which he complained were too long in the leg, and a safety razor, which he complained was behind the times. The Island's sunlight, the next morning, he complained was an escape from reality. He said that if he had only been able to meet Kipling, he thought Kipling would have declared him a 'pukka sahib'.

The rest of the visit was equally difficult, with Wells outraging some local guests by referring to the Royal Family as 'those rabbits and swine in Buckingham Palace'. One of those present asked why Wells felt such hatred for the monarch and his family. Wells replied that it was because his mother had adored them. J.B. Priestley, another island dweller, also visited the group and chatted with Wells. 'After a few minutes,' recalls Noyes, 'Wells closed his eyes and deliberately began to snore. Mrs Priestley, seated on the other side of Wells, gave a little start at the sound, looked with some amazement at the face of the sleeping beauty, then turned to her husband and said gently: "Surely, Jack, this is very rude of Wells?" Altogether I had a most enjoyable afternoon.'

Noyes should not have been unduly surprised at Wells' love of publicity and his ability to get it. He also recorded an incident in which Wells was hit in the nose by a ladder. 'The extraordinary thing about this accident was that although Wells was alone in the house, an account of the accident appeared in the London evening papers hardly more than an hour later. He must have staggered to the telephone with the blood streaming from his nose, and asked for either the Associated Press or Lord Beaverbrook.' Noyes collected a whole package of clippings about what had happened, some with headings such as 'H.G. Wells Gets Blow on Nose' and others with 'the injured novelists's rueful countenance peering out under bandages'.

Wells had had the idea and theme of *The Shape of Things to Come* in his mind for some years but only now, with the apparently insoluble problems of the thirties upon the world, did he put his thoughts to paper. He stressed that this was not supposed to be a volume of political statement or theoretical argument but a novel of prophecy – readers must be cajoled into action by frightening predictions rather than argued into change by considered accounts. 'It is as deliberate and laborious a piece of work as anything I have ever done and I took great pains to make it as exciting and readable as I could without any sacrifice of matter. There are one or two episodes of quite lively story-telling. I was becoming sufficiently sure of my ground to let my imagination play upon it.' This was humility beyond the call of memoir.

The Shape of Things to Come represented the culmination of Wells' opinions about where the world was going unless drastic steps were taken. Some of his optimism had faded away and it seemed that almost every political development in this new decade was potentially disastrous. Whereas in the past he had smiled while he read his morning newspapers, drinking milky tea and eating toast thick with honey as he did so, friends noticed that he now scowled throughout his read and drank only the blackest and most bitter coffee. Some of the pleasure of writing had left Wells, there was a dark urgency now about his working habits that left him feeling enervated and often completely exhausted. He was also feeling his age more, visibly grimacing when he walked up the stairs of the Reform Club. Whatever happened, though, he announced, *The Shape of Things to Come* must be read and must be taken to heart.

It was another book with a fictitious author, this time Dr Philip Raven. As a character Raven takes up hardly any space at all, being described quite simply as an official with the League of Nations who died in 1931 and who gave Wells his manuscript for the purpose of publication. Raven's history of the future begins with an analysis of the years readers already knew, from around 1900 to their own day. The book then proceeds through to the early years of the twenty-second century. The first major prediction from Wells is when he names 1939 as the year of the outbreak of the Second World War. More than this, Wells depicts Japan continuing its rape of China and a subsequent war with the United States which Japan eventually loses. Germany and Italy try to dominate and subdue most of Western Europe, while the Eastern European countries gradually fall into the Communist camp. Britain takes no part in any of these conflicts, economically barren and with no will to fight.

The various warring nations and alliances sign a peace treaty in Prague in 1949 but there is now a greater threat to humanity even than war. Bubonic plague and cholera have swept through entire countries and by 1956 almost half of the world's inhabitants have been killed. Wells' description of this holocaust is reminiscent of his evocative writing in *War of the Worlds*, bursting with claustrophobic horror. He then shows how a universal Air Dictatorship develops out of this chaos and leads to the first Basra Conference in 1965. Those at the meeting take decisive action, introducing elaborate and severe transport controls and a new, authoritarian state. The economy is still in ruins, with whole populations reduced to poverty. In spite of this various governments have been able to initiate large-scale arms build-ups and are clearly preparing for war. Another Basra Conference is called in 1978 and takes action to curtail such proliferation. It demands that no national government may make decisions on issues such as military expenditure and instead must let a Bureau of Transition decide on such matters. A Thirty Year Plan under the Air Dictatorship begins.

Wells also dwelt on his familiar theme of the future of religion and depicted a society where all forms of religious worship are illegal and the Pope is even gassed when he attempts to consecrate an airfield in Italy. This is a cold, clinical, terrifying police state where great works of literature are cleansed of their politically incorrect contents and individual freedoms are perceived as damaging and undesirable. The Air Dictatorship is concluded at the Conference of Megeve in 2059 and is superseded by a World Government. The next fifty years witness the world becoming more organized and controlled, and its inhabitants conforming to a universal norm. Problems of the environment have been solved and the weather is registered and supervised – eugenically improved men and women lead their lives in a garden-like world where material progress is the ultimate aspiration. All dissent, all eccentricities, most differences, are strictly discouraged and even language has been reduced to a phonetic English with no room for poetic variation or leaps of style or imagination. Indeed imagination is the last thing that this new state asks of its citizens, whose role is to limit population by rigid birth control, abstain from crime and live for the communal good with no interest in private or personal property or ambition. Life expectancy is increased to an average age of ninety and some seventeen million people are employed to research and write an enormous Encyclopaedia entitled 'The Memory of Mankind'. Philip Raven writes at the end of the book:

The body of mankind is now one single organism of nearly two thousand five hundred million persons, and the individual differences of every one of these persons is like an exploring tentacle thrust out to test and learn, to savour life in its fullness and bring in new experiences for the common stock. We are all members of one body. Only in the dimmest analogy has anything of this sort happened in the universe as we knew it before. Our sense of individual difference makes our realization of our common being more acute. We work, we think, we explore, we dispute, we take risks and suffer – for there seems no end to the difficult and dangerous adventures individual men and women may attempt; and more and more plain does it become to us that it is not our little selves, but Man the Undying who achieves these things through us.

The book was the latest, the last, Wellsian analysis of what could happen unless we were careful, what should happen if we were enlightened. The world state with its civil-minded citizens was for Wells, of course, highly desirable; not so the war that produced it. Wells had pursued similar themes in *A Modern Utopia* but this time, as he wrote in his autobiography, he used a different vehicle. 'The device of a partially deciphered transcription of a fragmentary manuscript got over a multitude of the technical difficulties that arise in an anticipatory history. I think I have contrived to set out my matured theory of revolution and world government very plainly.'

The book was received well enough but many critics believed it to be ground with which they were too familiar, old Wellsian territory that had nothing new to say. Sales were good, however, and a cheap paperback edition was eventually issued by Hutchinson. 'I don't want this book kept out of the hands of the earnest young men and women, the labouring men, schoolmasters, journalists and all those low-price readers for an interminable time,' he said. The real success of *The Shape of Things to Come* occurred about two years later when the film version of the book was released. Alexander Korda had contacted Wells shortly after the book's publication and the two men met at Bournemouth over cakes, sardine sandwiches and pots of coffee to discuss the script.[1] Wells' original treatment for a filmed version of the latter parts of his book was rejected by Korda but the second was adapted by Korda and director William Cameron Menzies.

Wells enjoyed and relished films, writing for them and being personally involved in them. He would be almost sleepless with excitement the evening before a project began filming and was often the first person on the set.[2] Of all of his books that were recorded on the big screen – including *The First Men In The Moon*, *The Invisible Man*, *The Passionate Friends*, *Kipps*, *The Wheels of Chance* – this particular piece of work was by far the most accomplished. Wells took his personal involvement very seriously, spending much time with Arthur Bliss on the music for the film and making constant suggestions and written amendments. The filmed version was eventually titled *Things to Come* and starred Raymond Massey, Ralph Richardson and Ann Todd. It differed from the book quite substantially but the underlying theme was the same. The depictions of a bombed and blitzed London were new

– and shocking – and the introduction of a terrifyingly efficient space-gun frightened even Wells himself. The film contains a flavour of pessimism and violence that surpassed that in the book, epitomized by the character Passworthy's rhetorical question, 'My God! Is there never to be an age of happiness? Is there never to be rest?'

Audiences were certainly shaken by the epic and it has been generally thought that the film added to the popular reluctance in Britain to rearm against foreign aggression. If future war meant such total destruction, some said, what was the point in building up an air force, army and navy against Germany or any other power? This is probably too simplistic an approach. Pacifism had many seeds in the 1930s, a willingness to trust German promises found supporters in many quarters, and confusion and fear after the carnage of 1918 silenced many former warriors. In his book on his father, Anthony West wrote that some people indicated that Wells

was one of the creators of the spirit of Munich. According to this thesis the fantasia in question, which first saw the light in 1933 and was very soon afterwards made into a film, with my father's active and enthralled participation, has to be considered as one of the many factors which created public support for the policy of appeasement because it featured a massive air attack on London, shrewdly previsioned as taking place in 1940.

West pointed out, however, that the book, and the film, were characteristic of the awful warnings his father was fond of producing. 'Its clearly expressed message can be summed up as: Watch out! This is the sort of thing you will more than likely be in for if you don't take a stand against Fascism now.' West also felt that the last thing that his father would ever have been able to produce was an anti-war tract, as some claimed was the intention of the film. 'His sentiment was that a stand had to be taken and the war fought sooner rather than later, since the free societies might become indistinguishable from the totalitarian ones if they were to become involved in the rigours of a fight for survival in the last ditch.' But, West wrote, 'In spite of the clarity of his intentions, his critics contend that he wanted to see the world plunged into a long, destructive period of war and anarchy, from which a puritan tyranny of technicians and scientists would emerge, because he was peeved with it for not listening to his own preachings. The thesis is that he wrote *The Shape of Things to Come* to punish his time for making him feel futile and insignificant.'

Anthony West is, however, too sanguine and just a little ingenuous; Wells' opponents too harsh and judgemental. Wells' book and film did contribute to British ambiguity about rearmament but this could only have happened if the tendency was already there. And as Wells always proclaimed, it is the job of the writer to provoke, annoy and, if at all possible, alter the way people think and act.[3]

Wells may have reacted badly to some of his critics and their criticism but attacks on him for being a pacifist and for promoting pacifism made absolutely no impression. Besides, by this time he had already been on his international tour and had other things on his mind. In 1934 Wells met and interviewed the two leaders of what he saw as the new world; on the one hand the American President who had introduced the New Deal and imaginative economic and social programmes; on the other the Soviet dictator who was both destroying and building a nation and an empire. Arranging the visits proved to be extremely easy – both politicians were eager to meet H.G. Wells.

When Wells met President Roosevelt in Washington in May 1934, onlookers were surprised at how nervous he seemed, how respectful and almost in awe of the man whom he had criticized many times in the past. Wells had long believed and long written that the New Deal could not possibly work. In the pages of *Liberty Magazine* in October 1933 he had dismissed Roosevelt's intentions and politics in a scathing article entitled 'The Place of Franklin Roosevelt in History' and as a consequence there were many within the inner ranks of the President's staff who were opposed to the visit. Yet in spite of all previous acrimony and suspicion the meeting was a model of its kind and Wells left the American capital a convinced man. Little of their conversation has been recorded and Wells refused to reveal very much as a point of principle. 'Even if my memory would serve for the task,' he wrote, 'I would not report the drift and shifting substance of our talk.' Roosevelt did apparently express his concerns about British diplomacy and Wells replied that the President was right to be so concerned.

Nor was Wells simply seduced by the power and glamour of the Oval Office. He had met three Presidents in the past – Theodore Roosevelt, Harding and Hoover – and had seen many errors in all of them. When he left the White House in 1934, however, he could write of Roosevelt:

He is bold and unlimited in his objectives because his mental arms are long and his courage great, but his peculiar equipment as an amateur of the first rank in politics keeps him in constant touch with political realities and possibilities. He never lets go of them and they never subdue him. He never seems to go far beyond the crowd as to risk his working leadership, and he never loses sight of pioneer thought. He can understand and weigh contemporary speculative economics, financial specialism and international political psychology, and he can talk on the radio – over the heads of the party managers and newspaper proprietors and so forth – quite plainly and very convincingly to the ordinary voting man.

It is difficult to believe that the astute and experienced Wells was here describing a consummate politician and one of the most accomplished managers of a political machine and party in recent American history. Wells was on firmer ground when he wrote of Roosevelt's listening and communicating skills: 'He is, as it were, a ganglion for reception, expression, transmission, combination and realization which, I take it, is exactly what a modern government ought to be.' Anthony West believed that his father came to 'almost revere Roosevelt as a hero'.[4]

Within two months, in July, Wells was in Moscow to meet Stalin. This was a very different interview from the one that had taken place in Washington. It was longer – eventually running to three hours – and was fully recorded. There were some similarities, however. As he was with Roosevelt, Wells was suspicious of Stalin and had every intention, he announced, to tell the Soviet leader what he thought of Russia, the Russians and the Russian dictator. Wells was also a wounded man, still smarting from the remarks made by Lenin when the two had met some years earlier. Wells had at one time placed most of his hopes in the new Marxist state, had 'talked of it, dreamt of it and, if it were possible, even prayed for it'.[5] Even now he longed to believe, and to find success and hope in the Soviet Union. He liked Stalin and thought him a greater and better man than Lenin. Stalin did not dislike Wells but he had little time for any intellectual, particularly when they came from the West. Some of Stalin's advisors on Britain had thought the meeting ill advised but Stalin himself insisted on it. For all of the potential difficulties the event looked promising.

Wells wrote in his autobiography that he had dismissed Stalin as a Georgian, a man of the clan and the village who had never quite emerged into the modern world. Wells admired Trotsky for his military achievements but he was uncertain about Stalin. Before the interview took place he had been sceptical, 'Yet I had to recognize that under him Russia ... was being governed and it was getting on. Everything I had heard in favour of the First Five Year Plan I had put through a severely sceptical sieve, and yet there remained a growing effect of successful enterprise.'

When they actually met the atmosphere was better than many had anticipated. A Soviet foreign office official, Umansky, made copious notes of what was said and then translated back and forth to each man. Stalin had no English and Wells had only a smattering of the Russian language. As the meeting progressed Stalin and Wells seemed to relax, even smiled and laughed at some of the delays in translation. Stalin smoked a great deal, Wells rocked on his chair. He later described Stalin as

one of those people who in a photograph or painting become someone entirely different. ... His limited sociability and a simplicity that makes him inexplicable to the more consciously disingenuous, has subjected him to the strangest inventions of whispering scandal. His harmless, orderly, private life is kept rather more private than his immense public importance warrants, and when, a year or so ago, his wife died suddenly of some brain lesion, the imaginative spun a legend of suicide which a more deliberate publicity would have made impossible. All such shadowy undertow, all suspicion of hidden emotional tensions, ceased for ever, after I had talked to him for a few minutes.

Stalin was dressed in his usual clothes for receiving official and semi-official guests. He wore a large, blouse-like white shirt, black trousers and his favourite knee boots; he thought the dress made him look exotic. 'He turned rather shyly and shook hands in a friendly manner,' remembered Wells. 'His face was also commonplace, friendly and commonplace, not very well modelled, not in any way "fine". He looked past me rather than at me but not evasively; it was simply that he had none of the abundant curiosity which had kept Lenin watching me closely from behind the hand he held over his defective eye, all the time he talked to me.'

They disagreed on many issues. Wells stressed that there was nothing specifically socialistic about long-term planning and that it was only a matter of time before the capitalist nations indulged in their own types of Five Year Plan. The conditions and the times demanded this, continued Wells, because of the nature of production and modern industry. Hence there should be no reason why Moscow, London, Washington and Paris could not cooperate and guarantee world peace. Stalin waved his hands after the translation was finished, then gave Wells a lecture reminiscent of Wells' meeting with Lenin. He took Wells through the history of revolutionary movements and the evolution of the Communist Party in the Soviet Union. Wells replied that times had changed and a new generation of scientific revolutionaries, technical experts with benign and radical intentions, could lead the world into a new dawn. No, said Stalin, it was the bourgeoisie, and these scientists were certainly members of the bourgeoisie, who had done so much damage to the Russian Revolution. They were not to be trusted. Stalin would not budge and neither would Wells.

Given this lack of agreement and given the authentic details of Stalin's Russia that Wells was hearing from those around him, it is difficult to understand why he was so positive about Stalin. 'I have never met a man more candid, fair and honest, and to these qualities it is, and to nothing occult and sinister, that he owes his tremendous undisputed ascendancy in Russia. I had thought before I saw him that he might be where he was because men were afraid of him, but I realize that he owes his position to the fact that no one is afraid of him and everybody trusts him.' And later: 'His unaffected orthodoxy is an assurance to his associates that whatever he does would be done without fundamental complications and in the best possible spirit' and, Wells continued, 'Later on we discussed liberty of expression. He admitted the necessity and excellence of criticism, but preferred that it should be home-made by the party within the party organization. There, he declared, criticism was extraordinarily painstaking and free.'

In 1936 Chatto & Windus published *The Croquet Player*, a short story. The book is narrated by a Mr Frobisher who is on holiday with his aunt in Les Noupets. He is a quite anonymous and unformed character, a man who will read only the sports pages of the newspapers and whose sole recreation is playing croquet. He meets Dr Finchatton in his hotel and is told of the man's terrible times as a doctor in England. The doctor believes that his patients are under the spell of an evil entity that inhabits the local marshes. He asks for Frobisher's opinion and Frobisher agrees to meet him the next day. When Frobisher arrives for the meeting he finds not Finchatton but the man's psychiatrist, Norbert, who explains that the entire story was a result of Finchatton's mental illness. Norbert then delivers a fustian lecture about the problems of society and how the caveman is returning and civilization coming to an end.

I made my break-away from Norbert's flooding eloquence that morning with some considerable difficulty. I stood up. 'I must be going,' I said. 'I have to play croquet with my aunt at half-past twelve.'

'But what does croquet matter,' he cried in that intolerable voice of his, 'if your world is falling in ruins about you?'

He made a move almost as though he would impede my retreat. He just wanted to go on being apocalyptic. But I had had enough of this apocalyptic stuff.

I looked him in the face, firmly but politely. I said: 'I don't care. The world may be going to pieces. The Stone Age may be returning. This may, as you say, be the sunset of civilization. I'm sorry, but I can't help it this morning. I have other engagements. All the same – laws of the Medes and Persians – I am going to play croquet with my aunt at half-past twelve today.'

The thrust of the book was an indictment of those people who simply did not want to know what was going on or refused to acknowledge that the world was drifting towards fascism; those who wanted to turn around and play croquet. The book deserved a wider reading than it actually received. Its poor reception hurt Wells, who was also now feeling the strain of his recent travels and consistently impressive output. He was determined, however, to visit Australia and in the summer of 1938 he arrived there to speak to the Australian and New Zealand Association for the Advancement of Science (ANZAAS).

The voyage to Australia was supposed to be restful for Wells but it proved to be the direct opposite. He sailed via Bombay and Sri Lanka, was sick for long periods and did not enjoy the company of the other passengers or the crew. He disliked the contrived snobbery of life at sea and would often sit on his own in a deck-chair looking out at the ocean.[6] At various stages of the trip he regretted ever setting out and was in a thoroughly bad frame of mind by the time he reached Australia. Yet the sight of the country cheered him up. His books sold well in Australia and he had always received fan mail and good reviews from Australians. He also liked the Australians he knew and was refreshed by the newness of their country and their attitudes and by what he saw as the possibilities of a new society in this far-away place.

Wells was feeling his age now; he was seventy-two years old when he set out for Australia. Nor was his health good; he found sleep increasingly difficult and his appetite seemed to become smaller each week. He was a scientist, he said, and knew what old age and the approach of death was all about. In spite of this he took few precautions and against the advice of his doctors accepted invitations to deliver several lectures in Australia, be interviewed by numerous journalists and then write a series of articles about his trip when he returned to Britain. In Adelaide he gave a radio talk entitled 'Fiction About the Future', in Perth he spoke at a dinner given by the West Australian Federation of Writers and in Melbourne he addressed half a dozen different meetings. It was all far too much. Added to this, the climate in Australia was more extreme than Wells had anticipated. When he arrived in Adelaide the temperature was 117 degrees Fahrenheit and Wells complained to one of his Australian hosts that he felt rather faint. Yet he rarely wore summer clothing and was only persuaded to remove his jacket and tie at the end of the first week. He explained that he had been to hot countries many times before but had never felt quite so oppressed by the climate.[7]

His first lecture was delivered in both Sydney and Canberra, and in it Wells argued that 'If the human race is not to go on slipping down towards a bottomless pit of wars, conquests and exterminations it must be through the rapid and zealous expansion of the intellectual organizations of the English-speaking communities.' In his second lecture he launched an attack on Judaism and Christianity as baleful mythologies which have caused far more harm than good. Some Roman Catholic bishops asked their priests to preach against Wells from the pulpits the following Sunday. Normally Wells would have ignored such an occurrence but he was unused to a Catholic Church as powerful and influential as that in Australia. Even some of his hosts were uncomfortable at his comments and told Wells so. He responded by telling them off and also complained that he had noticed a turning away from Britain towards the United States among some sections of the Australian population. They were ungrateful and foolish to do this, he said, and would only regret it later.

The last few days of the visit were difficult and uncomfortable, characterized by arguments and raised voices. On what was supposed to be Wells' last evening in Australia he went to sleep beneath an open window. When he fell asleep the temperature was extremely high but by the middle of the night it had plummeted to below freezing. He woke up feeling stiff and heavy, and within hours was shaking and vomiting. A doctor was called and after the briefest of examinations announced that Mr Wells was suffering from viral pneumonia. Wells' departure was delayed and when he did actually board his ship home he was a drained, wretched figure who needed a walking stick and moved painfully and with a pronounced stoop. He was in no state to argue much with anyone on the voyage home and stayed mostly in his cabin, dining on thin biscuits and a watery soup. When he finally reached England his friends thought he had aged ten years in as many months.[8]

As he recuperated from his Australian travels Wells oversaw the final stages of editing and publication of *The Holy Terror*. The book concerns Rudolph Whitlow, a 'holy terror' of a child who becomes World Dictator through a fascistic organization known as the Common-Sense Party. Wells depicts the paranoia and internecine squabbling of such a government and the eventual murder of most of those in command, including Whitlow himself. In the book's conclusion Wells wrote pertinently and incisively:

Queer lot these twentieth-century Dictators. They broke out like wasps in a dry summer. Conditions favoured them. A peculiar species they were. A crescendo of scavengers because the unadapted world was rotten with shabby evasions and make-believes. It asked for blow-flies and wasps. Not a loyalty, not a religion left that was not dead and stinking. These Dictators were master stinks, stinks like burning rubber and creosote, in a world of cowardly skunks.

When the real dictators did what they did best and war was declared, Wells was in Stockholm attending a PEN conference. He had planned to deliver a lecture on the subject of censorship and was upset when it was cancelled because of the outbreak of hostilities. He managed to get back to Britain in mid-September, via the Netherlands and after a close encounter with a German plane. Just a few months later, in February 1940, T.S. Eliot wrote an article in the *New English Weekly* that struck Wells very deeply. Eliot began by comparing Wells and Winston Churchill, and praising Wells' talents. He continued:

Mr Wells started as a popular entertainer, and his advantages of education gave him the opportunity to exploit 'popular science' for a generation all ready to suspend disbelief in favour of this form of romance. To this paying activity he brought imagination of a very high order . . . Through being a popular entertainer, he found an opening as a prophet – the nearest parallel in the last few years is Miss Dorothy Sayers. None of my contemporaries of a distinction at all comparable to that of Mr Wells has started by this popular appeal of entertainment. And I think that this is more than a personal difference; it is the difference of a generation.

The world into which Mr Wells – and the late Arnold Bennett – arrived . . . was a world of 'getting on'. For the ambitious youth of literary gifts and humble origins, the first thing – sensibly enough – was to make a living by giving the public its entertainment; when one had got sufficiently established, then one might be free, either to devote oneself to a work of literary art, or to preach openly to a public which is docile and respectful to success. In the course of this rough experience Mr Wells probably learned a number of things about writing – about 'putting over' ideas to the large public – which his juniors have never learnt. He also suffered, because of his period, in a way in which younger men have not suffered. He exhibits, for example, a curious sensitiveness about his origins: in a recent contribution to the *Fortnightly* he rebukes the younger generation for grudging him in middle age the modest competence which is no more than his due in consideration of his straitened youth . . .

The serious journalism of my generation is all minority journalism. That is more than a difference between Mr Wells and my contemporaries; it is a difference between the worlds into which they were born. The crowd of season-ticket holders is still there – it is bigger than ever – reading Mr Wells' latest in the first class as well as the third class compartment: he tells them what they are ready to accept, and part of what he says is true. His great imaginative gifts, and picture-book methods, make very real to his public the situation that he describes; and as he does not reason, or draw upon any kind of wisdom inaccessible to the common man, he imposes no great strain upon the minds of his readers. And as his proposals are always in world terms, he does not ask of his readers individually any great extension from which they would flinch. On the other hand . . . he is capable of a kind of bluntness which is far too rare among the loud-speaker voices of our time. Like Mr Churchill, he is capable of putting his foot into it again and again; and this capacity for rudeness is more endearing, in the long run, than the cautious, diplomatic politeness of the people who are so careful never to put their feet into anything. There is something very refreshing about Mr Wells's violent hostility to Christianity in general and to the Catholic Church in particular; and his words about the American attitude towards the war . . .

There is, I believe, no place for a modern Wells to educate the public in more modern opinions. Our public is not yet in existence. We can only hope to provide thought of a very different kind and very different tendency, formed in very different categories, for a small number of thinking people prepared for new 'dogma' . . . This is not to maintain an attitude of aloofness, but a realistic view of the limits of our possible effectiveness. We can have very little hope of contributing to any immediate social change; and we are more disposed to see our hope in modest and local beginnings, than in transforming the whole world at once. On the other hand, though the immediate aims are less glittering, they may prove less deceptive: for Mr Wells, putting all his money on the near future, is walking very near the edge of despair; while we must keep alive aspirations which can remain valid throughout the longest and darkest period of universal calamity and degradation.

According to J.B. Priestley, the article almost 'knocked Wells off his feet'.[9] Wells believed that Eliot represented the new and he the old and that the essay was a form of obituary. It appeared to him that he was an echo, a shadow from the past and could have no influence on the future. He read and re-read the piece, memorizing some of its passages and repeating them out loud to some of his friends. Was it true, he asked? Was H.G. Wells a spent force or did the article actually say that anyway? And the question that he asked over and over again remained with those who knew him. It was, 'Has my bloody life been worth a damn?'[10]

10 Enemies All Around

Although Wells had never seriously doubted that another war would break out, he was surprised at its timing and at the lack of military activity during the opening months of the conflict. He busied himself by writing letters to the newspapers and arguing with Bernard Shaw and others about the conduct of the war and the conduct of the inevitable peace. In 1940 he also brought out two books, *Babes in the Darkling Wood* and *All Aboard for Ararat*. The former opens in 1939 with a young publishing publicist named James Twain and his lover Stella Kentlake living in a Suffolk village. Their affair is smashed by Twain's father and the young man leaves England for Russia. Along with an American journalist, Gavin Peters, Twain witnesses the German attack on Warsaw and almost dies in an aerial bombardment.

He manages to make his way back to England but he has been so profoundly shocked by what he has seen that he is mentally ill. With medical care he recovers, marries his first love, Stella, and they devote themselves to the war effort. 'They will pass,' says Twain, 'all that will pass. We fight by the way. To get rid of a dangerous nuisance. It is not our essential business. Incidentally our world may be blown to pieces and we with it. That cannot alter what we are while we are alive, not what we have to do.'

All Aboard for Ararat features as its main protagonist Noah Lammock, a modern version of the Biblical character. He is a lonely, middle-aged writer who at the beginning of the Second World War starts an elaborate conversation with someone he first believes to be an insane escapee but then understands to be God. In typical Wellsian mode this modern-day Noah accuses God of betrayal and argues that he should never have disrupted the formation of a universal language that was attempted during the time of the Tower of Babel. God offers to return to Noah his estranged wife in a new and more acceptable form but Noah refuses the offer. If God wants to do anything for mankind, says Noah Lammock, again in true Wellsian style, it must be 'something quintessential for the elite and something very strong and clear and simple for the masses of mankind'.

The book then turns into a contrived and unconvincing discussion of Marxism and the state of modern socialism. When the ark does finally set sail, a stowaway, Jonah, is found on board and thrown over the side. He is, of course, swallowed by a whale, let free after three days and returns to the ark, where he is lazy and complaining. Noah Lammock resolves that in the new world and the new order such troublesome people as Jonah will not be allowed to live. The book has moments of delightful fantasy and intelligent analogy but this was 1940 and the German military was in the middle of preparing to invade Britain. There was little time and less leisure to read and discuss quite whimsical novels.

Late in 1940 an American journalist based in New York wrote to Wells and asked for permission to write his biography. It would be entirely sympathetic, he explained, as he was a great admirer of Wells and all Wells stood for.[1] Wells replied that he was not at all interested, and anyway he had no liking for the genre of biography and the modern biographer. Nor was Wells ever partial to biography, as Hesketh Pearson remembered. Pearson hoped to gain some insight from Wells into Shaw, for his biography of the latter; his memory of the meeting in August 1939 also reveals Wells' state of mind and temper at that period. 'Apart from his remark that he did not believe Shaw had ever slept with his wife "in the fullest sense of the word", I received nothing of interest from him. Mrs Shaw, he said, had had an unfortunate love-affair in early life which had put her against sex, and they made no secret of the fact that they had always occupied separate bedrooms.'

Over tea, in the company of one of Wells' sons, Wells said that:

people thought they were thoroughly educated because they had been to a public school or university. 'D'you think you can teach us anything?' was their attitude to him, said H.G. From the bootblack to the Master of the College, he continued, they were just as annoyed when accused of being under-educated as the poor were annoyed when accused of being

dirty, gross or inefficient. 'Yet what on earth is the use of an Oxford or
Cambridge education?' he asked. I replied that it helped one to take an
interest in the Varsity boat-race. This left him unsatisfied, so I thought
of something else.

'It produces our bishops,' I said.

'Is that a justification?'

'Well, they hand us at least one good laugh a day.'

'Is that their object in life?'

'I can't think of any other.'

At this point Wells' son chipped in, telling us that the Bishop of
London had once declared that he would like to make a bonfire of
all the contraceptives in the world and dance around it. 'Do you still
question the value of a Varsity education?' I asked Wells. He did not
seem much amused, but smiled wearily.

When Pearson then expressed interest in some of the people such
as Dickens and Wilkie Collins, who had lived in Hanover Terrace,
where they were meeting, Wells 'irritably exclaimed: "Why do
people live in the past?"' The argument continued:

'Because the past, which we know, is more interesting than the future,
which we don't know,' I replied.

'Isn't the present good enough for you?'

'Yes, quite; but one of its principal charms is that it enshrines
the past.'

'What's the use of biography, anyway?'

'What's the use of history, come to that?'

'History is a record of mistakes; it teaches people what to avoid.'

'Biography is a record of life; it shows people how to live.'

'I give it up,' said Wells with a tired laugh.

'I should,' said I, rather pleased with an easy victory.

Following the above spar we calmed ourselves over a cup of tea, and
he asked me what my next subject was to be. When I told him that I
hoped to write on Shakespeare, he said that the works of Shakespeare
had been produced by about a dozen people. In the argument that
followed each of us was able to prove to his own satisfaction that the
other was wrong. I closed the debate by saying that, whatever might
be urged against Frank Harris's book on Shakespeare, he had at least
made it clear that the creator of Falstaff and Cleopatra was a man, not a
committee. 'Harris', said Wells, 'was a blackguard, a blackmailer, a liar
and a bore, who would have murdered his grandmother for sixpence if
he had had the courage to do it.' Allowing for the fact that he was still a
little heated, I thought this concise summary a somewhat partial view of
Harris. Though possibly true, it was not the whole truth, and I begged
Wells to supply the proofs of the blackmailing and blackguardism. He
did not hesitate.

Between 1940 and 1943 Wells indulged in numerous petty, personal and ultimately pointless arguments and squabbles. He fell out with the editor of the *New Statesman*, Kingsley Martin, over a series of reviews of his work that had appeared in the magazine. Wells complained to Martin in such strident tones that Martin replied: 'With your note in front of me it takes some effort to recall that you are not really the vain and abusive little man that its petulance would suggest . . . I know well that by some inner compulsion you must work off your anger when anyone is in the least critical of you, but being a scientist and therefore interested in facts, you will realize after a minute's thought that on this occasion you have been more than usually hot-tempered.'

But Wells had greater enemies to attack than mere magazine editors. With the forces of Nazism expanding into most of Europe and parts of Africa, and their allies conquering large chunks of Asia, Wells could have found targets easily enough in Berlin or Tokyo. Instead he looked to Rome.

In 1941 Secker and Warburg published *You Can't Be Too Careful: A Sample of Life.* This was Wells' last novel of the 'small man', the figure he had perfected so many years earlier in *Kipps* and *The History of Mr Polly*. Edward Albert Tewler is a powerless young man, put upon and somewhat pathetic. He is brought up by his mother, spoiled by her and then given as a ward to an uncaring schoolmaster. Tewler is later pressurized into an unwanted marriage which dissolves soon after the birth of the couple's child. When the Second World War begins Tewler joins the Home Guard and wins the George Cross by disposing of a group of Germans. Throughout all of this Wells' creation becomes more and more conservative and complacent, and insists on quoting the words of the book's title, 'You can't be too careful'.

The book was notable, however, not for its lacklustre setting and characterization but for its quite gratuitous attack upon the Roman Catholic Church. Catholicism, we are told, is 'the most evil thing in the whole world . . . Wherever the Catholic priest prevails, among the decadent pious (French) generals of the surrender, in Croatia, in Japan, in Spain, in that spite-slum Eire, in Italy, in South America, in Australia, there you will find malicious mischief afoot against the enlightenment of mankind.'

Yet Wells was being dishonest when he claimed that his fear, suspicion and hatred of the Catholic Church was based on its alleged hostility towards 'progress'. He had been a vehement anti-Catholic since a child, imbibing bigotry from his evangelical Protestant mother from his earliest days. As Anthony West states: 'As a provincial, and a Protestant, my father had gone to Rome with a certain inner queasiness. He had . . . been raised to think of the church synonymous with the city as The Scarlet Woman, and of its Pope as Anti-Christ, or even as The Beast of the Revelation.'[2]

Wells had attacked the Catholic Church for decades in his novels and in his journalism, and there is nothing surprising in the intensity of Wells' views and their stubborn longevity. 'The entire issue was very far from our thoughts in 1942,' said J.B. Priestley. 'There was something peculiarly personal about Wells and the Catholics, especially after the war began. Not sure what it was.'[3] The attacks reached a crescendo in 1943 with the publication by Penguin of *Crux Ansata: An Indictment of the Roman Catholic Church.* Consisting of only ninety-six pages, the booklet must be considered one of the most irresponsible polemics written by an influential author. With chapter titles such as 'Why Do We Not Bomb Rome?', 'The Struggle For Britain' and 'Christendon Marches East', it was a catalogue of imagined and real crimes committed by Catholicism and Catholics. In his opening essay Wells wrote:

On June 1st, 1942, the enemy bombed Canterbury and as near as possible got the Archbishop of Canterbury. But what is a mere Protestant Archbishop against His Holiness the Pope?

In March 1943 Rome was still unbombed . . . Not only is Rome the source and centre of Fascism, but it has been the seat of a Pope, who, as we shall show, has been an open ally of the Nazi-Fascist-Shinto Axis since his enthronement . . . Why do we allow these open and declared antagonists of democratic freedom to entertain their Shinto allies and organize a pseudo-Catholic destruction of democratic freedom? Why do we – after all the surprises and treacheries of this war – allow this open preparation of an internal attack upon the rehabilitation of Europe? The answer lies in the deliberate blindness of our Foreign Office and opens up a very serious indictment of the mischievous social disintegration inherent in contemporary Roman Catholic activities.

The book was a rant, exhibiting extraordinary paranoia from a man who prided himself on being well read and informed. 'Everywhere the Church extends its tentacles and fights to prolong the Martyrdom of Man . . . it dominates the policy of the British War Office and Foreign Office, and through these the B.B.C. and the press; by a disciplined Catholic vote, a casting vote in endless elections and a sustained organization of menace and boycott, it silences the frank discussion of its influence.' Wells explained what he believed to be the sinister history of the Jesuit order, the attempt by the modern Church to create a new Holy Roman Empire and how the story of Catholicism had been one of murder and persecution. When discussing Ireland, for example, he virtually ignored the Catholic sufferings under Oliver Cromwell but spent pages discussing the massacres of Protestants during the reign of Charles I.

No American company would publish the book at first — Wells saw conspiracy rather than repugnance behind this — and when a publisher was at last found it was a meagre organization notorious for publishing anti-Catholic tracts. It was, according to J.B. Priestley, a humiliation that Wells should never have tolerated and did his reputation incalculable damage.

The editor of the *Catholic Herald*, Michael de la Bedoyere, had been in correspondence with Wells for some time over his anti-Catholicism. He finally recorded the exchange in a short book entitled *Was It Worth It Wells?*.[4] The author explained how he had been telephoned one day by a colleague who said that Wells had published a 'vulgarly abusive' attack on the Catholic Church. The fear of the concerned caller was that cheap edition Penguin books were sent in great numbers to the British armed forces as part of an education package, and for armed soldiers about to enter Roman Catholic countries to be reading such violent propaganda was very dangerous. De la Bedoyere wrote to Wells, stating that 'you are so frightfully ignorant about us. Before attacking a person or an institution it is only common sense — as well as normal courtesy — to inform oneself about him or it. I suppose you rely on books, and probably those kind of popular, horizon-sweeping efforts of the imagination for which you have become famous since you gave up writing first-rate novels. This is a tragedy, because as an experienced novelist you are certainly capable of judging the worth and soundness of a man.' He went on to describe the book as 'vulgar, abusive, ignorant and badly written' and to list the errors within it and the fundamental misunderstanding of Catholicism that the book exhibited; in all de la Bedoyere listed forty-four major mistakes.

In spite of the disagreements between Wells and the editor of the *Catholic Herald* the two men agreed to meet and Wells also accepted that a priest, Father Heenan, would be present. They even fixed a date, time and place – Pagani's restaurant in Great Portland Street – for the discussion. But shortly before the day of the meeting Wells pulled out, claiming that he required more information concerning de la Bedoyere's objections. The meeting was rearranged and then cancelled again, and so the pattern proceeded. It became very clear that Wells did not want to meet with an authority on the history and structure of the Church and had no intention of so doing. Finally de la Bedoyere was forced to write an open letter to Wells which ran to over 10,000 words and in which he challenged Wells' arguments and itemized his criticisms point by point. He concluded:

But I am much more worried and sorry about you than about the book. I am worried to think that you can be so blind, so prejudiced. I am worried at the thought that you want to indulge this phobia of yours – a phobia which others might very reasonably call a peevish spite. I am worried that you can choose this time of all times to try and increase the hatred and misunderstandings which must inevitably make shapeless the things to come.

Please think it over once again. Was it worth it? Was it, Wells?

Wells was not only hostile towards Roman Catholics and Roman Catholicism. He also had an antipathy and antagonism towards the Jews. Such feelings were largely disguised within Europe, but when Wells travelled to the United States such a philosophy could not be hidden for very long. In New York, for example, with its large, vociferous and politically organized Jewish population Wells found it impossible to avoid controversy.[5] Then, as today, proponents of anti-Semitism were taken to task in a public and publicized manner.

The matter has to be placed in context. As has already been noted, Wells was a social engineer. He was an advocate of forced societal change, of restructuring populations and places by means of government fiat, relocation, punishment for deviants and, if we are to take his writings at face value (and so we ought), the murder of those races and sub-groups who stood in the path of a rigid utopia. Interwar anti-Semitism is one of the best yardsticks we have to measure social engineering, in that it was ubiquitous and perennial within those parties which demanded such policies, and is one of the few that united the Nazis on the right and the Stalinists on the left.

British anti-Semitism in the 1920s and 1930s has been explored, expatiated and expunged to such a degree that further investigation seems almost redundant. Studies of anti-Semitic attitudes have, however, frequently taken aim at individuals who have been relatively free of anti-Jewish sentiment and feeling, while failing to place some of the more invidious malefactors in their sights. Wells' opinions on the Jewish people were not unrecorded during his lifetime, but they have been conscientiously ignored since his death. The reasons for such an oversight owe more to misplaced affection than sinister revision. Yet others have been less fortunate, and hence the balance of blame and approbation of individuals, and subsequent understanding of ideologies, is perverted.

G.K. Chesterton and Hilaire Belloc for example, who together composed the literary spearhead of the Roman Catholic revival of the interwar years, are assumed to be anti-Semitic. Chesterton made occasional remarks which were ill conceived, hurtful and provocative; he also wrote pamphlets which exposed and condemned Nazi racism as early as 1934, and was honoured after his death by the leaders of the American Jewish community.[6] Belloc dedicated his work *The Jews*[7] to his amanuensis, Ruby Goldsmith, one of the two Jewish women who served him as secretary throughout his working life. Belloc's polemics did periodically drift into the realms of bigotry, but he was invariably a tenacious opponent of philosophical anti-Semitism, ostracized friends who made attacks upon individual Jews, and was an inexorable enemy of fascism and all its works, speaking out against German anti-Semitism before the National Socialists came to power. A recent study of the Kristallnacht massacre tidily grasps the situation when it states that 'Belloc, like his friend Chesterton, like so many of the English middle class, was prejudiced against Jews. . . . Nevertheless, he was not anti-Semitic . . . and the idea of employing physical brutality against a single Jew would have appalled him.'[8]

Similar cases of defence may be made for the novelist and politician John Buchan, assumed to be an anti-Semite. He was sometimes ambivalent on the subject, but was honoured by inclusion in the Golden Book of the Jewish National Fund for his advocacy of Jewish causes whilst he was a Member of Parliament.[9] T.S. Eliot would apologize for any distress he had caused amongst his Jewish readers, Evelyn Waugh largely toned down the sardonic, somewhat contemptuous attitude he displayed towards the Jews. Mitigation, ambiguity and circumstance do not, however, flavour or dilute the stance of Wells on the Jewish people and anti-Semitism. His position was as constant as it was consistent.

Late-Victorian Kent contained few Jews, and in the London of the 1890s the Jewish population was most noticeable for its novelty and recent arrival. Between 1890 and 1905 the major pogroms of Ukraine and Poland sent hundreds of thousands of Jews to Britain, the majority settling, as have all waves of immigrants to the British capital, in London's East End dock area.[10] The Jewish influence on socialism was immediate and fundamental. Jewish radical movements were established, employing East European ideas in an English ambience, and reflecting the left-Zionist and Bundist or mainstream Jewish socialist ideas. As Jews became more assimilated, and more interested, in the host culture, they became active in the Independent Labour Party, the Labour Representation Committee and the Fabian movement. It was within these organizations that Wells encountered most of those few Jews whom he knew.

Wells differed from Chesterton and Belloc in his lack of intimate contact with, and consequent personal ignorance of, Jewish people. Chesterton attended St Paul's school, which had a large Jewish minority, and during his teenage years at least half of his regular companions were Jewish; Belloc always appreciated the company of Jews, though never properly understanding Jewish ambitions and valid insecurities. Wells did form a relationship with the noted novelist and Zionist campaigner Israel Zangwill,* though they would part company over anti-Semitism in later years. His other Jewish friends were few. Degree of friendship with a minority does not, of course, necessarily dictate one's views towards that

---

* Zangwill (1864–1926), author of *Children of the Ghetto* (1892) and *The King of Schnorrers* (1894), was the leading English Jewish writer of the Edwardian era. He coined the phrase 'The Melting Pot', and was a tireless campaigner for Jewish and Zionist causes.

minority; tolerance is not shaped merely by propinquity. Motives are speculative by their very nature, aetiology is a dangerous discipline, and it is impossible to explain why Wells became so splenetically hostile to the Jews. That he was so, however, appears to be irrefutable.

In his fictional writings, Jewish characters occur in surprisingly large numbers, and are invariably stereotypical villains or base caricatures. The first such depiction is in *The Invisible Man*, published as early as 1897. Here we encounter the Jew as landlord, man of property. He is 'an old Polish Jew in a long grey coat and greasy slippers'; one of his two Yiddish speaking stepsons possesses 'staring eyes and thick-lipped bearded face'. The Invisible Man is tempted to 'hit his silly countenance', but instead sets fire to the entire house. Griffin, the Invisible Man, is nowhere described as a man of heroic or noble principles, but it is surely pertinent that such personal venom is reserved for the landlord and his unfortunate family.

In *Tono-Bungay* of 1909 Wells propounded much of his personal philosophy in the guise of a novel. This England is decadent, even moribund, and at the heart of the flaccid chaos is the Lichtenstein family, symbolizing modernity and corruption. The extent to which Wells echoed the fears and proclivities of the more traditional anti-Semites is surprising, considering that he advocated a revolutionary society. His anxieties centred on the alien nature of the change he sometimes observed; alien to his notion of Britain, alien to him. For all of his internationalist polemics, Wells remained a parochial figure. In recent wealth Wells perceived the 'slow decay of the great social organism of England'. The author of *Tono-Bungay* is intrinsically ill at ease with the 'new unhappy Lords':[11]

Bladesover House is now let furnished to Sir Reuben Lichtenstein, and has been since old Lady Drew died; ... It was curious to note then the little differences that had come to things with this substitution. To borrow an image from my mineralogical days, these Jews were not so much a new British gentry as 'pseudo-morphous' after the gentry. They are a very clever people, the Jews, but not clever enough to suppress their cleverness.

The New Machiavelli, which included amongst its major characters a figure based on the Jewish Liberal politician Sir Herbert Samuel, appeared in 1911, just as the Marconi scandal was gaining public attention.[12] Samuel was a key player in the scandal, and Wells was to attack him incessantly for the next three years. As Postmaster-General Samuel had been offered and had accepted a tender from the English Marconi Wireless Telegraphy Company for the construction of a chain of wireless stations throughout the British empire. There was of course a sudden and dramatic rise in the price of Marconi shares, particularly since the recent tragedy of the *Titanic* sinking had revealed the importance of wireless communications. The managing director of the English Marconi company was Godfrey Isaacs, whose brother Rufus was also a successful Liberal politician. Rufus Isaacs had been told by his brother to buy Marconi shares, before the public knew of the government contract and subsequent expansion of the Marconi company. Money was made and lost, the scandal became known, and a court trial would eventually ensue.

Jew and Gentile were involved in the corruption, but it was the Jewish ministers who received most of the acrimony. G.K. Chesterton, his brother Cecil and Hilaire Belloc led the literary campaign against the guilty men, and some of Cecil Chesterton's attacks bordered on hysterical Judaeophobia. Wells threw himself into the ranks, supporting his erstwhile enemy Belloc and distinguishing himself by being one of the few socialist writers to support virtually every lunge made by *The Eye-Witness*,[13] the magazine of Chesterton/Belloc. The entire escapade, and both sides, were ignoble and tainted. Wells' description of Lewis, the Herbert Samuel parody, kills with kindness: he is 'a brilliant representative of his race, able, industrious and invariably uninspired'. He believes in a mandate which 'is sacred to his system of pretences'.

The next year witnessed publication of *Marriage*, in which Wells devoted more time to the Jewish question than in any other work of fiction. Marconi was still in full fury, and both sides believed *Marriage* to be a partisan contribution to the debate. The married couple of the title are divided by belief: the husband, Trafford, is an idealist with scant regard for finance; his wife, Marjorie, is an irresponsible materialist. Richard Trafford is forced to sell his abilities as a scientist to Sir Rupert Solomonson, a patently unlikable entrepreneur. Terms such as loss of 'honour', the seduction of 'Orientalism' disguised in tweeds, and cosmopolitan contempt, especially from the character of Lady Solomon, abound.

The early part of the book bristles with fatuous and damaging caricature:

Of course this was the clue to Lee and Solomonson. How extremely happy Lee appeared to be! Enormous vistas of dark philoprogenitive parents and healthy little Jews and Jewesses seemed to open out to Trafford, hygienically reared, exquisitely trained and educated. And he and Marjorie had just one little daughter – with a much poorer educational outlook. She had no cloth elephant to ride, no elaborate cubby-house to get into, only a half-dozen picture books or so, and later she wouldn't when she needed it get into that linguistic Swiss.

He wasn't above the normal human vanity of esteeming his own race and type the best, and certain vulgar aspects of what nowadays one calls Eugenics crossed his mind.

A writer cannot, or should not, be judged merely on the evidence of his fictional work, but Wells provided a multitude of examples in his non-fiction of his attitudes towards the Jews. In a series of essays he lambasted Zionism, even going so far as to describe Nazism as 'inverted Judaism'. In *Travels of a Republican Radical In Search of Hot Water*, published in 1939, he explained how the national egotism of the Jewish people was responsible for so many of their sorrows and sufferings, claiming that 'no people in the world have caught the fever of irrational nationalism that has been epidemic in the world since 1918, so badly as the Jews'. He went on to say: 'But throughout those tragic and almost fruitless four years of war, Zangwill and the Jewish spokesmen were most elaborately and energetically demonstrating that they cared not a rap for the troubles and dangers of English, French, Germans, Russians, Americans or of any other people but their own. They kept their eyes steadfastly upon the restoration of the Jews.'

It was laboriously explained to Wells that the first American to volunteer for the European conflict was a Jew, that entire regiments of Ukrainian and White Russian Jews fought on the Eastern Front, that the number of German Jews to be decorated was far greater than their proportion in German society, and that French and British Jews died side-by-side with their Gentile colleagues in France and Belgium. Wells refused to alter his thesis.

The idea of a Jewish minority having no loyalty to its host nation, but simply exploiting a transitory home, was and still is the fundamental stuff of anti-Semitism. It is a facetious proposition, in that Jews have long desired to assimilate into virtually any nation which would accept them, and by 1939 the most accepted Jewish community in the world was in Germany. The establishment of Israel, and the subsequent fact that only a small minority of world Jewry is willing to live in the country, destroys the myth of rootlessness in all but the most intransigent of minds. It was seldom the Jews who rejected the host nation, but the host country which rejected, in varying degrees of violence or discrimination, the Jews.

Wells boasted of one conversation with a Jewish acquaintance which occurred shortly before the Second World War. He was asked what he thought would happen to the Jews of Europe. He told the man that he would rather be asked, 'What is going to happen to mankind?' 'But my people . . . ' 'That,' he interrupted, 'is exactly what is the matter with them.' Such smugness, at such a time, cannot be lightly dismissed. Nor was it by contemporaries. Israel Zangwill, in his *The Voice of Jerusalem*, condemned Wells' 'conscious prejudice against Judaism and unconscious prejudice in favour of Christianity'. Wells' response was to intensify his attacks. In *The Shape of Things to Come: The Ultimate Revolution*, published in the year the National Socialists came to power in Germany, he was pessimistic about the future of the Jews after the war ended, and the toil of renaissance began in earnest:

It might have been supposed that a people so widely dispersed would have developed a cosmopolitan mentality and formed a convenient linking organization for so many world purposes, but their special culture of isolation was so intense that this they neither did nor seemed anxious to attempt . . . the orthodox Jews played but a poor part in the early attempts to formulate the Modern State, being far more preoccupied with a dream called Zionism . . . Only a psychoanalyst could begin to tell for what they wanted this Zionist state. It emphasized their traditional wilful separation from the main body of mankind. It irritated the world against them.

During the 1930s Jewish organizations and individual Jews were more concerned with simple survival than with the foundation of a national homeland. Before the Nazi Holocaust a high percentage of Jews were indifferent to Zionism or even, as in the case of the British politician Edwin Montagu, actively antagonistic towards the philosophy. Wells did not confine his attacks to Zionism and Zionists. In the essay 'The Future of the Jews',[14] he dismissed the 'lies and delusions of mankind', and continued: 'The accepted tradition of the Jews is largely nonsense. They are no more a "pure" race than the English or the Germans or the hundred per cent Americans. There never was a "Promise"; they were never "Chosen"; their distinctive observances, their Sabbath, their Passover, their queer calendar, are mere traditional oddities of no present significance whatsoever.'

For many people, Jew and Gentile, this was too much. Eleanor Roosevelt initiated a series of attacks on Wells, including an article entitled 'Mr Wells is Wrong'. Leon Galman, President of the Mizrachi Organization of America, a religious union, wrote that: 'H.G. Wells is brazenly spreading notorious lies about the Jews. His violent language betrays a streak of sadism that is revolting. If any man who professes to be an enlightened human being can preach such heinous distortions then mankind is doomed to utter darkness.'

The noted journal *Liberty*, for which Wells wrote one of his central articles on the Jews, was inundated with letters; most reprimanded the author, a small number congratulated him for his 'delightfully interesting' essay.[15] One intriguing aspect of the entire episode is that seldom did Wells attempt to escape the issue of the Jews, rarely employing euphemism and only occasionally painting his remarks with a thin gloss of affection. Correspondent Harold Brown wrote from Paterson, New Jersey:

Popular novelists as well as morons have the privilege of making stupid statements. If Mr H.G. Wells would only think a little before he writes, he would observe that it is not the Jews who make anti-Semitism but it is anti-Semitism that makes Jews. If it weren't for persecution, the Jews would have disappeared hundreds of years ago.

These people have been trying to assimilate with their neighbours since the time of the great Greeks. Wherever and whenever Jews are allowed to love as equals they adopt the habits and customs of the majority, they intermarry and merge with the population. In Germany they became so Germanized that they completely forgot they were Jews until Hitler came along and reminded them of it.

If Mr Wells is right, then Germany should have been the last place in the world for anti-Semitism to have arisen.

The British section of the debate had been in progress for over a decade. The *Jewish Chronicle* reacted with severity to Wells' fulminations in the 1936 work *The Anatomy of Frustration*.[16]

Wells had written of the 'essential parasitism of the Jewish mycelium upon the social and cultural organisms in which it lives'. The term parasite is a reliable stand-by in the anti-Semitic lexicon, and the mainstream Jewish newspaper charged him with vulgar abuse. Wells responded to the editorial, wondering why the Jews demonstrated no gratitude for his revelations, and essential altruism towards their people. Elements of the Jewish community believed his protestations, and solicited his help when early signals of the Holocaust began to reach Britain, particularly as he had repeatedly predicted an organized slaughter of European Jewry. When Jan Karski told Wells in late 1942 that he had seen at first hand a Nazi extermination camp, Wells' response was that 'there is room for very serious research into the question why anti-Semitism emerges in every country the Jews reside in'.[17]

Wells lived to learn of the Holocaust, and to realize that some of his predictions were accurate, most of his theories nonsensical. Retractions were not forthcoming, even after a number of fellow travellers of the far right, and literary figures who had flirted with fascism, expressed contrition. The best that may be said of Wells is that he desired peace for the Jews on his own terms, in a Wellsian Utopia where all ethnic and religious divisions would be expunged from the human mentality. The worst that may be said about him is probably the worst that may be said about any figure of the mid-twentieth century. As he said himself in his autobiography, 'I have always refused to be enlightened and sympathetic about the Jewish question.'

11 Man at the End of His Tether

W ells showed physical courage during the bombing of London in 1943 and 1944, and refused to abandon his home in the centre of the city. He wrote to a friend complaining of hysteria in the country because of the new V-bombs the Germans were sending to London. He spoke of 'panic-stricken bores, who when they get to the country lie & exaggerate to justify their own disgraceful cowardice. Here I am in the middle of it all & only one window cracked by the concussion of an AA gun on Primrose Hill. Do show people this letter & shut up the pro-German panic-mongers. We stood up so well to the Blitzkrieg at the beginning of the war & now this silly behaviour is disgracing the country in the eyes of the world.'

He spent much of his time on his balcony in Hanover Terrace drinking weak tea and reading the newspapers. He wore his favourite panama hat to shield his face from the sun; he complained to friends and to his doctor that he burned easily nowadays.[1] He slept a great deal, often dozing in his deck-chair and waking up with a start, wondering where he was and shouting for help. He was an old, tired man. He read aloud to J.B. Priestley the final paragraph of his autobiography, written over ten years earlier: 'So ends this record of the growth and general adventure of my brain, which first squinted and bubbled at the universe and reached out its feeble little hands to grasp it, eight and sixty years ago, in a shabby bedroom over the china shop that was called Atlas House in High Street, Bromley, Kent.' Usually when he had finished this passage he would laugh out loud but on one occasion Priestley saw him cry.[2]

There was one book to come, however, one final statement from the man who had said and written so much. *Mind at the End of Its*

Tether was published in 1945 by William Heinemann and included the final chapter of the 1945 revised edition of *A Short History of the World*. Its despair seemed apt.

The writer finds very considerable reason for believing that, within a period to be estimated by weeks and months rather than by aeons, there has been a fundamental change in the conditions under which life, not simply human life but all self-conscious existence, has been going on since its beginning. This is a very startling persuasion to find establishing itself in one's mind, and he puts forward his conclusions in the certainty that they will be unacceptable to the ordinary rational man.

If his thinking has been sound, then this world is at the end of its tether. The end of everything we call life is close at hand and cannot be evaded. He is telling you the conclusions to which reality has driven his own mind.

Wells continued:

Our universe is not merely bankrupt; there remains no dividend at all; it has not simply liquidated; it is going clean out of existence, leaving not a wrack behind. The attempt to trace a pattern of any sort is absolutely futile . . . He would rather our species ended its story in dignity, kindliness and generosity, and not like drunken cowards in a daze or poisoned rats in a sack. But this is a matter of individual predilection for everyone to decide for himself.

And so the sorry book went on. While others were celebrating victory over an enemy whom they once thought would return the world to another dark age, Wells lamented his own personal failures. Critics were ashamed and outraged at the timing of publication and thought the book a waste of time. Friends attempted to change the subject when the book came up for conversation. Wells stayed on his balcony.

He now had cancer and his liver was not functioning properly. There was occasional pain but usually the rapid disintegration of his body caused Wells merely to sleep. The end was obviously near and people had begun to call to see Wells for what they knew would be the last time. Wells knew it too and said very little to these late visitors.

On 13 August 1946, only weeks short of his eightieth birthday, Herbert George Wells died. There was so much happening in the political and military world that his death did not cause as much of a ripple as some had expected. He was cremated three days later at Golders Green, as he had requested.

J.B. Priestley knew Wells as a friend, an associate, a rival and an occasional enemy. He delivered an address about Wells at the Golders Green service that is worth quoting in full. Priestley was nervous, noticed his hands shaking a little and steadied himself by taking a deep breath and swallowing hard two and then three times. He thought about Wells for a moment and recalled the man laughing so hard on one occasion that he fell off his chair. Priestley was now relaxed.[3]

We have come together here today to say goodbye to our friend, Herbert George Wells. All of us here were privileged to know him — and some were so close to him that it is not possible for any one of us outside his family circle to express their sense of loss — and I think that all of us, knowing how great was his work and how worldwide his influence, realize that at this moment we represent millions of men and women of all races who found in him a counsellor and friend. For this was a man whose word was light in a thousand dark places. Since the beginning of this century, whenever young men and women, from the Arctic to the Tropics, were determined to free themselves from mental squalor, from superstition, ignorance, cruelty and fear, there was H.G. Wells at their side, unwearying and eager to instruct and inspire. They turned to him to help them in their struggle for knowledge, insight and courage, and they never asked in vain. His literary genius was rich and rare — the best of his novels and short stories are among the finest creations of our time — but he belongs not only to English literature, but also to world history, as a great educator and as the chief prophet of this age of transition, long foreshadowing, with pity and passion, the shape of things to come. [A few polite chuckles, embarrassed laughs and smiles.]

And now we live indeed, with our rockets and atom bombs, in a Wellsian world. We hover at the crossroads, leading either to a real world civilization or to the possible extinction of our species; and nobody would be foolish enough now to say that Wells was an idle prophet. He saw further than other men did. His unique combination of literary power and intuition, social experience, and early scientific training, gave him a profound insight into the strange historical dramas of our time. He worked with a double vision, both his own, but one long-range, the other short-range.

At this there was a ripple of approval from the company followed by some gestures of disapproval from those who thought that this was not an occasion for any sort of public commentary on a speech.

His long-range vision, born of his biological studies and his vivid imagination, showed him Mankind as a species, struggling through darkness and slime, cruelty and fear, towards truth and beauty, freedom and joy. So he worked with a passionate loyalty for the whole toiling, contriving, endlessly hopeful family of Mankind. His other – and short-range – vision, which made him the chief prophet of our age, and gave him the pattern of many of his best stories, was a vision of some ordinary little citizen – bewildered but hopeful, baffled but touchingly gallant – being swept along by forces he could not understand into a world of gigantic conflict and sinister changes, the very world in which H.G. found himself in these last years, old and often ailing, but still indomitable, refusing to leave his ruined terrace and the London folk he knew so well. The age of total and terrible war, against which he had warned us so often, had arrived; but he was still there to share it with us. And looking back, and remembering what little comfort his strange insight could give him, we can marvel now at his buoyancy, his vast geniality, his glorious intellectual high spirits. For, as all of us here can testify – this was no gloomy prophet, turning his back on us for his private wilderness, disdaining friendship and fun. [A ripple of agreement and a shout of approval from someone not recognized by Wells' closest friends.]

This was the man who could write *Kipps* and *Mr Polly* and *Tono-Bungay*, the man who could invent uproarious family games, whose blue eyes twinkled with mischief and whose famous voice, which never lost a kind of reedy Cockney impudence, rose higher and higher in friendly mischief; who was not only a tremendous character, but also a most lovable man. Of course, he could be prickly, rather intolerant, easily exasperated, but there was not a single streak of hard pride in his nature. When he was angry, it was because he knew, far better than we did, that life need not be a sordid greedy scramble; and when he was impatient it was because he knew there were glorious gifts of body, mind and spirit only just beyond our present reach. And always the greatness was there; the immense range of his mind, the astonishing fountain of ideas, the devastating or illuminating judgement, and the unwearying sympathy with us all, of every colour and race, in our bewilderment, despair and hope. He was a world-famous figure, the great prophet of our time, but always, from first to last, one of our friends, who only asked to talk with us truthfully, eagerly and vividly. At his worst he never diminished and hurt us. And at his best he made us feel, as he did, that we live on a star.

Priestley paused at this point, drank from a glass of water at his side and cleared his throat. Somebody had begun to cry.

'His body vanishes from our sight as it goes towards the comsuming flames. But we shall remember him with gratitude and affection – he will live on in our hearts and still light our minds – as, I trust, we try to serve his vision of one world, the home of the whole human family, free at last from ignorance, cruelty and fear.' Another pause, this time in preparation for the conclusion of the tribute.

So, remembering to hold his noblest vision as a legacy and a trust, let us say goodbye to our friend in his own words and not in ours: 'So far and beyond, this adventure may continue and our race survive. The impenetrable clouds that bound our life at last in every direction may hide innumerable trials and dangers, but there are no conclusive limitations even in their deepest shadows, and there are times and seasons, there are moods of exaltation – moments, as it were, of revelation – when the whole universe about us seems bright with the presence of as yet unimaginable things.'

Priestley was, of course, a judge lacking in objectivity. *The Times Literary Supplement* got nearer the truth when four days after Wells' death it devoted its lead article to him. The tribute was heartfelt and moving but it also stressed that Wells had been a star in an earlier firmament, and it understood some of his undoubted flaws. After a paragraph of praise the author of the piece continued:

The magic faded. The single conviction that possessed Wells lost its spell, and the more impatient, more emphatic tone of voice in which he preached salvation through the orderly planning of the progress of mankind did not secure greater attention for him. The world moved on . . .
   Today it is not difficult to recognize his limitations as an artist and as a thinker . . . Wells, it need hardly be said at this time of day, is a popularizer and educator rather than a thinker, and as such he belongs somewhat narrowly to his time and place. Boldly conceived though they are, *The Outline of History* and *The Science of Life* do little more than infect one with the author's own tireless curiosity of mind. Even so, moreover, they exhibit the fatal touch of philistinism in his thought and his still more fatal utopian positivism. Wells's faith in knowledge and reason, in brief, excluded too large, too central a part of human experience.

Malcolm Muggeridge was another who commented on Wells after his death. Muggeridge had been asked to attend the funeral but declined. Instead he wrote his own of form of obituary of Wells some years later:

Poor, squeaky H.G. Wells, ardent evolutionist and disciple of Huxley, with his vision of an earthly paradise achieved through science and technology; those twin monsters which have laid waste a whole world, polluting its seas and rivers and lakes with poisons, infecting its very earth and all its creatures, reaching into Man's mind and inner consciousness to control and condition him, at the same time entrusting to irresponsible, irresolute human hands the instruments of universal destruction. It must be added that, confronted with this prospect when, at the very end of his life, the first nuclear explosion was announced, Wells turned his face to the wall, letting off in *Mind at the End of Its Tether* one last, despairing, whimpering cry which unsaid everything he had ever thought or hoped. Belatedly, he understood that what he had followed as a life-force was, in point of fact, a death wish, into which he was glad to sink the little that remained of his own life in the confident expectation of total and final obliteration.[4]

So what of Wells' true legacy and genuine achievements? He was without doubt a writer touched by genius and capable of work that will for ever delight those who read it. That he was a novelist of overwhelming abilities is beyond argument. But through his political writings Wells helped create an intellectual climate in the 1920s and 1930s that – though not leading directly to the social-engineering horrors of Hitler and Stalin – certainly gave credibility to the atrocities of the dictators that were to take place in the coming years. He injected permissibility into political eugenics, varnished murderous ideas with respect and reputation. At its most simplistic level the belief of the social engineers was that by exterminating or incarcerating perhaps one half of the world's population the remaining half would enjoy unparalleled benefits. Wells not only went along with this, he encouraged it. Thus there is a stain on his writing and on his character that is indelible.

Anthony West was asked to read and reconsider some of his father's writings on social engineering, eugenics, the Jews, the new utopia. After he had done so he shook his head several times, read some of the passages again and held them up to the light. Then he paused and said quite simply: 'It is for the past and in the past.' He then placed the papers carefully and calmly on the table in front of him and left the room.[5] He was wrong, however. H.G. Wells' writings are still with us and are very much part of the present.

Sources

Introduction

1 Author's interview with Earl of Longford.
2 Somerset Maugham, *A Writer's Notebook*, 1949.
3 Harry Ransom Humanities Research Center, Austin, Texas.
4 Ibid.
5 Author's interview with J.B. Priestley.
6 Harry Ransom Center.
7 Ibid.

1 Early Days

1 H.G. Wells, *Experiment in Autobiography*, London, 1934.
2 Mile End Museum Archives, London.
3 Anthony West, *H.G. Wells: Aspects of a Life*, London, 1984.
4 Interview with J.B. Priestley.
5 *Experiment in Autobiography*.
6 Ibid.
7 G.K. Chesterton papers, British Library.
8 Wells Collection, Bromley.
9 Sir John Betjeman, *Summoned By Bells*, London, 1960.
10 Author's interview/correspondence with J.B. Priestley.
11 Wells Collection, Bromley.
12 Ibid.
13 *Experiment in Autobiography*.
14 Wells Collection, Bromley.

2 The Shaping of a Life

1 Arthur Conan Doyle, *A Study In Scarlet*, London, 1888.

2 Henry Mayhew, 'London Labour and the London Poor', London, 1851.
3 *Experiment in Autobiography*.
4 G.K. Chesterton's *Weekly*, 1927.
5 G.K. Chesterton papers, British Library.
6 *Experiment in Autobiography*.
7 Local History papers, Wrexham Public Libraries.
8 Wells Collection, Illinois.
9 Ibid.
10 *Certain Personal Matters*, London, 1897.
11 Wells Collection, Illinois.
12 *Experiment in Autobiography*.
13 Wells Collection, Bromley.
14 *Experiment in Autobiography*.
15 L.C. Cornford, *William Ernest Henley*, London, 1913.
16 Wells Collection, Bromley.
17 Wells Collection, Illinois.
18 Author's correspondence and interviews with J.B. Priestley.
19 Author's correspondence and interviews with Anthony West.
20 Ibid.
21 Ibid.
22 Wells Collection, Illinois.

3 Anticipating Utopia

1 Author's correspondence and interview with J.B. Priestley.
2 Author's correspondence and interview with Malcolm Muggeridge.
3 Houston Chamberlain, *Rasse und Personlichkeit*, Munich, 1925.
4 Houston Chamberlain, *Grundlagen*, Munich, 1899.
5 Author's correspondence and interview with Malcolm Muggeridge.
6 Letter to Miss Healey, Wells Collection, Illinois.
7 Wells Collection, Illinois.
8 G.K. Chesterton papers, British Library.
9 Wells Collection, Illinois.
10 G.K. Chesterton papers, British Library.
11 Wells Collection, Illinois.
12 Ibid.
13 Ibid.
14 London School of Economics & Political Science.
15 G.B. Shaw, *The Christian Commonwealth*, London, 1909.
16 *Experiment in Autobiography*.
17 Anthony West, *H.G. Wells: Aspects of a Life*.
18 Wells Collection, Illinois.
19 G.B. Shaw, *New Statesman*, 1946.

4 The Man of Substance

1 Author's interview with Anthony West.
2 *Experiment in Autobiography*.
3 Ibid.
4 G.K. Chesterton papers, British Library.
5 Ibid.
6 *Experiment in Autobiography*.
7 *Daily News*, 2 April 1915.
8 Anthony West, *H.G. Wells: Aspects of a Life*.
9 Author's interview with Anthony West.
10 *Experiment in Autobiography*.
11 *H.G. Wells in Love* (supplement to *Autobiography*), London, 1984.
12 Author's interview with J.B. Priestley.
13 Wells Collection, Bromley.
14 British Library.
15 Ibid.
16 *Experiment in Autobiography*.
17 British Library.
18 Author's interview with J.B. Priestley.

5 A Woman of Some Importance

1 Anthony West, *H.G. Wells: Aspects of a Life*.
2 *H.G. Wells in Love*.
3 *H.G. Wells: Aspects of a Life*.
4 Rebecca West's letter to Gordon N. Ray.
5 Wells Collection, Illinois.
6 Ibid.
7 G.K. Chesterton papers, British Library.
8 *H.G. Wells: Aspects of a Life*.
9 Wells Collection, Illinois.
10 Wells to West, June 1915, Wells papers.
11 Author's interview with Martha Gelhorn.
12 Wells to West, October 1920, Wells papers.
13 Wells to West, 20 March 1922.
14 Rebecca West's diary, 5 April 1944.
15 Wells to West, September 1922, Wells papers.

6 Sniffing at the Heels of Reality

1 *Experiment in Autobiography*.
2 Leo Szilard, *Perspectives II* (Cambridge, Massachusetts, 1969).

3 *Daily Chronicle*, 30 December 1914.
4 H.G. Wells, *The War and the Future*, 1917.
5 Bertrand Russell, *Portraits from Memory and other Essays*, London, 1956.
6 Frank Swinnerton, *An Autobiography*, London, 1937.
7 Wells Collection, Bromley.
8 Wells Collection, Illinois.
9 Ibid.
10 Author's interview with J.B. Priestley.
11 Ibid.
12 Jerome K. Jerome, *My Life and Times*, London, 1926.
13 A.L. Rowse, *Glimpses of the Great*, London, 1985.
14 Wells Collection, Illinois.
15 *Experiment in Autobiography*.

7 History and Mr Belloc

1 Author's interview and correspondence with J.B. Priestley.
2 Bennett papers, University of Texas.
3 London School of Economics Library.
4 Wells Collection, Illinois.
5 Wells Collection, Bromley.
6 Reginald L. Hine, *Confessions of an Un-Common Attorney*, London, Dent, 1945.
7 Author's interview and correspondence with Anthony West.
8 Philip Guedalla, *A Gallery*, London, Constable, 1924.
9 Wells Collection, Illinois.
10 Ibid.
11 Author's interview and correspondence with Anthony West.
12 *Experiment in Autobiography*.
13 Basil Joseph Mathews, *The Young Man*.
14 Author's interview and correspondence with Gregory MacDonald.
15 Philip Guedalla, *The Missing Muse*, Harpers, 1930.
16 Belloc papers, Boston College.
17 H.G. Wells, *Mr Belloc Objects*, London, Watts, 1926.
18 *London Mercury*, November 1920.
19 G.K. Chesterton papers, British Library.
20 Wells Collection, Illinois.
21 G.K. Chesterton papers, British Library.
22 H.G. Wells, *Mr Belloc Objects*.
23 H. Belloc, *Mr Belloc Still Objects*, London, Sheed & Ward, 1926.
24 G.K. Chesterton papers, British Library.
25 Author's interview and correspondence with J.B. Priestley.

26 G.K. Chesterton papers, British Library.
27 *Mr Belloc Still Objects*.
28 G.K. Chesterton papers, British Library.
29 Ibid.
30 H. Belloc, *A Companion to Mr Wells's Outline of History*, London, Sheed & Ward, 1926.
31 G.K. Chesterton papers, British Library.
32 Ibid.
33 Author's interview and correspondence with J.B. Priestley.

8 Debates and Farewells

1 *H.G. Wells In Love*.
2 Author's interview with J.B. Priestley.
3 G.K. Chesterton papers, British Library.

9 The Shape of Things

1 Author's interview with Anthony West.
2 Ibid.
3 Ibid.
4 Ibid.
5 Author's interview with J.B. Priestley.
6 Ibid.
7 Ibid.
8 Ibid.
9 Ibid.
10 Ibid.

10 Enemies All Around

1 Author's interview with J.B. Priestley.
2 Anthony West, *H.G. Wells: Aspects of a Life*.
3 Author's interview with J.B. Priestley.
4 Michael de la Bedoyere, *Was It Worth It Wells?*, Paternoster Publications, 1944.
5 Estimates place the Jewish population of New York City as high as forty per cent in the 1930s (Archives, B'nai B'rith, New York).
6 Weiner Library Archives, London.
7 *The Jews*, Constable, London, 1922.
8 Anthony Read & David Fisher, *Kristallnacht*, Random House, 1989.

9 Janet Adam Smith, *John Buchan: A Biography*, London, 1965.
10 Canadian Jewish Congress, Toronto.
11 The eponymous line from a poem by G.K. Chesterton which bemoans the new, alien nature of stewardship.
12 Frances Donaldson, *The Marconi Scandal*, London, 1962.
13 Personal interview with Gregory MacDonald, journalist on the Chesterton/Belloc magazines.
14 *Travels of a Republican Radical In Search of Hot Water*, London, 1939.
15 Ibid.
16 *Jewish Chronicle* archives, London.
17 'Messenger from Poland', Channel 4 Television, May 1987.

11 Man at the End of His Tether

1 Author's interview with J.B. Priestley.
2 Ibid.
3 Ibid.
4 Malcolm Muggeridge, *Conversion*, London, Collins, 1988.
5 Author's interview with Anthony West.

Bibliography

The papers of H.G. Wells are mostly to be found in the University of Illinois, Champaign-Urbana, but also in the H.G. Wells collection in Bromley Central Library, Bromley, Kent. Other collections I used included the Hilaire Belloc papers at Boston College and the G.K. Chesterton papers, then in Top Meadow, Beaconsfield, Buckinghamshire, but now in the British Library and the Chesterton Study Centre, Bedford. Other source material may be found in the book's references. Below is a list of secondary sources:

Archer, William, *God and Mr Wells* (London, 1917)
Baring, Maurice, *Puppet Show of Memory* (London, 1922)
Belgion, Montgomery, *H.G. Wells* (London, 1933)
Belloc, Hilaire, *A Companion to Mr Wells's Outline of History* (London, 1926)
Belloc, Hilaire, *Mr Belloc Still Objects* (London, 1926)
Belloc, Hilaire, *The Jews* (London, 1922)
Bergonzi, Bernard, *The Early H.G. Wells* (Manchester, 1961)
Brome, Vincent, *H.G. Wells* (London, 1951)
Brooks, Van Wyck, *The World of H.G. Wells* (London, 1915)
Brown, Ivor, *H.G. Wells* (London, 1923)
Chaplin, F.K., *H.G. Wells. An Outline* (London, 1961)
Costa, R.H., *H.G. Wells* (New York, 1967)
Crauford, A.H., *The Religion of H.G. Wells* (London, 1909)
Dark, Sydney, *The Outline of H.G. Wells* (London, 1922)
De la Bedoyere, Michael, *Was it Worth it Wells?* (Paternoster, 1944)
Dickson, Lovat, *H.G. Wells. His Turbulent Life and Times* (London, 1969)

Gettman, Royal (ed), *George Gissing and H.G. Wells* (London, 1960)

Guyot, Edouard, *H.G. Wells* (Paris, 1920)

Holroyd, Michael, *Bernard Shaw* 3 vols (London, 1980–91)

Mackenzie, Norman and Jeanne, *The Time Traveller. The Life of H.G. Wells* (London, 1973)

Nicholson, Norman, *H.G. Wells* (London, 1950)

Newell, Kenneth B., *Structure in Four Novels by H.G. Wells* (The Hague, 1968)

Pearson, Hesketh, *By Himself* (New York, 1965)

Pearson, Hesketh, *Thinking it Over* (London, 1938)

Ray, Gordon N., *H.G. Wells & Rebecca West* (Yale, 1974)

Smith, David C., *H.G. Wells. Desperately Mortal* (Yale, 1986)

Speaight, Robert, *The Life of Hilaire Belloc* (New York, 1957)

Vallentin, A., *H.G. Wells: Prophet of Our Day* (New York, 1950)

Wagar, W. Warren, *H.G. Wells and the World State* (New Haven, 1961)

Ward, Maisie, *Gilbert Keith Chesterton* (New York, 1944)

Wells, Frank, *H.G. Wells. A Pictorial Biography* (Jupiter Books, 1977)

West, Anthony, *H.G. Wells. Aspects of a Life* (London, 1984)

West, Anthony, *Heritage* (New York, 1955)

Wilson, Harris, *Arnold Bennett and H.G. Wells* (London, 1960)

Index